Techniques of Archaeological Excavation

'We owe the dead nothing but the truth'
Voltaire, *Letters on Oedipus*

To all who have dug with me

Overleaf Part of the plan of the Romano-British Village at Rotherley, Wiltshire, excavated by Lieut.-Gen Pitt-Rivers in 1886-7 (Pitt-Rivers, 1888)

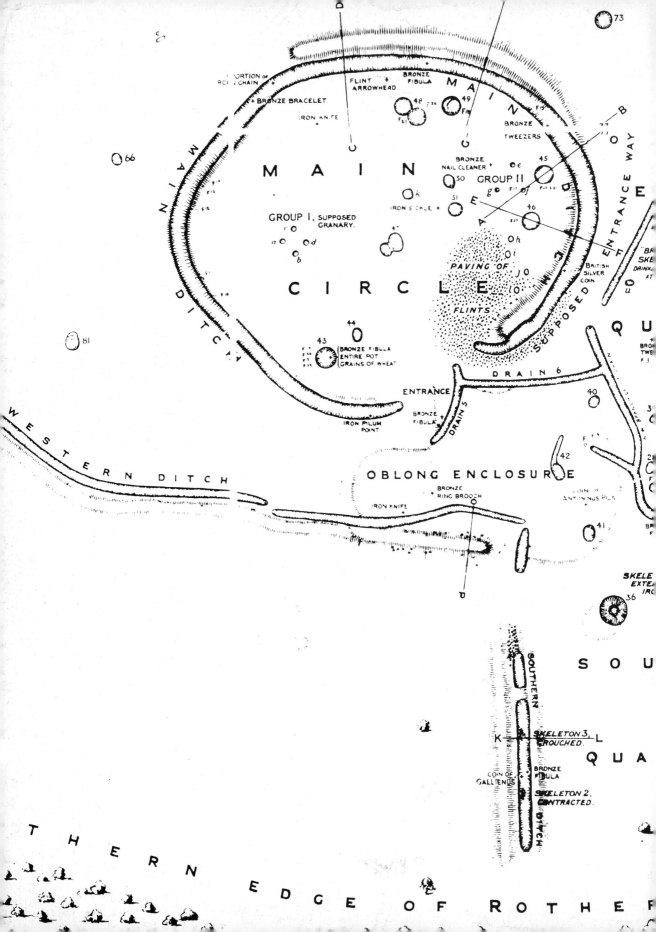

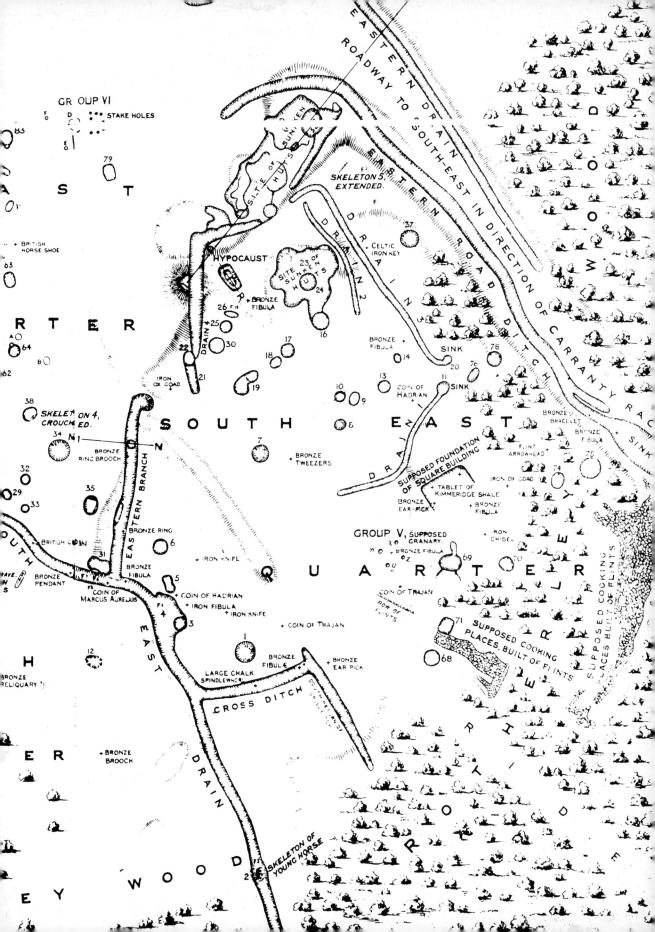

GR OUP VI

F D ⊙ ••• STAKE HOLES
E

EAST

GROUP VI

SITE OF SUNKEN HUTS

SKELETON 5, EXTENDED.

+ BRITISH HORSE SHOE

HYPOCAUST

SITE 23 OF SUNKEN HUTS 24

+ CELTIC IRON KEY

37

+ BRONZE FIBULA

26 FIB

+ 25

30

18 17

22

IRON OX GOAD

21

19

BRONZE FIBULA

SINK

78

14

20

QU A RTER

64

62

SOUTH EAST

10

9

13

8

7

COIN OF HADRIAN

11 SINK

+ BRONZE TWEEZERS

SKELETON 4, CROUCHED.

38

34 NI

N

BRONZE RING BROOCH

SUPPOSED FOUNDATION OF SQUARE BUILDING

BRONZE BRACELET

BRONZE FIBULA

FLINT ARROWHEAD

74

75

+ IRON OX GOAD

TABLET OF KIMMERIDGE SHALE

BRONZE EAR-PICK

+ BRONZE FIBULA

+ IRON CHISEL

32

29

33

35

EASTERN BRANCH

BRONZE RING

+ BRITISH COIN

6

+ IRON KNIFE

GROUP V, SUPPOSED GRANARY.

⊙

NO ⊙ + BRONZE FIBULA

OZ

69

70

QUARTER

31

BRONZE FIBULA

RAVE NS

BRONZE PENDANT

COIN OF MARCUS AURELIUS

F

5

+ COIN OF HADRIAN

+ IRON FIBULA

+ IRON KNIFE

+ COIN OF TRAJAN

+ COIN OF TRAJAN

ROW OF FLINTS

3

SOUTH

H

12

BRONZE RELIQUARY ?)

1

LARGE CHALK SPINDLEWHORL

BRONZE FIBULA

+ BRONZE EAR PICK

71 SUPPOSED COOKING PLACES, BUILT OF FLINTS

68

SUPPOSED COOKING PLACES, BUILT OF FLINTS

CROSS DITCH

ER

+ BRONZE BROOCH

DRAIN

EY WOOD

SKELETON OF YOUNG HORSE

RIDE ROW

Techniques of ARCHAEOLOGICAL EXCAVATION

Philip Barker

Second Edition, revised and expanded

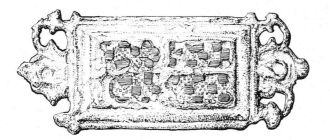

Universe Books New York

Acknowledgments

First I must acknowledge the help and advice of my colleagues Peter Addyman, Ken Barton, Martin Biddle, Peter Fowler, Brian Hope-Taylor, John Hurst, Philip Rahtz, Axel Steensberg and Graham Webster. From them, either by example or argument, I learned how to excavate.

I must also gratefully acknowledge the help, encouragement and advice I have received from the Directorate of Ancient Monuments through its Inspectors, and from the Department of Extra-Mural Studies, The University of Birmingham, through its Director Allen Parker.

My thanks are also due to all those who have assisted, in whatever capacity, on excavations which I have directed, and particularly Bob Higham, Charles Hill and Peter Barker at Hen Domen, and Kate Pretty and Clive Partridge at Wroxeter, from all of whom I have learnt much.

Thanks are due also to the following colleagues and institutions for permission to reproduce illustrations: Det Kongelige Danske Videnskabernes Selskab for figs. 1 and 2; Professor Axel Steensberg, fig. 3; The Society of Antiquaries of London, figs. 4 and 5; Philip Rahtz, figs. 15, 16, 37 and 75; Christine Mahaney, fig. 17; William Britnell, fig. 19; Sue Hirst, figs. 44 and 45; Grahame Guilbert, fig. 38; John Hurst, fig. 39; Brian Hobley, Tevor Hurst, and the Department of Urban Archaeology, Museum of London, figs. 41, 46, 54, 55, 56 and 72; Professor Dr W.A. van Es, figs. 42, 43 and 74 and back endpapers; Richard Bradley, figs. 58 and 59; Edward Harris, figs. 67 and 68; The Ashmolean Museum, Oxford, fig. 69; Peter White and Richard Lee, fig. 73; Dr John Kent, fig. 79; Peter Addyman and the York Archaeological Trust, figs. 80 and 81; Peter Reynolds, figs. 85 and 86.

In addition, I am most grateful to Edward Harris for permission to quote him in the section on the use of a feature matrix; to Professor R.J.C. Atkinson for permission to quote *in extenso* from his article 'Worms and Weathering'; to Sue Hirst for permission to paraphrase parts of her pamphlet *Recording on Excavations: I The Written Evidence*; to John Greenwood for the section on the immediate treatment of coins; to Grahame Guilbert for Appendix A and to Sidney Renow for appendix B; and to J.W.W. Morgan for permission to quote from his article on the rate of decay of posts.

Martin Biddle, Philip Rahtz and Graham Webster read much of the typescript and made many helpful suggestions, most of which I gratefully incorporated.

My thanks are due particularly to Graham Webster, who initiated the book, to Diana Webster, who read the script and improved the English, to Robert Boyle, Jeremy Barker, and Ros Styles, who drew the bulk of the illustrations, and to Jane Field who typed the evolving manuscript many times.

Finally, my thanks are due to my wife for her continual encouragement.

Frontispiece Work in progress on the site of the Baths Basilica, Wroxeter, in 1976. The post-hole building in the foreground overlies the mosaics of the north aisle of the basilica (Photo Sidney Renow)

Title-page decoration A military belt ornament from Wroxeter (Drawn by Rachel Askew)

Published in the United States of America in 1983 by Universe Books
381 Park Avenue South, New York, N.Y. 10016

© 1977, 1982 by Philip Barker

ISBN 0-87663-414-5 (cloth)
ISBN 0-87663-587-7 (paper)

83 84 85 86/10 9 8 7 6 5 4 3 2 1

Printed in Great Britain

Contents

Acknowledgments 6

Prefaces 8

1 Introduction: the Unrepeatable
 Experiment 11

2 The Development of Excavation
 Techniques 13

3 Fieldwork 26
 The site's setting 26
 Aerial photography 33
 Geophysical prospecting 34
 Fieldwalking and soil-sampling 35
 Previous work on the site 35

4 Problems and Strategies 37
 Sample trenching and gridding 44
 Choice of site and methods 54
 Excavation of timber and
  stone buildings 58

5 The Processes of Excavation 68
 Tools 69
 Sections 81
 Special problems 91
 Site organization 104

6 The Soil 116
 Worms and weathering 121

7 Rescue and Salvage Excavation 126
 Rescue excavation of crop-
  mark sites 131
 Salvage excavation and
  recording 136

8 Analysis, Recognising and
 Recording the Evidence 143
 Data retrieval 146
 The site grid 150
 Site planning 150
 Photography 158

9 The Recording of Pottery and
 Small Finds 173
 Uses and limitations of
  pottery as evidence 175
 Residual pottery 181

Recording of pottery and
 animal bones 182
Recording of small finds 185
Value of coins as
 archaeological evidence 188

10 The Interpretation of the Evidence 192
 Dating 197
 Limitations of archaeological
  evidence 203
 Importance of negative
  evidence 204
 Alternative explanations of
  excavated phenomena 205

11 Scientific Aids 207
 Use of scientific evidence 210
 Excavation and environment 212
 Study of building materials 215

12 Synthesis: the History of the Site 216
 Archaeological evidence and
  historical documents 218
 A model interpretation 219
 Covergence of varying kinds
  of evidence 220
 All excavations are local
  history 222
 Works of art as
  archaeological evidence 223

13 Publication — an Obligation 226
 What to publish, and where? 227
 The lay-out of the report 232
 The illustrations 233
 The text 247
 Interim reports 248
 Data storage as an alternative 250
 Pottery and small finds
  publication 251

14 The Theoretical Reconstruction of
 Buildings 254

Appendix: Treasure Hunting and
 Metal Detectors 268
Glossary 270
Bibliography 272
Index 281

Preface to the First Edition

A number of good introductory books on the practicalities of excavation have been published in Britain since the war. Earliest of these was R.J.C. Atkinson's *Field Archaeology*, 1948, 2nd., edition 1953, for long the standard primer. Sir Mortimer Wheeler's *Archaeology from the Earth*, 1954, while not setting out to be a handbook, contains much sound advice. Graham Webster's *Practical Archaeology* followed in 1963 (2nd., revised edition 1970) and in its turn became the standard textbook. (Dame) Kathleen Kenyon's *Beginning in Archaeology*, 1964, is a useful guide to those wishing to take up the discipline, though job opportunities have changed a good deal in the last twenty years. John Alexander's *The Directing of Archaeological Excavations*, 1970, takes a world view and a specifically problem-oriented stand. John Coles' *Field Archaeology in Britain*, 1972, is principally confined to prehistoric archaeology, but contains much that is relevant to all periods of excavation. David Browne's *Teach Yourself Archaeology*, 1975, is the most recent handbook and contains the fruits of the author's acquaintance with the 'New Archaeology'. In America, Heizer and Graham published *A Guide to Field Methods in Archaeology*, 1967, which, though somewhat old-fashioned, has sections which are relevant to European archaeology.

This book does not seek to repeat the advice and information given in these earlier publications and it is assumed that the reader will become acquainted with them. Today, no one book can embrace all the complexities of even a short excavation, and the would-be director or supervisor needs a small shelf-full of reference works. The most essential of these are noted throughout the text and in the bibliography.

The simpler pieces of advice given here may seem too obvious to be worth repeating. However, I believe that many excavators get into difficulties because they ignore some of the basic precepts, such as keeping excavated surfaces meticulously clean, or measuring always in the horizontal plane. Other practical hints are included because they help the excavation to run faster, or more smoothly and economically and thus increase its effectiveness in time and labour.

Inevitably, the book has a somewhat autobiographical air, since I believe that it is more valuable to speak from first-hand experience when this is relevant than to try to preserve a colourless neutrality. I hope that readers will forgive the repetition of examples from sites which I have either dug or with which I have been involved.

Preface to the Second Edition

In the five years since the first edition of this book was written field archaeology in Britain has changed perceptibly. Excavation has become concentrated more and more in the major units, both urban and regional, and it is from these that the principle advances in techniques have stemmed. The recent reductions, in real terms, of government and local authority finance have led to fewer excavations (often, however, on a larger scale) rather than a multiplicity of small ones. This lack of resources has led, beneficially, to a sharpening of the arguments for and against excavation, to the discussion of sampling strategies and to closer long-term co-operation between archaeologists and planning departments, in order that the most effective use shall be made of what money there is.

At the same time, the number of excavations directed by amateurs has declined, due principally to their recognition of the expense and complexity of effective excavation even on a small scale, and the inadequacy of excavation not backed up by laboratory facilities, the proper conservation and storage of finds, and the funds (and time) necessary for post-excavation analysis and publication. Increased professionalism results in higher standards of excavation, analysis and synthesis, but runs the risk that field archaeology, and particularly excavation, will become more and more remote from the experience of the interested layman (as it is already in most European countries). Happily, many amateurs are willing to work under professional direction, and particularly to carry out or take part in field surveys, so that the link between the highly specialised major excavation and the historic base of British archaeology, the dedicated amateur, is still maintained.

A recent book central to the subject of excavation recording is Edward Harris' *Principles of Archaeological Stratigraphy*, 1979, while there is a number of important papers, among them, J.S. Jeffries, *Excavation Records, Techniques in use by the Central Excavation Unit*, 1977; *The Scientific Treatment of Material from Rescue Excavations*, D.O.E., 1978; P.J. Fasham, *et al., Fieldwalking for Archaeologists*, 1980, and the essays in the section 'Strategies for sampling Infra-Site Variability' in J.F. Cherry *et al.* (ed.), *Sampling in Contemporary British Archaeology*, 1978.

The most important statement on excavation techniques made since the publication of the first edition of this book will be found in Chapter 2 of Brian Hope-Taylor's *Yeavering*, HMSO, 1977, pp. 31-45. If this report had not been delayed, but had been published ten years earlier, the art of excavation would have been immeasurably advanced and the present book scarcely needed.

This second edition has benefitted from discussions of the first with many friends and colleagues. I am grateful to them all.

Worcester 1982

1

Introduction: the Unrepeatable Experiment

Excavation recovers from the earth archaeological evidence obtainable in no other way. The soil is an historical document which, like a written record, must be deciphered, translated, and interpreted before it can be used. For the very long prehistoric periods of man's history excavation is almost the only source of information and for the protohistoric and historic periods it provides evidence where the documents are silent or missing. The more we can refine our methods and techniques the more valid will be the interpretations which we derive from our results.

This book does not pretend to be the *Compleat Excavator*. It does not describe the way to dig every variety of site on every kind of sub-soil. But it is written as the result of hard thinking, in the field and at the drawing-board, about the inadequacies of our excavation techniques and the possible ways in which we might refine them. However, each refinement will produce more complicated evidence, which, in its turn, will bring greater difficulties of observation and recording, more data to be sorted, more intricacies to be interpreted and more detailed plans and sections to be published. Yet, however complex and detailed excavations may become, we must always keep the wholeness of archaeology in mind. Excavation is only a method of producing evidence about the past, a means to an end, akin to surgery in that it is drastic, unlike surgery in that it is always destructive.

The whole of our landscape, rural and urban, is a vast historical document. On its surface has accumulated a continuous accretion of hundreds of thousands of small acts of change, both natural and human. The purpose of excavation is to sample the sequence and effect of these surface changes at a chosen point. Such samples will, inevitably, always be very small since even the largest excavation covers only a tiny fraction of the landscape it studies. The point chosen will ideally be one which promises to give the maximum information about the things in which we are interested: periods of occupation, types of structure, burial practices, a social unit, past environments or, happily, all of these and more on one site.

Every archaeological site is itself a document. It can be read by a skilled excavator, but it is destroyed by the very process which enables us to read it. Unlike the study of an ancient document, the study of a site by excavation is an unrepeatable experiment. In almost every other scientific discipline, with the exception of the study of the human individual and other animals, it is possible to test the validity of an experiment by setting up an identical experiment and noting the results. Since no two archaeological sites are the same, either in the whole or in detail, it is never possible to verify conclusively the results of one excavation by another, even on part of the same site, except in the broadest terms, and sometimes not even in these.

In the case of an urban excavation it may be feasible to confirm a defensive sequence or the broad stratigraphy revealed on one site, by excavation on another nearby, as equally it may be possible, on a site in which a sequence of stone buildings has been preserved after excavation, to re-examine the evidence as one would a written document. But generally, excavation is destruction, and often total destruction.

Our responsibility therefore is very great. If we misread our documents as we destroy them, the primary evidence we offer to those interested in the past will be wrong, and those following us will be misled and will have no way of knowing it.

The excavator's task is to produce new evidence that is as free as possible from subjective distortions and to make it quickly and widely available to other specialists in a form which they can use with confidence in their own research. This, however, is not enough. There is an increasing number of people who take a highly intelligent interest in the past. To these, the results of excavations, and the integration of these results into local, national and continental history must be presented in different, but equally valid, forms, such as museum displays, synoptic books, lectures, television and radio programmes.

The evidence uncovered by an excavation and the reasoned deductions which can be drawn from it, using all the parallel evidence from other sources, documentary, linguistic, scientific, epigraphic or whatever, enable us by acts of sober imagination to recover fragmentary glimpses of the past, like clips from an old silent film, badly projected.

Slowly we are building up a fuller and more accurate edition of the film. It will never be complete, and like any film will always be subject to the distortions of cutting and editing, and the viewpoint not only of the director but of the audience.

Our task is to minimise the distortions, to bring into focus the unclear images and to discern the converging patterns which over the last fifty millennia have brought us to the point where I write, and you read, this book.

2

The Development of Excavation Techniques

The growth of archaeology, and with it the techniques of excavation, have been outlined, with many contemporary quotations and a bibliography, by Professor Glyn Daniel (1950 and 1967) and its more recent aberrations castigated by Sir Mortimer Wheeler (1954). Our modern techniques stem from the fifteen years between 1881 and 1896 during which Lieut.- General Pitt Rivers carried out a series of masterly excavations on Cranborne Chase (Pitt Rivers, 1887–98) where he had inherited estates, and was therefore able to work with unhurried care, with adequate finances and labour, but, above all, to publish with a lavishness which we can now rarely hope to emulate. As he tells us (Vol. 1, 1887, xix), his first lessons as an excavator were derived from Canon Greenwell, the opener of Yorkshire barrows, but he far transcended his tutor, and dug with a breadth of vision and a grasp of detail which were quite unprecedented. It was this meticulous attention to detail that was, and is, important, together with his realisation that all the observed evidence should be recorded, even if its meaning is not understood at the time. Two short quotations will put his point of view:

> Excavators, as a rule, record only those things which appear to them important at the time, but fresh problems in Archaeology and Anthropology are constantly arising, and it can hardly fail to escape the notice of anthropologists . . . that on turning back to old accounts in search of evidence, the points which would have been most valuable have been passed over from being thought uninteresting at the time. Every detail should, therefore, be recorded in the manner most conducive to facility of reference, and it ought at all times to be the chief object of an excavator to reduce his own personal equation to a minimum. (Pitt Rivers, vol I, 1887, xvii)

I have endeavoured to keep up in the present volume the minute attention to detail with which the excavation commenced. Much of what is recorded may never prove of further use, but even in the case of such matter, superfluous precision may be regarded as a fault on the right side where the arrangement is such as to facilitate reference and enable a selection to be made. A good deal of the rash and hasty generalization of our time arises from the unreliability of the evidence on which it is based. It is next to impossible to give a continuous narrative of an archaeological investigation that is entirely free from bias; undue stress will be laid upon facts that seem to have an important bearing upon theories current at the time, whilst others that might come to be considered of greater value afterwards are put in the background or not recorded, and posterity is endowed with a legacy of error that can never be rectified. But when fulness and accuracy are made the chief subject of study, this evil is in a great measure avoided . . . (Pitt Rivers, preface to Vol II, 1888)

As a result of his 'fulness and accuracy', the General's excavations can be reinterpreted in the light of our much more extensive background knowledge (eg. Hawkes, 1948). Similarly, a large-scale excavation of his assistant's, Harold St George Gray, has recently been fully published for the first time by Richard Bradley (Bradley, 1976). This was only possible because Gray kept detailed records in the manner of Pitt Rivers. The General also realised that area excavation was the only way to understand the structures and sequences of settlement sites (see front endpapers). His chief weakness was his summary treatment of layers above the natural chalk. They tended to be ignored except in ramparts, ditches and pits, so that only major features cut into the subsoil were seen and recorded. It may be a platitude to say that the General was in advance of his time, but it is true that the lessons implicit in his work were not fully appreciated for many years. Even Flinders Petrie, writing in *Methods and Aims in Archaeology*, published in 1904 (quoted in Daniel, 1967, 233-6), betrays a complete lack of understanding of Pitt Rivers' example. And Sir Leonard Woolley modestly describes his first experience of digging when, in 1907, the great Haverfield agreed to supervise an excavation at Corbridge on behalf of the authors of the *Northumberland County History*. It was considered that 'a small-scale dig' would 'settle the character of the site' and Woolley, with an assistant, some volunteers and labourers, taught himself by trial and error. '. . . we were all', he says, 'happily unconscious of our low performance, nor did anyone from outside suggest that it might have been better . . . .' British field archaeology was at a low ebb. (ibid, 246)

In the years leading up to the first world war Harold St George Gray modelled his own excavations on the General's. In fact, as Richard Bradley says, 'His actual digging was cleaner and more orderly than his mentor's, and some of his photographs must rank among the best of all time' (Bradley, 1976). But the publication of Maumbury Rings has had to wait until 1976, and, as a result, Gray's work did not have the influence on British excavation techniques that it deserved.

Since the late nineteenth century there have been significant shifts of emphasis in excavation techniques, first towards horizontal, then to vertical, and now again towards horizontal methods. The earliest excavators of our Roman towns, such as Caerwent, Silchester and Wroxeter, excavated horizontally in large areas, attempting to see the sites as a whole, but failing to observe the subtleties of stratification which are necessary not only for the understanding of the chronology of the site but even for the recognition of more tenuous evidence (e.g. fig. 18). One result was that these sites, among many others, appeared to contain only stone buildings, whereas we now know that almost all have long sequences of timber buildings, some earlier, some contemporary with and some later than the stone buildings. Thus the chronological and structural sequences were distorted by this summary digging, which, though fundamentally the right method, was crudely applied. The plan was dominant. In both the Silchester and the earlier Wroxeter reports for example there are large diagrammatic plans but very few sections (Fox and Hope, 1891; Fox, 1892; Fox and Hope, 1893; Bushe-Fox, 1913, 1914, 1916).

In Britain, reaction came in the 1930s, mainly under the powerful influence of Sir Mortimer Wheeler, when the section, the grid system and three-dimensional recording became paramount, and as a result the importance of the plan decreased.

Sir Mortimer, like many innovators, transcended the limitations of his innovations. This is perhaps because he worked on the grand scale, and because he was aware of the need to see the evidence horizontally as well as vertically (Wheeler, 1956, 149, 246), so that he usually finished up with a large open area. His followers — that is, nearly all excavators working in Britain between the 1930s and the 1960s — usually worked on a much smaller scale. As a result the *sample* was too small, often no more than one or two trenches or a small grid of boxes, even, on occasions, tiny trenches leap-frogging in a line across large and complex sites.

Sections were now drawn in the greatest detail, whereas plans, even of totally excavated features, were recorded much more summarily, and where structures disappeared under the frequent baulks, they were completed with conjectural dotted lines. The section seemed to offer an economical, swiftly obtained microcosm of the site's development and this led to the trial trenching of hundreds of sites, with the results being used as the basis for generalised statements about the whole site, and often of other, unsampled sites.

These techniques were used particularly on Romano-British sites. Because it is possible to separate the four centuries of Roman rule from the rest of our history there have been, and are, a considerable number of 'Romano-British archaeologists' both professional and amateur, whose interest waxes *c.* AD 43 and wanes *c.* AD 410. Archaeologists in the countries of north-west Europe outside the Roman Empire are fortunate in that they are much freer of these period divisions, so that their archaeology is seen as a continuum to be studied naturally as a whole.

The Roman occupation was a period of building in stone and timber sandwiched between periods of timber building in the prehistoric period and the immediate post-Conquest years and again in the so-called sub-Roman period. Since stone buildings can more easily be dug in trenches and boxes, it can reasonably be argued that the isolation of the Roman period by scholars, coupled with the widespread use of stone buildings in Roman times, led to the general adoption of the grid system, even on sites where it was unsuitable.

Prehistorians were the first to become aware of the limitations of this method (eg. Case, 1952), chiefly because they were more often dealing with structures which simply cannot be understood in trenches or boxes, if they are seen at all.

Pioneer work, notably by Dr van Giffen in Holland (van Giffen, 1958), Professors Gudmund Hatt and Axel Steensberg in Denmark (Hatt, 1957, Steensberg, 1952, 1974) and Professor Gerhard Bersu in Britain (Bersu, 1940, 1949), showed that the only way to elucidate the intricate patterns of the timber buildings found on by far the majority of ancient sites is to combine highly detailed observation of the layers in plan with a study of their composition in depth; a fully three-dimensional approach in which every cubic centimetre of soil is made to yield the maximum information.

Professor Hatt's last excavation, that of the Iron Age village of Nørre Fjand in Jutland, carried out between 1938 and 1940 (Hatt, 1957), was his most highly developed and influential (figs. 1 and 2).

Professor Steensberg has described, in a letter to me, the evolution of Hatt's technique in the 1920s. He writes:

However, Hatt realised — being a geographer — that in the case of indistinct sites it would be necessary to uncover bigger areas in order to follow the edge of the houses. The break came in 1927 when he had to excavate a house site in Tolstrup, Himmerland (south of Ålborg). The local archaeologist, S. Vestergaard Nielsen, who had found the site, could not be present all the time, because he was a school teacher. He told me later on, that the following day he came out to the site and found that Hatt made use of wheelbarrows and uncovered a considerable area before he started the real digging. This amused Vestergaard Nielsen, and he threatened Hatt saying: 'I am going to write a letter to the National Museum's First Department telling C. Neergaard, that you are excavating like a peasant's servant!' The method proved, however, to be very profitable. But as can be seen from Hatt's publications in *Aarboger for nordisk Oldkyndighed*, 1928 and 1930, he still made use of the traditional measuring tapes from two main points A and B. Therefore the features had a rather awkward outline which irritated Hatt. He wished to uncover the features according to their real shape, and what is very important he wished to remove layers just as they had been deposited, not taking away a layer of 5 or 10 cm. everywhere. This must have been due to his geological training. And he did not use sections where it was not necessary, though in his investi-

Pl V (House II and VIII).

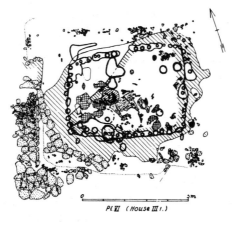

Pl VI (House III 1.)

1 Nørre Fjand: this is the plan of two houses from this Iron Age site in Jutland. Each stone is drawn to scale and the outlines of layers of burnt and unburnt clay show the positions of the clay walls.

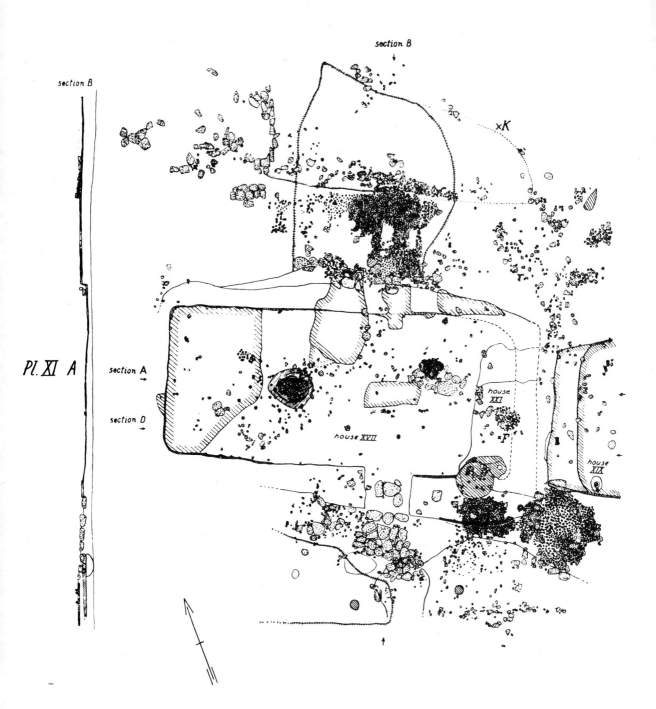

section B

Pl. XI A

section B

×K

section A

section D

house XXI

×Γ

house XVII

house XIX

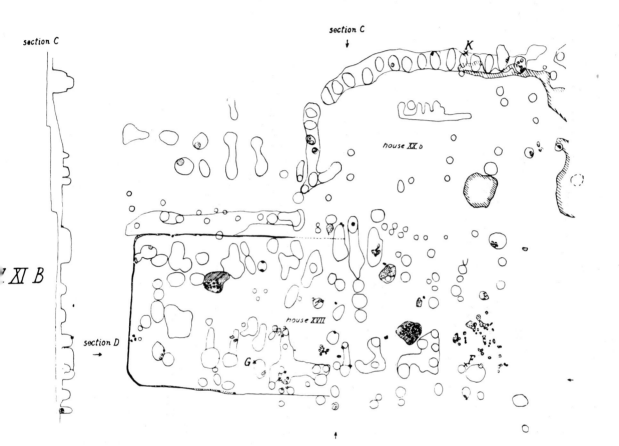

section C

section C

K

XI B

section D

house XX b

house XVII

G

2 Nørre Fjand: this drawing shows the plan of a series of houses, XVII, XXI, XIX, as first discovered, and, right, the pattern of underlying post-holes revealed when the uppermost layers were removed. At this point house XXb was revealed.

gations of pre-historic fields he dug sections through the low division walls and analysed them as other geologists would have done.

Hatt realized that sections cut across the very flimsy and discontinuous floors and superimposed hearths of Iron Age houses would destroy them unseen, so in order to keep vertical records he levelled-in layers, features and finds on the assumption that a notional section could subsequently be drawn across the site wherever required. This method was adopted and refined by Steensberg, who had assisted Hatt at Nørre Fjand, in a series of excavations on farm sites in Denmark (Steensberg, 1952), and reached its fullest development at Store Valby, (Steensberg 1974). Fig. 3 shows the successive buildings of Farm 3 at Store Valby.

The internment of Professor Gerhard Bersu in the Isle of Man during the War was an ill wind which blew good for British archaeology, for while there Bersu dug a number of sites (Bersu, 1949 and 1977). Outstanding among them, technically, was the excavation of a Viking camp at Vowlan (Bersu, 1949) where it is clear from the plan along (fig. 4) that a system of grids with intervening balks would seriously have hampered the understanding of the site (op. cit., 67). Though Bersu's section drawing has sometimes been criticized for its excessive naturalism and over-elaboration, the naturalistic technique of the plan of Vowlan is there most appropriate, showing, as it does, the soil-changes which were the sole evidence for the buildings.

The lessons implicit in excavations such as Vowlan were slow to be understood but are now the basis for the very large investigations of sand and gravel sites which form a great proportion of the rescue excavations in the lowlands of Britain.

Two crucial excavations of this type were carried out by Brian Hope-Taylor from 1953-58 at Yeavering (Hope-Taylor, 1977) and by Philip Rahtz in 1960-62 at Cheddar (Rahtz, 1964, and in press). Both as it happens, were on the sites of Anglo-Saxon palaces. The excavation of Yeavering, though only recently published, has had a profound influence on the standards of excavation in Britain, due to the exceptional acuteness of the observation, the precision of the recording and the beauty of the draughtsmanship, which led to a depth of interpretation beyond the capacity of most previous excavators. Rahtz, working on the grand scale at Cheddar, demonstrated conclusively that very large sites cannot be understood unless they are excavated totally.

There is, of course, a fundamental difference between those excavations in which the sole evidence consists of horizontal changes in the colour and texture of the soil and those where there are superimposed levels, complicated by the presence of vestigial stone walls, pebble surfaces and other fragments of structures. The latter type of site is immeasurably more complicated to dig, especially if the superimposed layers are very thin, and if subsequent structures have removed parts of even these thin layers, their discontinuity making them yet more difficult to trace and interpret.

In England, research in the 1950s on the peasant houses of deserted medieval villages faced just this sort of problem. The excavation of the now classic site of Wharran Percy, begun by Professor Beresford, was continued in 1955 by J. G. Hurst and J. Golson, using techniques derived from those of Steensberg. The account of the development of the excavation (Hurst, 1956, 271-3 and 1979), with its cautious beginnings, using balks which were abandoned when they proved to mask vital evidence, records a turning point in British archaeology. The methods used at Wharram have since been further modified, the levelling in of all finds being discarded in favour of the recording of finds within their layers. This continuous modification of techniques during the course of long-term excavations is one of the principal ways in which the science, or art, of excavation advances. In addition, techniques developed on one type of site have been tested on other sites of quite different character. It is now clear that the methods used at Wharram Percy are equally valid on sites containing major stone buildings and that if such sites, which once might have been thought to contain only the stone buildings, are excavated horizontally and in great detail, the plans of unsuspected timber buildings may well emerge.

During the 1950s and '60s urban excavation was developing in parallel with the rural excavations of prehistoric and medieval sites. Professor Sheppard Frere's excavations at Verulamium in 1955-61 (Frere 1959 and 1971) pointed the way towards Martin Biddle's rapidly expanding excavations at Winchester in the early 1960s. It is very instructive to follow the development of Biddle's techniques through the series of interim reports which began in 1962 and continued until 1975 (Biddle, 1962-1975).

On many sites timber and stone buildings were intermixed or followed one another in varying sequences. It is in those areas and periods in which timber buildings follow stone that the elusive evidence of wooden structures is most vulnerable, either to later disturbance, or to the excavator's desire to get at the underlying stone buildings. How many Roman villas have been dug with the possibility in mind that later occupants of the site might have used the destruction rubble as foundation rafts for timber buildings? Similarly, the final phases of Roman towns and the 'Dark Age' layers of our cities have been neglected in the past partly because they require the uncovering of large areas if they are to be understood, but partly also because they require a different attitude of mind, one that is open to any form of structural evidence which presents itself, and does not look simply for preconceived features, such as walls and post-holes, and ignores the unexpected.

We are only just beginning to realise the potential of excavated evidence, especially the wealth of information which might be revealed by a really detailed analysis of every aspect of the soil removed in the dissection of the structures we are excavating.

Techniques in the past have often been too panoramic, too clumsy to reveal more than the broadest outlines of the more obvious structures. The excavation

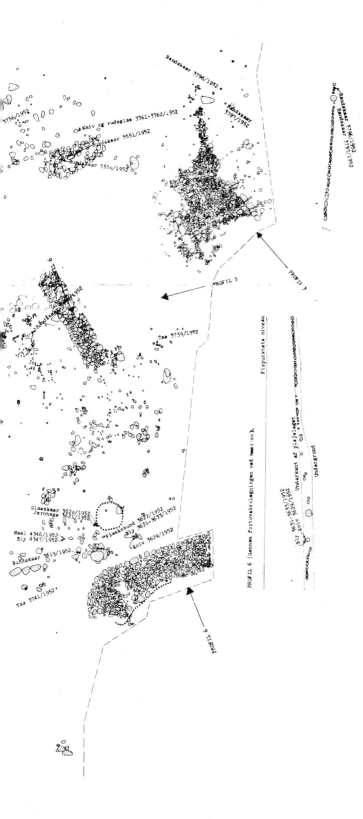

3 Store Valby: part of the highly detailed plan of farms 3 and 4 at the medieval Danish site. The position of each find with its number is included. Schematic sections are printed at the side of the plan.

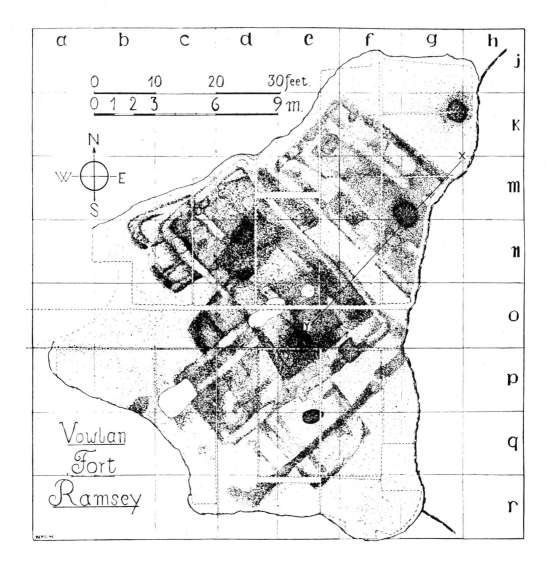

of the Roman town of Silchester is an often-quoted example, where it is suspected that the published plan, showing, as it does, only a scatter of stone buildings in a sort of garden city, may be quite misleading, the gaps being filled by undiscovered timber buildings. This is an old and obvious example; what is much more worrying is that it is at least possible that the majority of all published (or, for that matter, unpublished) excavations may be misleading in that, either by taking too small a sample of the site in boxes or trenches, or by digging too insensitively, especially in the upper levels, whole periods of the site's occupation have been lost, ignored or distorted.

The consequences for the history and prehistory of Britain are far-reaching. If I am right, the syntheses made from these excavation reports and integrated

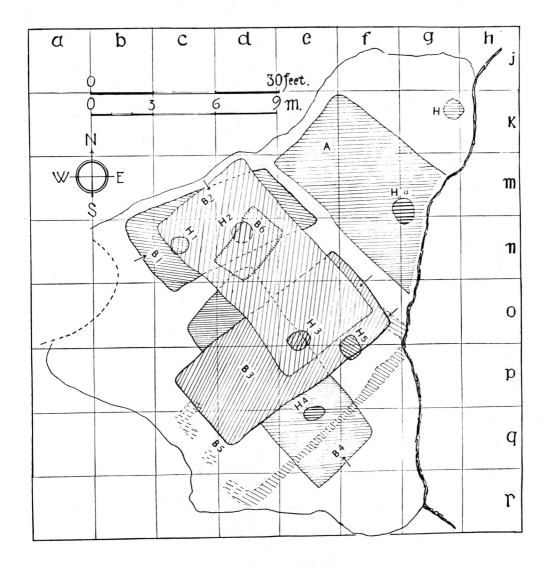

4 *opposite* Vowlan, Isle of Man: excavated area inside the promontory fort at the level of the untouched soil. The drawing indicates, by means of differential shading, the varying colours and shades of the surface of the sand revealed when the turf and topsoil were removed.

5 *above* Vowlan: diagram of houses inside the promontory fort. This drawing is a simplification and interpretation of the plan shown in fig. 4. It is clear from both plans that a system of trenches or grids cut across the site would not have uncovered an understandable pattern. If the reader doubts this, he can play a salutary game by taking a piece of cardboard and cutting in it holes to represent any desired system of trenches or grids (to scale), laying it over the plan, and then attempting an interpretation from the visible areas. A similar game can be played with any of the other area excavations here reproduced e.g. figs 1, 2, 3, 17, 19, 38, 70, 71, 76, 82, 83 and 84.

with other forms of evidence will be falsified because the distortions and missing phases, being unknown, cannot be taken into account.

It is sometimes argued that, if an excavation is published as fully as possible, the evidence should be sufficient for re-interpretation by future workers in the light of their greater background experience. However, if the evidence from the original excavation was mistakenly observed or inadequately recorded in the field, the inadequacies will lie further back than the published drawings and lists of finds, however plausible they may seem; and the more skilful the drawings, the more convincing they will be. There is no absolute safeguard against this since excavation can never be completely objective, but we must be constantly aware that all interpretation is, in a sense, a personal opinion, and be careful, as far as possible, to keep the interpretation separate from the evidence on which it is based. Naturally, the more detail there is in the publication, the more confidence the reader will have that the losses of evidence are minimal; although this in its turn brings further difficulties. In an age of larger and more complex excavations drawings must now be published at a much greater scale if the mass of significant detail is not to be lost, and here the problems of ever-increasing printing costs become a major factor in the adequate publication of excavations (see below p. 222). Yet it may well be that greatly increased attention to detail is the key to all improvements in excavation techniques.

The archaeological dilemma of our age is that just as it is becoming necessary for us to excavate more slowly, and in much greater detail, we are beginning to realise the full extent and speed of destruction of sites and whole settlement areas which is going on around us. How can we justify months spent on the *minutiae* of part of a small site when the hearts of great cities, such as London, Lincoln, York and Gloucester, are being torn out in a matter of weeks and when square miles of prehistoric settlement are being totally removed in a matter of months? There is no single, simple answer, but the dilemma must be faced and a solution attempted.

3

Fieldwork

The site's setting

It is a platitude worth repeating that the landscape is a palimpsest on which all man's activities have left some trace. The earth's surface, particularly in intensively occupied countries such as Britain, is a floor on which men have carved and scratched a mesh of superimposed *graffiti*. The form which these patterns take is not accidental; it is the resultant of converging forces such as the shape of the land surface, the underlying geology, the soil cover, micro-climates, and the evolution of agriculture, as well as the expansion and contraction of settlement and the necessities of defence. Recognition of meaningful sequences among these patterns can be intensely gratifying, so that for some archaeologists fieldwork becomes an end in itself. However, archaeological conclusions based merely on the inspection of earthworks or crop-marks can be very misleading, and in many cases excavation has shown that previous assumptions have been wrong. In addition, sites, when dug, almost always prove to be much more complex than their surface indications suggest.

Excavation must be seen as the culmination of the investigation of a site. We should only resort to surgery after intensive preoperative examination. The process of investigation must be complete — an amalgam of fieldwork (that is, the non-destructive examination of the site and its surroundings), excavation, the study of past work not only on the site but in the region, and, in the case of sites of the historic period, a close and specialised study of the documentary evidence.

The site must be seen in its setting. The geology of the region is literally and metaphorically fundamental. From it the landscape has evolved. It has determined the nature of the soil and thus the nature of the primal vegetation, and ultimately the pattern of agriculture.

It is useless for the field archaeologist to try to work in isolation from the geologist, the geographer, the pedologist, the climatologist or the ecologist. It is, on the other hand, depressing to read settlement studies by geographers or historians which completely fail to take into account the work of archaeologists in the same region. Just as excavation should ideally be the work of a team of specialists, so should the preliminary fieldwork. It is becoming more and more necessary for the field archaeologist to be an *entrepreneur*, an intermediary between a whole range of disciplines which can be brought to bear on the problems posed by archaeological investigation.

Although the complex discipline of fieldwork in archaeology is dealt with at length in a volume in this series (Taylor, 1974), and has an exemplary introduction in Aston and Rowley, 1974, it cannot here be passed over without mention since sites must be dug in their context as part of the landscape, not as isolated detachable phenomena. In addition, the publication of the excavation must include location and area maps, and at least one map which relates the site to its immediate surroundings. This will usually require fieldwork more detailed than that to be found on Ordnance Survey maps, so that the survey becomes the excavator's responsibility.

There is no doubt that some archaeologists have a better 'eye' for the ground than others but fieldwork is an art which can be transmitted by experienced and perceptive teachers, and developed by practice. Often only long acquaintance with a site and the area in which it is set will reveal the subtle indications of former earthworks, roads or buildings. A well-known field, seen daily under all conditions of light and shade, damp and drought, will quite suddenly, on a day of thawing snow, reveal for the first time, and for a few hours only, that it is full of the most ephemeral traces of ridge and furrow. On other occasions a summer of exceptional drought will bring out the parch-marks of a totally unsuspected building.

The slight undulations of ploughed-out or eroded earthworks are concealed by long grass and weeds, so that the winter and early spring are the optimum seasons for field-walking. Even with conditions at their best, with the grass short and with glancing light, one can often only sense very slight earthworks by walking across them in different directions; and when one stands still they seem to vanish. The enhanced three-dimensional sense which movement gives, revealing these subtleties, makes oblique stereo-photography, taken from the optimum angle to the earthworks, the best way of recording them pictorially. Aerial or terrestrial photogrammetry, if the contours are drawn at small enough intervals, would be the most satisfactory way of recording large areas; but for smaller areas ordinary contour surveys, drawn at intervals of 20cm. or less, will not only reveal the earthworks but enable them to be understood in a way impossible on the ground, just as the aerial photograph draws together the visible evidence within the compass of a glance. The aerial photogrammetric surveys carried out in advance of major developments can often be made available to the archaeologist, especially if he is engaged in rescue excavation prior to the develop-

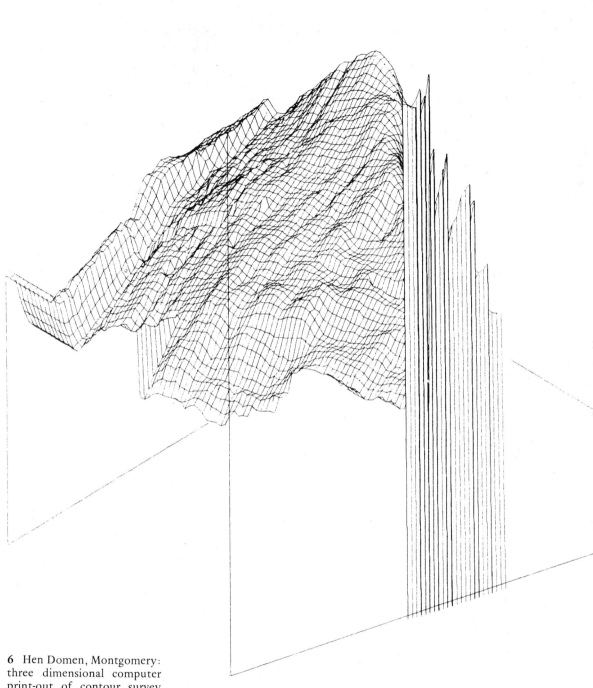

6 Hen Domen, Montgomery: three dimensional computer print-out of contour survey of pre-Norman field system (by Susan Laflin, University of Birmingham). The vertical scale is exaggerated to emphasise the very slight ridges, which were only a few centimetres high.

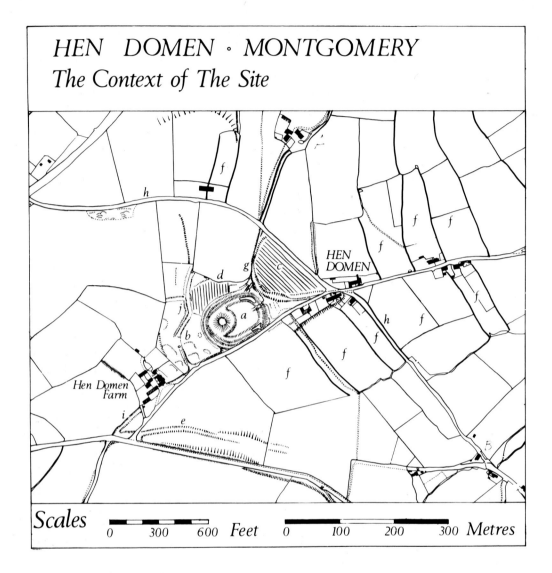

HEN DOMEN · MONTGOMERY
The Context of The Site

HEN DOMEN

Hen Domen Farm

Scales

0 300 600 Feet   0 100 200 300 Metres

7 Hen Domen, Montgomery: the Context of the Site.

Key: a. The Motte and Bailey Castle
b. Earthworks of settlement possibly connected with pre-Norman field system
c. and d. Pre-Norman ridged fields
e. Former road to Montgomery

f. Medieval strips (notice reversed S shape)
g. and j. Pre-Norman hollow ways
h. An early road leading to the ford at Rhydwhyman
i. An earlier alignment of the present lane

ment. Not only is the stereoscopic mosaic of photographs (usually of the highest quality) likely to be full of information but the contoured maps derived from the mosaic will often reveal slight earthworks, such as eroded ridge and furrow, which cannot be seen on the photographs. It is now possible to feed the raw data of a grid of levels into a computer programmed to provide a three-dimensional print-out in which earthworks or other remains are viewed from any desired angle. This has been done for the survey of the pre-Norman ridged field system at Hen Domen, Montgomery (Barker and Lawson, 1971). A grid of levels was taken at 1-metre horizontal intervals over the field, and the resulting contours were interpolated by eye. At the same time a three-dimensional computer plot was made to provide a more objective interpretation (fig. 6).

The more rapid type of survey, based on a series of measurements made at points chosen by the surveyor along the tops of banks or in the bottoms of hollows and then drawn as a series of hachures or 'tadpoles', is more easily 'read'; it is, however, inevitably simplified and runs the risk of being subjective, since some surveyors will have a more acute awareness of the subtleties of earthworks than others. The accuracy of this kind of survey is very considerably reduced by long grass and weeds, but on the other hand it may be the only practicable method in wooded scrub country where the theodolite or the level cannot be used. Aston and Rowley, 1974, fig. 46, p. 156 shows a fine survey of this kind, of the earthworks surrounding the Cistercian Abbey of Bordesley in Redditch, Worcestershire. They show how such a plan can reveal the fact that the earthworks are of many periods. The surveyors have distinguished four phases in the development of the site and the exploitation of the water resources provided by the nearby River Arrow. While this interpretation may be modified by the long-term excavations now being carried out there, it provides a good example of this comparatively rapid method of planning complex earthworks. Clearly surveys of this or any other kind will be more accurate if carefully measured with tape or chain, but if speed is necessary because of the imminent destruction of the site, a paced survey is better than nothing. However, there is no need here to describe surveying methods in detail, since a number of good textbooks are available (e.g. Fryer, 1966 and 1971; Coles, 1972; Taylor, *op. cit.* 1974).

The basis of the site fieldwork will, of course, be the Ordnance Survey maps of the region and the immediate locality. Contemplation of the 2½-inch or 6-inch maps will very often reveal patterns of field boundaries, roads or tracks, which are the fossilised remnants of deserted settlements or superseded field systems. For example, fig. 7, prepared as part of the publication of a long-term excavation, shows the area round the small castle at Hen Domen, Montgomery, Powys. On this old superseded road lines (g, j, e and i) can be seen together with curving field boundaries (f) which are almost certainly the result of enclosing strips in the open fields. This example could be paralleled in differing forms almost anywhere in rural Britain, and often (except where development is total) in urban areas as well — in cities such as Lincoln or Gloucester where the skeletal remains of their Roman ancestry can still be seen, or in Ludlow, where eighteenth-century streets preserve a twelfth-century plan.

The older editions of the Ordnance Survey, beginning with the first edition of 1801-05, are invaluable, and many public libraries have sets of the 1:2500 sheets published in the nineteenth century, which show a great deal of information that has since been lost. The 1:500 sheets of towns are a unique record which is a necessary tool for the urban archaeologist, as are the early town maps of Speed, Roque and others. The splendid collection of the King's maps in the British Museum is also invaluable. The Public Record Office and most libraries and county archive collections have estate maps, terriers and tythe maps which may contain a scrap of information about a long-vanished site, trapped like an insect in amber. Field names from early sources may lead to the discovery of lost sites, or to sites peripheral to the one under excavation. Many collections of documents in libraries and museums include topographical drawings of the sort popular in the eighteenth and nineteenth centuries. These are often the only record of prehistoric monuments, castles, churches and other subjects suitable for the Romantic pencil, showing them in less weathered or damaged condition than they are today.

As more county and regional archaeological units are formed the cumulative storage of all known information about the archaeology of the district concerned is becoming normal practice. Many of these site and monument records are designed to be compatible one with another and the information, stored on cards or tape, with accompanying maps, is readily retrievable, and is normally available to the public for consultation.

Except in the case of the most unexpected emergency excavation, the area in which the site lies should be intensively examined by field-walking and the study of maps and aerial photographs, as well as in discussion with the local farmers and other residents who may remember earthworks now ploughed out, or finds adorning mantelpieces. The results of this examination should, as far as possible, be incorporated into the area map published with the excavation report. More than this, the study of the surrounding landscape inevitably illuminates the excavation and brings greater understanding to the interpretation of the site in its wider sense.

Too many excavators in the past have treated sites almost as though they were portable objects which just happened to be in the field where the excavation was to take place. It is obviously insufficient to dig a deserted medieval village without identifying and examining the field system on which its economy depended; or to dig a Roman fort without attempting to trace the roads which served it, temporary camps which may have preceded it or the civil settlements attached to it which may have continued in existence. Barrows, perhaps more than any other monument, have been dug in isolation, probably because they are small and seem self-contained. Only rarely has the archaeologist widened the excavation to include the surrounding area with its possibly related structures or peripheral burials, or attempted to identify the settlement site from which the buried people came. Happily, one of the benefits of the large-scale destruction caused by mineral extraction and ploughing is that in a few cases whole ancient landscapes are being examined by excavation (e.g. Jones, 1968; Cunliffe, 1973). Much more often, excavation is confined to a single site or even to part of a site. In these cases the results of digging will be stultified if the surrounding landscape is not studied as fully as possible, both by fieldwork and, as described below, by the environmental sciences.

Aerial photography

It is of the greatest value to have access to aerial photographs of a site and its surrounding landscape as a complement to the study of maps and to fieldwalking.

The major collections of archaeological aerial photographs are held by the National Monuments Record and the Committee for Aerial Photography at Cambridge, though large collections are held by some of the major museums and universities, and by a number of private flyers. Not all of these collections are easily available for inspection, even to scholars, and there is no doubt that an immense amount of information, much of it unique and unprecedented, awaits assessment. Unfortunately, one might almost say, disastrously, many of the sites newly revealed from the air will have been destroyed before their existence is known to more than a very few. The problem, which is primarily one of man-power and money in storing, cataloguing and making available the prints, is beyond the scope of this book, but is under active consideration by a Committee of the Council for British Archaeology. The papers read at a symposium entitled 'Aerial Reconnaissance for Archaeology' have been published by the C.B.A. under that title (Wilson, ed., 1975). This volume forms an excellent summary of recent developments, while the realization of the importance of aerial photography has led to the founding, in 1971, of the *Journal of Aerial Photography*.

The Royal Air Force cover is an invaluable source of high-level photographs, though not, of course, taken with archaeology in mind. Sometimes it happens, however, that the circumstances are favourable. For instance, part of the second world war Royal Air Force cover for Shropshire was taken when light snow covered the ground — the conditions could not have been better for the definition of earthworks and the series has produced much new evidence. Many Development Corporations and Road Construction Units have commissioned photo-grammetric surveys made from vertical mosaics of photographs. Both the surveys and the photographs are usually available if an approach is made through the proper channels.

Aerial photographs, vertical, oblique or stereoscopic, may reveal earthwork or crop-mark sites related to the site to be excavated. The site itself, if it has been, or can be, photographed from the air before excavation, may reveal details of earthworks within it not otherwise visible, and there is no need to say that very many archaeological investigations are carried out on sites which would not be known without aerial photography. If aerial photography can be arranged during or immediately after the excavation, the resulting photographs will greatly enhance the published report. By giving a panoramic view, they may also reveal patterns in the excavated surface not readily seen from the ground.

This is not the place to discuss either the techniques of aerial photography or its specialised interpretation. The best introductions to the subject are: J.K.S. St Joseph, *The Uses of Aerial Photography* 1966, and Wilson, *op. cit.*, together with M.W. Beresford and J.K.S. St Joseph *Medieval England, An aerial survey*, 2nd ed., 1979 and J. Bradford, *Ancient Landscapes*, 1957.

Geophysical prospecting

The various forms of geophysical prospecting (for an introduction to geophysical prospecting see Brothwell and Higgs, 1969, Chap. 60 and 61, and see also the volumes of the Journal *Archaeometry*) give, under optimum conditions, a broad picture of the potential of the site before excavation, a picture comparable with that given by crop-mark photographs. Geophysical prospecting shares the limitations of aerial photography in that a negative result does not mean that archaeological features are not present. On the positive side, however, the evidence provided by a magnetometer or resistivity survey may be invaluable in planning the excavation in those cases where the whole site cannot be dug. Where it *is* intended to dig the whole site, geophysical surveys may be of value to the scientists involved in developing the equipment and interpreting its results when, ultimately, the survey is compared with the excavated evidence. Obviously a total excavation should be conducted as methodically as possible, and the temptation to divert the excavation on to some massive magnetic or other anomaly must be avoided, allowing the excavation to reach it in due course. In cases such as this it will be of great interest to see how the excavated results compare with the plot of anomalies. But, in the case of a rescue excavation, which is working against time, or where a site is so large that total excavation cannot be contemplated, geophysical surveys can be of great use in planning the course and size of the excavation. An excellent account of the use of geophysical evidence to determine the areas to be excavated within a large site will be found in Alcock, 1972, 54ff. and the use of a magnetometer to determine the strategy of excavation of a small site in Barker, 1966.

Geophysical prospecting will always be more useful on sites without deep stratification, since on stratified sites not only may deep structures escape detection, but with a whole sequence of structures and occupation levels lying one below another, the geophysical record will inevitably be confused. Nevertheless, even under these circumstances, over a large site the general areas of occupation may be very clearly defined, even if the details are not clear (Alcock, 1972, figs. 6 and 8).

The apparatus used in both resistivity and magnetic prospecting is continually being modified and techniques refined. An account of recent developments will be found in Vol. II of the *Journal of Archaeological Science*. Experiments are at present being carried on applications of radar and sonar scanning which may be able to scan to successive depths (at, say, 10 cm. intervals) in the hope of detecting major stratigraphic changes.

Many small groups have constructed their own resistivity meters, which often give remarkably accurate results, and the Department of Physics at Bradford University has developed and marketed the Bradphys, which is a compact resistivity machine costing £595 plus VAT (in 1980). Some C.B.A. groups and other confederations of societies own a magnetometer which enables individuals or groups to carry out independent surveys while the Department of the Environment Laboratory has a geophysics section which carries out major surveys on threatened sites in advance of their excavation. Magnetic scanning with a fluxgate gradiometer has proved the most successful in surveying large areas in a comparatively short time, and is undoubtedly the most useful technique for rescue work.

Field-walking and soil sampling

A good deal of thought has been given recently to the problems of field-walking, to evolving methods which will minimize the effects of the weather, the light and the varied abilities of the walkers on the recovery of finds. A most useful booklet, Fasham *et al.*, *Fieldwalking for Archaeologists* (1980) has been published by the Hampshire Field Club and Archaeological Society, while the Department of the Environment has published a series of papers arising from a seminar held in 1976, under the title of *Fieldwalking as a method of Archaeological Research*, Occasional Paper No. 2, 1980.

Both of these publications describe and assess the various methods of field-walking, though detailed guidelines for standardized methods have not yet been agreed, the variables being so numerous and difficult to assess. In spite of this, field-walking is an essential supplement to all the other methods of site discovery and assessment.

If the site or sites to be excavated are under the plough intensive field-walking for pottery, tile or burnt daub scatters may limit the likely occupation areas, particularly if these coincide with areas of darker soil or burning.

Field walking in times of drought will often discover areas of parching, revealing former roads or stone buildings, sometimes in great detail, or, alternatively, the darker green lines of ditches, pits and wells can be seen as distinctly from the ground as from the air. For example, the ripe corn over the Roman fort at Duncot in Shropshire grows three to four inches higher over the silted-up ditches than it does elsewhere, an effect which can be clearly seen from ground level, and enables the site to be plotted with great accuracy.

Farmers often know a good deal about earthworks and cropmarks on their land, and will equally often be interested to hear archaeological explanations for them. Conversely, they may explain the real origins of earthworks which wishful-thinking archaeologists might otherwise make into ancient sites. I was once saved by a farmer from considerable embarrassment when showing two eminent field-workers round the site of a deserted medieval village. A splendid platform close to the farm house promised to be the site of one of the major buildings of the abandoned settlement until the farmer told me, *sotto voce,* that it was the plat-form for a long-disused tennis court, levelled-up by terracing.

A grid of soil samples tested for phosphates may also delimit occupation areas, though this method has had only variable success, probably because it is dependent on a number of other factors apart from ancient occupation, factors such as intensive fertilising which may obscure or eliminate the detectable chemi-cal differences.

Previous work on the site

It is essential, before beginning the excavation, to discover if possible, the extent and nature of any previous work on the site. Search should be made in national and local journals, in the records of local museums (where chance finds from the site may also be encountered), in bibliographies both general and specialist (see Grinsell, Rahtz and Price Williams, 1974, 31 for a list) and the topographical and subject card catalogues of the Society of Antiquaries of London.

Too often, however, earlier work is not recorded at all, or, if it is, the location of the trenches is not illustrated, and the excavator has to discover the earlier trenches during the course of the excavation, and treat them simply as recent features. It should be observed that many earlier excavators did not take their trenches down to the undisturbed subsoil but stopped when they reached floors or similar levels. It should not, therefore be assumed that a pattern of early trenches or areas has necessarily been totally destructive.

The positions of earlier excavations should be shown on the general plan of the excavation included in the final report. In addition, finds from earlier work may still be available in museums, or in private possession, for illustration in the report, when they can be integrated with more recent material.

4

Problems and Strategies

There is a continuing debate on the strategies to be adopted when designing an excavation. Some archaeologists, using the parallel of scientific experiments set up to prove hypotheses, would advocate specifically problem-orientated excavations designed to throw light mainly, or sometimes only, on the questions which are uppermost in their minds at the time. The danger of this procedure is that, by investigating one period or aspect of a site single-mindedly, other periods or aspects will be ignored, or given scant treatment, and any remains belonging to them may well be destroyed in the course of the excavation. The grossest examples of this approach were the unconsidered bulldozing or summary digging of the medieval and post-medieval levels of towns in order to get at the underlying Roman levels.

Apart from the problems of the size of the excavated samples of a site, discussed below, p. 54, archaeological excavation differs from other scientific research in that postulated theories cannot be proved by the setting up of duplicate experiments. Each part of every site is unique, so that the results obtained on one part of a site cannot, except in the broadest sense, be demonstrated to be correct by reference to work on another part of the same, let alone a different, site. Moreover, archaeological experiments cannot be set up to investigate isolated problems, since every site is not only unique but complicated and above all unpredictable. An excavation designed to answer a specific question will almost certainly run into completely unexpected evidence, in all probability tangential to, or even entirely unconnected with, the problem to be solved, evidence which is likely to raise more questions than it answers and which should certainly not be ignored.

It may be useful to cite some examples of mistakenly conceived problem-orientated digs. A long trench was dug, under my direction, across the ditch and part of the inner bailey of a castle in Shropshire not otherwise threatened (Barker, 1961). This excavation was specifically planned to recover a pottery sequence dating from between 1115-1225, dates suggested by the documentary evidence.

It not only produced a plausible and entirely misleading pottery sequence (Barker, 1961, 76, 77) but, though care was taken to do as little damage as possible, the trench destroyed parts of timber and stone buildings of the inner bailey without producing enough evidence to understand them. When eventually the castle is properly excavated the missing evidence may prove to have been vital, and I shall rightly be castigated.

I also directed a limited excavation on the castle mound at Hastings (Barker and Barton). The work was initiated principally to prove whether or not the mound was that built by William I and which appears in a famous scene on the Bayeux Tapestry. The excavation showed, among other things, that the primary mound was probably of near-Conquest date (it contained a large unabraded sherd of c. 1050-1100, which strictly only gives a *terminus post quem* of that date), but it is now clear that it is impossible to prove by excavation that this is the mound depicted in the Tapestry. Even if coins of William I were found in the mound, or its make-up proved to be banded like that shown on the Tapestry, it could still be the castle said to have been built at Hastings by the Count of Eu a year or so after the Conquest. It is extremely improbable that any dating methods capable of a precision of ± one year will be evolved, methods moreover which would date the construction of a mound and not simply the objects or other material found in it. There is some reason to believe that William's castle was sited on the beach to protect his ships, in which case the present mound on the cliff-top cannot be the one shown on the Tapestry. But there is now no way of establishing this, especially as the coastline on which William landed has long been eroded away. In retrospect this was a piece of problem-orientated excavation, which, although producing interesting results, did not, and I believe could not, have satisfactorily answered the question posed.

Trenching the ramparts and ditches of a series of individual classes of earth-works, such as Roman forts or medieval moats, in order to obtain a sequence of dated periods of occupation, will almost certainly fail to produce reliable informa-tion, either because the whole sequence is not present at the point or points chosen, or, if it is, it cannot be shown to be so without very much more extensive excavation. Such trenches are also notoriously liable to destroy other unsought-for and unexpected evidence.

A dig which aims to shed light on a particular problem or period in a town's history is also liable to run into similar difficulties since towns are probably the most complicated and unpredictable of all archaeological sites. A long-buried castle ditch, of great interest to the student of the Norman period, may be over-lain by a series of seventeenth-century industrial buildings, unique in the region and of great importance to the industrial archaeologist. The Roman and medieval town nuclei may sandwich between them the much more elusive evidence of the immediate post-Roman centuries. In the past, holes carefully sited to determine the extent of the forum or the *principia* or other monuments of Roman town or forts have been dug oblivious of a host of overlying problems.

What questions can be asked about a deserted medieval village which do not require virtually the total excavation of the village? Sampling trenches will certainly not give answers relevant to dates or structures except in a purely general sense. Such trenches may show that occupation extended beyond the period suggested by the documentary evidence, or that the village overlay an earlier sequence of settlements, that the houses were of wood, or clay or stone; but the price paid for this information may be the mutilation of the site to the extent that the structures trenched may never be subsequently understood. Even the total excavation of one or two house sites will only give answers which relate to those houses, which may be, for some reason, anomalies in the village, either in date or function, and cannot, in any case, be *proved* to be typical without further excavation. For example, at Abdon in Shropshire, R.T. Rowley excavated two house sites at opposite ends of the complex of earthworks which filled the large field in which stood an isolated church. One house proved to date from the thirteenth century, the other from the late eighteenth. Without extensive excavation it would be hazardous to assign a date to any of the other houses which may be there (personal communication).

Such examples could be multiplied tenfold. What questions therefore should we ask of our sites and what sampling units might be considered valid? No-one, presumably, plans an excavation without some inkling of what he is likely to find and some reason for digging this, rather than another site. Even under emergency conditions, or perhaps especially under emergency conditions, excavation is selective, dependent on the predicted richness of the site in structural or material evidence, or its importance in the area, or its rarity, its availability, its degree of preservation or the particular interests of the excavator or a controlling academic committee. In the absence, as yet, of any planned and coordinated strategy of investigation of our sites on a national scale all these factors may, or may not, be considered before digging, but usually some of them are.

M.O. Carver has admirably expounded the problem and suggested solutions in 'Sampling Towns, an optimistic strategy' in Clack and Haselgrove, 1981. He argues that one should concentrate on those areas of a town where the archaeological deposits are deeper, or more intact, and preferably waterlogged, especially if these coincide with good documentary and architectural evidence. Thus, the effectiveness of the excavation will be at its maximum at these points. This strategy is in contrast to that which advocates either digging wherever opportunity occurs within a town, or digging only in those places where one expects to solve specific, often isolated, problems.

Such an approach, can, of course, be extended into the countryside. If it is, it follows that untouched earthworks will take precedence over crop-mark sites, that, by definition, have been damaged by the plough, which, in many cases, will have churned up or removed all the superficial layers. Again, Hen Domen, Montgomery illustrates this point. One nine-inch ploughing of that site would have destroyed the last two periods of occupation, leaving only the deeper, post-hole structures (which may well have appeared as marks in a subsequent crop). Clearly, therefore, if there is a choice between a ploughed and an unploughed site of the same type, excavation of the second will be likely to be more productive. It follows that, in general, intact earthworks deserve more protection than crop-mark sites, as they are likely to embody more (and more reliable) evidence.

Any excavation strategy should therefore include intensive site evaluation by all the non-destructive methods available. The decision to excavate one rather than another site can then be made on more strictly archaeological grounds than has often been the case in the past. Such site evaluation may, of course, result in the site's preservation rather than its excavation, since the best and richest of our sites (in terms of surviving evidence) should be protected from destruction by excavation and should be conserved as part of a rapidly diminishing resource.

Nevertheless, we seem to be moving towards a more coherent research/rescue policy, in which non-archaeological factors, such as individual interests, local availability of funds or manpower, as well as the patterns of destruction are minimized. The question has recently been discussed in relation to the Anglo-Saxon period (Wade, 1974) where, after the very great practical difficulties of statistically random sampling of sites are acknowledged, cogent arguments are put forward for a mixed strategy of large-scale excavations together with small-scale sampling based on extensive fieldwork. It is an open question whether fieldwork on the scale needed, particularly the assessment of the vast back-log of aerial photographs, can be made before a large proportion of the sites here have disappeared or been deeply damaged. It is also open to question whether one should pursue the study of settlements of a particular period, since unless they happen to be founded on virgin territory, and to have had no successors, other periods of occupation will be drawn into the enquiry, and may receive less than their due from the single-minded worker. So we are brought back to the relationships of sites to their setting and the concept of landscape archaeology, in which it is the landscape which is sample, rather than a series of sites; Wade's discussion of sampling criteria and strategies is therefore as applicable to the landscape as to Anglo-Saxon settlement research (*ibid.* p. 88).

There are two levels of sampling: since all known or suspected sites cannot be sampled, some must be selected for large-scale work, some for small-scale sampling, and others either left to be eroded by natural processes or destroyed by development or ploughing, or preserved intact for future investigation. The difficulties of making such a selection are formidable and liable to the grossest errors of judgement, especially if the only criteria are crop-mark photographs, scatters of pottery (with their bias toward ceramic periods in regions which have long aceramic periods), field names and other imponderables. To this must be added the complication that many village, town and city sites overlie sites of the period or period under consideration. The Deserted Medieval Village Research Group changed its name and its objectives to the Medieval Village Research Group because by definition it had been studying failed settlements. The successful villages had flourished and are now under expanded settlements. Beormas-ingham is a notable example.

To all the difficulties of statistical sampling of the population of sites must be added the continuing distortions due to the fact that they are not a static, fossilized entity but a rapidly changing and diminishing asset, disappearing, like the expanding universe, at a rate faster than we can overtake.

If we can envisage an Ideal Excavation, in which every scrap of the evidence which survives is recovered, from complete plans of major buildings to the total pollen count (and if it is remembered that all of this will only be a small fraction of what existed during the occupation of the site), then it will be clear that this ideal level of recovery would give us the best chance of interpreting the site most fully and that anything less than this ideal situation would give us progressively less information down to the point where much of the structural and stratigraphic evidence could not be understood. Since the Ideal Excavation is unattainable we have to decide what the acceptable levels of recovery are. In the case of structures and buildings I believe that total recovery should be the aim. Only in a very few special cases, where the structures are known beforehand to be repetitive and the stratification simple (as, for example, at Trelleborg or Fyrkat) can sampling provide valid and satisfying evidence. The case of Chalton may here be cited. Champion (1978) has shown that a 20 percent random sample using 8 m. quadrats covering no more than 30 percent of the site gave a fair estimate of the total number of buildings (60 against an observed total of 57) and some information about the nature of the structures. However, Chalton is an exceptional site consisting of many buildings of roughly similar size, and with little, if any, superimposed stratification. In addition, this exercise was retrospective and sampled an excavation rather than an untouched field. The difficulty is to know beforehand what the size and variety of the structures present are likely to be, so that a sampling strategy can be devised. Aerial photographs and geophysical surveys are notoriously deceptive, detecting the major structural features such as walls, floors and large post-holes, but failing to detect those more tenuous sorts of evidence such as pebble spreads, lines of stones, shallow post-sockets and discolorations of the soil which may, nevertheless, indicate the presence of major buildings. In addition, a large proportion of sites are vertically stratified, with the sizes and distribution of structures changing through time and the nature of the occupation. The writer knows of no sampling strategies which would be adequate for the excavated evidence illustrated in figures 1, 2, 3, 4, 15, 18, 70, 76, 82, 83, 84 and the end papers of this book.

Nevertheless, it would be patently ludicrous to take a total sample of every type of evidence. A total soil sample would mean keeping the whole spoil heap, while the labour involved in recording a total seed or pollen sample can be demonstrated statistically to be pointless. The problem then resolves itself into a determination of the size of sample of each type of evidence which is valid. For example, at Wroxeter all pottery sherds are kept, as are all animal bones, because specialist opinion is currently divided on the validity of sampling such assemblages, and we are only at the beginning of a very long-term investigation of the site. It may well be that, when this pottery is well known and a large collection has been made, sampling strategies will be initiated. Similarly, it may one day be considered unproductive to keep and examine all the animal bones, and sampling strategies for these will be devised. However, sampling for organic remains like seeds and charcoals, insects, snails etc. is based on criteria such as the apparent importance of the feature, e.g. a buried soil, a hearth, the filling of a pit, or a waterlogged context, together with a horizontal distribution which covers the various areas of the site with their varied structures and uses. Here the sampling is carried out within the context of a total excavation.

The case is different if the site is to be destroyed and a rescue excavation is mounted. Here, a whole range of sampling techniques may be deployed, aimed at the site's subsistence, economy, diet and industry, technology, trading links as evidenced by pottery and other artefacts, animal bones and other faunal remains, together with the evidence for the natural and man-made environment. Such sampling is, however, less likely to answer questions of the site's structures and their inter-relationships, nor to relate the sampled evidence to the structures.

Faced with the destruction of a large and complex site a number of interrelated decisions have to be made. These will be based on the expected survival (or not) of the structural remains and their nature, the likely survival of organic material, the expected density of artefacts such as potsherds (a Roman site as opposed to a Bronze Age site, for example), and the amount of information already available about this type of site in the region — an early Anglo-Saxon site is proportionately more important in the West Midlands than in East Anglia (see Ellison, 1981, p. 11, for a suggested rank order of sites in Wessex).

Intensive and extensive sampling should be preceded by site evaluation which uses all means of archaeological prospection. (See Carver, 1981, for a discussion of the problem in the context of a town, and Cherry, Gamble and Shennan eds., 1978 for a comprehensive discussion of sampling methods and strategies.)

Nevertheless, when a site has been selected for excavation, whether total or partial, I believe that the questions should be widened as far as is possible to include all aspects of the site which might be recovered.

I am becoming more and more convinced that the only valid questions to ask of a site are 'What is there?' and 'What is the whole sequence of events on this site from the beginnings of human activity to the present day?' Any other question must only be a part of this all-embracing one. (See Collingwood, 1939, Chap. V, and particularly the example of the non-starting car and the spark-plug.) If one asks, 'Was there prehistoric occupation here?', an excavation designed merely to answer this question will probably do so fairly quickly but perhaps at the expense of later occupation levels. Or if one asks 'What is the date range of the occupation of the site?' then a series of cuttings through the whole sequence of deposits may answer this but only for those parts of the site tested; there may be other periods of occupation in the untested areas. One might ask 'Does this site contain a sequence of imported pottery?', or 'Is it a deserted medieval village?', or 'Was it a ring-work before it achieved a motte?', or 'What is the extent of the suspected mesolithic occupation area?'. In obtaining answers to all these perfectly reasonable questions, other aspects of the site may, and probably will, be ignored and perhaps irretrievably damaged. If, however, while keeping firmly in mind the questions which prompted the excavation in the first place, together with all the myriad subsidiary questions which are posed by the emerging evidence, we are alert to the possibility of the unexpected — the medieval cottage built into the Roman fort, the motte encapsulating a bronze-age barrow — we shall avoid finding only what we set out to find rather than what is there. On this point Collingwood's advice is less than sound (*ibid*. p. 124) and runs counter to the considerations that prompted this book.

If a trial excavation is required for some overriding reason, to produce evidence of dating of the structures rather than simply the fact that they are there and something of their nature, it will be necessary to empty features, and remove floors, foundations and other structural remains in the hope of recovering stratified datable material. In such a case, the recording must be especially rigorous. Only if each surface, layer or feature is precisely levelled and drawn with an accuracy of ± 1 cm. will it be possible for a subsequent excavator to be certain of correlating his results with those from the trial trench.

However, no excavation can be totally neutral in its approach. We inevitably enter a site with some preconceptions as to what we hope to find and we constantly formulate questions and as constantly abandon them. The evidence as it emerges will pose new questions of tactics, and may even alter the course or strategy of the whole excavation. Whatever major problems we may have uppermost in our minds we must always be prepared to encounter entirely unexpected (perhaps unwanted) evidence, which must be treated comprehensively, and not given scant attention or even swept away as irrelevant. What is more important is that the unexpected evidence may present itself in an unexpected form, one with which we are not familiar or which does not fit in with our preconceptions of what might or should be there.

The scale and complexity of all but the smallest sites may deter us from total excavation, especially when the increasing refinement of excavation techniques can turn the study of one quite small site into a lifetime's work. Almost always in the past, research by means of excavation has been aimed at solving the problems of a site as quickly as possible, within a year or two, or at least within the lifetime of the excavator. Now, however, complete excavation is necessarily such a slow process that we shall not know within our own lifetimes the answers to many of the questions we ask about single sites, let alone complexes of related sites. Research excavations, therefore, must be planned for posterity, eschewing the quick answer and setting up a framework of excavation and recording which can be handed over, extended, modified and improved over decades, and in some cases, centuries.

I have in mind particularly the case of the Roman City at Wroxeter, where some 150 acres are being preserved for the nation. Total excavation of the city, spreading out from the central area which has been the focus of most previous excavation, would occupy at least two centuries even if the present rate of progress were to be doubled. Since all previous work has shown that each area of the city is radically different from its neighbour, the results of the work at present being carried out there cannot be extrapolated to any other part of the site. The whole will have to be dug in the greatest detail if the rise, heyday and decline of the city are to be fully understood. The same applies to many other complicated and comparatively unthreatened sites, such as deserted medieval villages, hill forts, and motte and bailey castles. We must be patient and work for the future, so that we do not leave our prospective colleagues a legacy of mutilated indecipherable monuments.

Sample trenching and gridding

To dig holes, however well recorded, in an ancient site is like cutting pieces out of a hitherto unexamined manuscript, transcribing the fragments, and then destroying them, a practice which would reduce historians to an unbelieving stupor, but whose counterpart is accepted by the majority of archaeologists as valid research. A single section, even of a ditch, can be grossly misleading, as anyone who has cut multiple sections will know. Many layers are discontinuous, appearing in one side of the section only or changing in composition across the cutting to re-appear in a different form on the opposite face. Clearly it is not sufficient to dig a section either by hand or with a machine and attempt an interpretation on the basis of the observed vertical surfaces. The old archaeological maxim 'it will all come out in the section' is simply not true. Extensive excavations on sites previously trenched (eg. Dorestad, van Es, 1969, 183 ff.) have so often shown that the earlier conclusions have been completely misleading, that it is now clear that only total, or near-total, excavation will yield results which are not deceptive. One possible exception is the more formalised, stereotyped Roman building which may be dug in small areas, the plan then being extrapolated from them with some confidence, but this presupposes that there are no anomalous or unexpected buildings above or below the stereotype. Even Roman forts are now seen to contain so many unconventional, even eccentric features, that argument from the part to the whole is becoming increasingly hazardous in an area of investigation once thought to be comparatively simple (e.g. The Lunt Roman Fort, Hobley, 1973).

Too often a trench cut across the defences of a site has been held to reveal, in concise form, the whole sequence of events on the site. Subsequent area excavation usually shows that the facts are much more complex. One section of the ditch of the outer bailey at Hen Domen, Montgomery showed the ditch there to have been dry, V-shaped, and once recut; another section, 15 metres away, showed that there the ditch was of at least three periods, flat-bottomed and wet. It might have been assumed from these cuttings that there were three phases in the life of the castle, but five sections of the motte ditch, all different in their evidence, showed a minimum of seven phases. In some of these sections, drawn within a few metres of each other, varying depths of recutting had removed almost all traces of two or three of the earlier ditches; and careful collation of all the sections was needed to produce a solution which total excavation of the whole ditch system might yet modify (figs. 8 — 11).

It is astonishing how close a trench can be dug to a stone or brick structure without revealing its existence. Take, for example, two short emergency excavations on moated sites in Shropshire (Barker, 1958 and 1964). In both, trenches passed within a metre or two of the foundations of brick or stone buildings, in one case the foundations of the Manor House at Shifnal, without encountering any evidence such as fragments of tile, brick, stone or mortar which would have suggested the imminent presence of a major building. At Shifnal, a subsequent trench cut at right angles to the first, encountered the massive sandstone foundations of the house. In both these cases, geophysical prospecting would probably have discovered the structures in advance, in which case the trenches would not have been needed, or could have been sited more usefully.

The problem for the prehistorian interested in the earliest periods of man's activities is a very difficult one, since structures are unlikely to be discovered, partly because they were flimsy and partly because they will have suffered far more from weathering than later structures (see Atkinson, 1957, 219-33). Localising scatters of palaeoliths or mesolithic flints depends more often than not on recent ploughing or other disturbance, and the element of chance introduced here may be compounded by test holes sited in the wrong places, where perhaps the flints were nearer the surface and were therefore more disturbed by the plough, giving a false emphasis to the scatter. There is no easy solution to this problem.

A further form of sampling excavation may seek to obtain environmental evidence from a sequence of waterlogged ditches or drainage channels. I have in mind the investigation of, for instance, a system of medieval fish ponds. Total excavation would be impossible, even ludicrous, but a series of trenches across the ditches, leats and pools might produce very valuable and valid environmental samples. Even here however any structures on the islands surrounded by these pools and ditches will have to be given the full treatment. (See reports on excavations on a fishpond site at Washford, Worcestershire, M. Gray, forthcoming and at Bordesley Abbey, S. Hirst and P.A. Rahtz, 1976.)

Nevertheless, trenches often give immediate and apparently satisfactory results. The broad dates of the site, the nature of its occupation; whether it had timber or stone buildings; the richness of its deposits and the wealth of its preserved finds may quickly become apparent. Thereafter the law of diminishing returns rapidly begins to operate. Six trenches will not give three times as much informa-

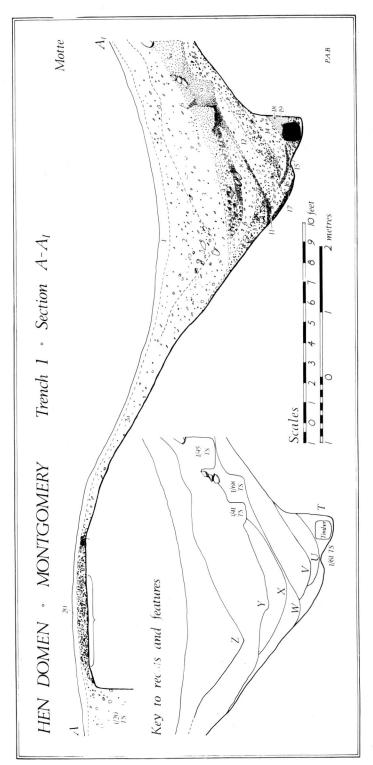

8 - 11 Four sections of the motte ditch at Hen Domen cut within a length of 20 metres. As will be seen, each section is different so that only correlation of all the sections produces a reliable picture.

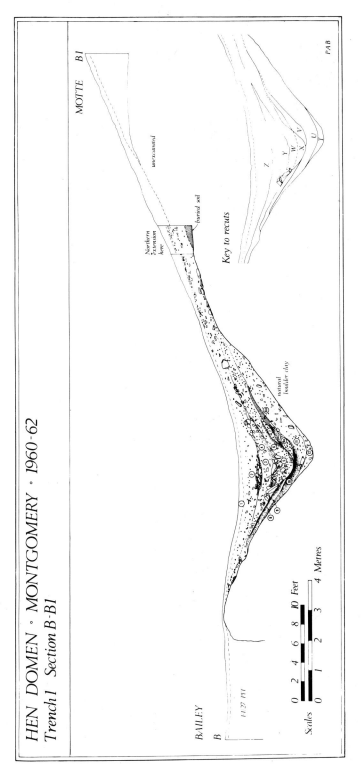

HEN DOMEN · MONTGOMERY · 1960-62
Trench 1   Section B-B1

BAILEY

B

MOTTE

B1

Northern
Extension
here

buried soil

unexcavated

natural
boulder clay

Key to recuts

Z   Y   W   X   V   U   T

PAB

Scales

0   2   4   6   8   10 Feet

0   1   2   3   4 Metres

9

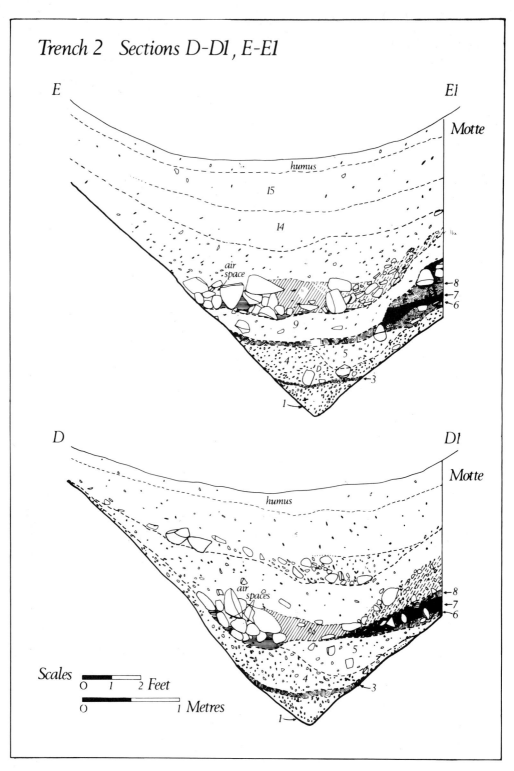

Trench 2   Sections D-D1, E-E1

E

E1

Motte

humus

15

14

air
space

9

←8
←7
←6

4

5

←3

1→

D

D1

Motte

humus

air
spaces

←8
←7
←6

5

4

←3

1→

Scales

0   1   2 Feet

0   1 Metres

10

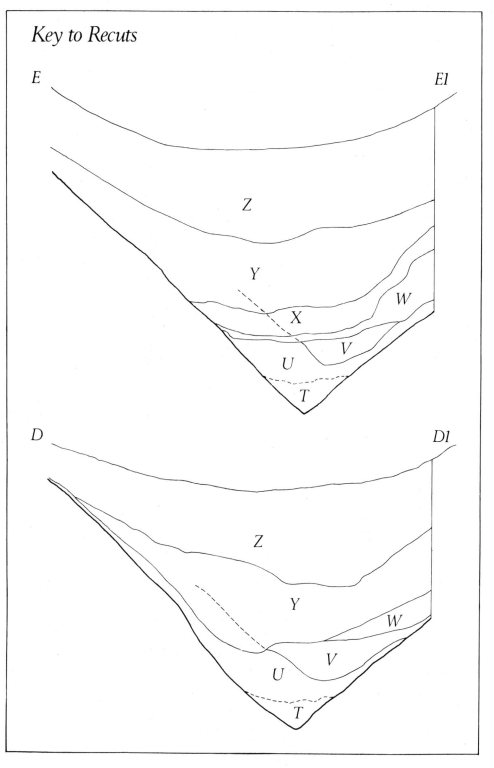

Key to Recuts

11

tion as two, and the second, third and fourth weeks' work will not quadruple the information of the first.

What, then, is the value of the trench? It can test the site's potential for future exploration and it can check the results of geophysical surveys, or establish the depths of deposits and the nature of the subsoil. Although this information may be of considerable value, and although trial trenching may be unavoidable in the planning of some emergency excavations, I believe that if possible trenches should not be dug below the surface of the first archaeological layer encountered, that is the latest occupation layer. Only an excavator who has dug on a site already riddled with trial trenches from previous excavations will know how almost inevitably these trenches destroy areas of vital evidence; sometimes in the only places where relationships between structures can be tested. On other occasions they will have removed parts of timber buildings, unrecognised because the trench was too small in area.

It may be useful here to use an analogy. Imagine a room the floor of which is covered to some depth by an assortment of carpets, rugs, blankets, newspapers, magazines and sheets of cardboard, the whole covered with a wall-to-wall carpet. A person wishing to understand fully the layers covering the floor will naturally begin by rolling back the uppermost carpet and then recording the surface revealed beneath. He will then remove one by one each overlying rug, newspaper or blanket, recording its removal and the layers revealed beneath, until he reaches the floor. Surely no one faced with this problem would take a knife and cut a rectangular hole in the carpet and then continue this hole downwards to the floor removing the partial layers of paper and cloth as he went. How could he in this way know that, though he has recovered a portion of yesterday's *Times*, a whole Persian rug may lie a little to his right?

This seems a fair parallel to the archaeological situation, even down to the fact that, on most sites with timber buildings, the layers will be as difficult to see and interpret in section as the layers in my analogy.

There are some occasions, of course, when for sheer practical reasons a trench is all that is possible. This is particularly likely to be the case in towns, where the work has to be confined to the space between two buildings, or along a sewer trench, or to the hole dug for a manhole or so forth. Classic examples of such trenches on the grand scale are those dug by Dame Kathleen Kenyon in Jericho and Jerusalem where, short of a nuclear holocaust, it will never be possible to dig very large areas. The restrictions here are extra-archaeological, so to speak, and they are not trial trenches dug into sites which could, and might in the future, be dug more extensively.

It is argued also that there is some value in knowing the depth of the deposits before work starts. If this is really felt to be necessary then an auger hole or a mechanically bored test-hole will do much less damage than a 2-metre square trench. Such exploration only gives very limited information, perhaps determining the eventual size of the spoil heaps, or the number of lorries required to remove the spoil. Nor can it give a clear idea of the time needed to excavate the site, because it cannot give any indication of the site's complications, which will only be revealed when an area is stripped. In the course of an excavation, it sometimes happens that a deep pit of one of the latest periods is cleared of its infill revealing the stratification of the underlying and hitherto unseen layers in its side. This is of interest but must not be allowed to alter the strategy of the excavation, which should continue to concentrate on the uppermost layers.

Still less should holes be dug into the site to determine the nature of the subsoil. If the subsoil is homogeneous over the whole area it can be examined at a point away from the site; but if this is not the case, in drift deposits, for instance, there is no point in taking a sample at one or two points within the site; it will have to be recognised afresh everywhere it is eventually encountered. In many areas of Britain the subsoil changes so rapidly that is is pointless to examine it except within the area of the excavation.

In a recent excavation, directed by the writer, on the floor of an occupied thirteenth-century timber-framed hall, there was some doubt as to the nature of the subsoil on which the yellow clay floor was based. The subsoil under the garden immediately outside the house, and no more than 20 m. from the excavation, was dark red marl. This marl was therefore expected under the floor. The excavation showed, however, that the house was built on an outcrop of grey-green lower lias, a fact which caused some confusion at first. In this case examination of the surrounding subsoil had not been helpful but the reverse.

A way of examining the depth and nature of deposits on town sites, particularly large ones, without damaging intact archaeological layers, is to remove modern recognisable surfaces, such as concrete platforms, rubble foundations, floors and so forth, and then identify recent wells, pits and other intrusions into the underlying layers. If these are emptied it will be possible to observe the stratification in section at a number of places around the site. Cellar walls can be selectively removed and the stratification behind them examined. In this way assessments of the depth and nature of deposits can be made, and costings estimated without damage to the site. Since, in towns particularly, vital evidence often survives only in small 'islands' or 'peaks' left between pits and other disturbances, it is vital that these should not be lost in blind trial trenching, or their understanding jeopardised by digging them in trial holes, where their context cannot be appreciated. Only if such methods of prior examination fail should one resort to trial trenching, and especially to trial trenching by machine.

The problem is more difficult in the countryside, where recent holes are likely to be fewer, or non-existent. It may be possible to trace field drains (by magnetometer, resistivity meter, or even dowsing) and empty them as a first stage. Where stratified sites survive they are so precious that we should exhaust all non-destructive methods of examination before we begin to destroy them.

However, all these methods will only give a broad picture of the depth and nature of the thicker deposits at the places examined — they will not reveal the existence of the thin or discontinuous layers which are often of crucial importance and may even represent whole periods of occupation. It is, perhaps, safe to say that any site is likely to be at least three times more complex in plan than it appears in section, so that when estimates of time and money are being calculated a multiplier of at least three should be used.

A stronger case can be made out for trenching linear features, such as ramparts, dykes, and roads. Obviously it would be impossible to excavate Offa's Dyke or the Fosse Way completely, so a series of carefully selected sections across such monuments will give a great deal of information about their construction; and, if circumstances are fortunate, about their date. However, the same limitations which apply to all excavations do still apply here. A trench cut across an undated dyke may recover Iron Age pottery from the old ground surface beneath it, and if no other sections are cut a post-Iron Age date can correctly be assumed for the dyke. But for how much of it? It may not all be of one build; centuries may separate two periods of its construction, or two short portions of pre-Roman dyke may have been joined together in Saxon times. The evidence from the section only relates to the sectioned part of the dyke, and cannot be projected to a point two or three miles away unless very careful fieldwork makes it virtually certain that the dyke is all of one build (for a good example which illustrates this point see Hill, 1974).

However, a section cut only a few metres away from our original section may recover a medieval sherd from the lower layers of the dyke's make-up. Are we then justified in putting the whole earthwork into the medieval period? Is it perhaps a park boundary? Or is this section a late infill? Only more extensive work can hope to provide a satisfactory conclusion. Furthermore, sections cut across ramparts and dykes will not provide answers to important questions such as the existence, or not, of a palisade. Even Sir Cyril Fox, in his great work, did not advocate the stripping of a length of Offa's Dyke to see if it was palisaded although this would be the only way to find out.

In the case of Roman (or any other) roads the limitations of sectioning can be reduced by cutting wide trenches which enable each road surface to be seen in plan before it is removed. In this way a great deal more will be learned about the road than from a narrow vertical trench. The existence of buildings on its latest surface, or the traces of cart ruts, will be much easier to discover in a wide section, dug layer by layer.

The choice of site to be dug and methods used

With limited time and resources, all excavations cannot be total, so that partial investigation of many of our sites must be planned to give optimum results, and, to that end, must be problem-orientated, and the limitations of such excavations realised and accepted.

The factors which govern the choice of sites to be dug vary enormously. They will include purely practical considerations, such as the availability of money, and, more important, of competent directors and site supervisors, the length of time the site is available (which will determine the strategy of the digging) and its size and probable complexity. If the dig is to be financed by public funds then the site's relative national importance *vis-a-vis* sites not only of the same type and period, but of a totally different kind must be assessed. To make a decision on the importance of a small but complex and apparently unique crop-mark site in rural Shropshire relative to a development in the centre of a well-known Roman town in Warwickshire is difficult almost to impossibility, but is the kind of choice which is being constantly forced upon us. If neither can be dug completely, the amount of information likely to be achieved by a partial excavation of one or both must be estimated (perhaps incorrectly), and a strategy for each devised. This strategy will itself depend on a number of factors. It may be agreed, however reluctantly, that some aspects of the site must be abandoned if we are to shed light on those aspects which we consider the most important. In the case of the crop-mark site these may be its dates, and its length of occupation rather than the details of its structures. In the case of the town site it may be suspected that an earlier defensive line runs through the available site and therefore that this, rather than any overlying or underlying buildings, should deserve the highest priority. Note that in both these cases, and in many others which one could postulate, it is the *buildings* that take the most time to elucidate, and thus tend to be abandoned first. Broad dating ranges and defensive works (together with massive stone buildings) can be more rapidly dealt with.

Other factors which may affect the decision to dig entirely, or to sample, or abandon, perhaps with a watching brief, are the uniqueness, or conversely the ubiquity of the type of site in the region — whether it is an anomaly or representative of a common, generally recognized type; the paucity in the region of previous studies of the period thought to be represented by the site; its degree of preservation or its apparent relationship with structures of other periods which seem to overlie or underlie it, promising a relative stratigraphy. These are the considerations which will affect problem-orientated *strategy*. Problem-orientated *tactics* will depend on the practicalities outlined above, such as time, and the availability of finance and skilled labour. If these are not sufficient for a full-scale excavation, yet the site is irrevocably to be destroyed, painful decisions will have to be made as to what will be sacrificed and what, if possible, recovered. All such decisions, made before the start of the excavation, are liable to drastic modification within hours of the commencement of the dig, since the immediate results may be quite unexpected. It is, therefore, necessary to maintain a flexible approach and not to plough on, determined to solve only the problems discussed round the committee table. New, more important, problems may be revealed by the emerging evidence, or it may transpire that the evidence for the solution of the original problems is not there.

Sometimes we are faced with the situation, such as the construction of a motorway, where many sites will be destroyed or damaged, and only one or two can be dug. Here the decision may well be based on gaps in our knowledge of a particular kind of earthwork or crop-mark site, rather than on other more practical considerations such as the longer availability of another site or its clearer indications on the ground, or its state of preservation. The decision to dig one site rather than another having been made, the question of techniques will then depend on the time, money and other resources available. If there is only time for a short excavation it will be necessary to decide whether to dig a number of trenches across the site in the hope of establishing a chronological sequence, to strip off the top-soil over a large area in order to recover a broad plan of the structures; or whether to use geophysical methods, basing one's decision as to the method of excavation on magnetic anomalies or other similar evidence. If, in the latter case, magnetic or resistivity anomalies indicate the existence of a building in one area of a complex of earthworks, the decision to recover the plan of this building rather than attempt, in the time available, to sample the whole site for other equally interesting information will be a conscious decision based on what is currently needed in the archaeology of the region, or of that class of earthwork. If the opposite decision is taken, to strip the site summarily in order to recover the broad picture, losses of detail and perhaps some confusion of chronology must be expected.

To summarize: it seems to me that where ten sites are to be destroyed it is far better to dig two of them totally and salvage-excavate the others than trench or partially excavate all ten. Of course, the choice will be a difficult one and mistakes are inevitable; but the principle should stand in spite of this.

Total excavation of a non-threatened site, which inevitably means its destruction, must not be undertaken lightly. Trenching will mutilate it, and extensive trenching will make it virtually impossible to excavate the site properly in the future. Total excavation of half a site, leaving the other half for future more refined excavation is a solution that has been suggested, although the two halves of even a small site may be very different from one another in the length, intensity and nature of their occupation.

This my colleagues and I have found to our cost at Hen Domen (Barker, 1969a) where the quarter of the bailey now under excavation has presented quite different problems and a different sequence of events from the immediately adjacent area, excavated earlier. Another team of excavators, digging the new area independently some years after the end of the first stage of the excavation, would have been baffled (as we were) by the results, and would probably have concluded that our earlier conclusions were totally mistaken. It is only because we have much the same personnel digging the site in exactly the same way as in the first stage that we know that it is the site which is changing across the width of the bailey (a mere 30 or 40 metres) and not the result of a different technique.

The problem of sampling resolves itself ultimately into the question of the *size* of the sample. Ideally the smallest valid sample is a complete site, or better still a whole area of ancient landscape, but since we do not live in an ideal world, we have to compromise and accept all the external constraints which leave us with far smaller samples than we would wish for; and we must be wary of projecting those aspects of the excavated evidence which cannot justifiably be extended into the surrounding undug areas on whatever scale we may be digging.

Only full, highly-detailed excavation will yield all the available evidence, itself only a fraction of what was originally there. Anything less than total excavation must be problem-orientated if it is to give the maximum results, and, in my view, is only justified if the site or part of it is to be destroyed, or if it is too vast to be dug completely, when the excavation must be planned on the assumption that the rest of the site may one day be dug.

If a site is inevitably going to be destroyed, and time, finances or other considerations forbid excavation on a large scale, then it may be decided to sample for particular aspects of the total evidence which is assumed to be present. For example, it might be considered that the most important aspects of a large multi-period prehistoric site are not the structural sequences, but the environmental changes which have occurred since before the site's occupation up to the present day. A sampling strategy, based on extensive bore-holes and test pits may answer these questions in a very economical way, though other questions which may be asked will evade such a strategy.

Other strategies may be devised to sample pottery scatters over a large site, to determine the lengths of phases of occupation or shifts in their nuclei. A difficulty here is that aceramic phases will escape this net, and the picture thus become distorted.

Patterns of sampling pits and trenches are described by Champion in Cherry, Gamble and Shennan, 1978, pp. 207-226. To the present writer, who still remembers vividly the impossibility of understanding the evidence produced by the not dissimilar trenches and pits of the 1950s, such techniques must be used with great caution and their limitations fully appreciated.

So far it has been implied that all sites should be excavated in the same way, regardless of date or type of structure or function, that is, whether they are military, religious, secular, domestic or palatial.

To take first the question of period. It has often been maintained that excavations should only be carried out by specialists in the particular period of the site concerned, and there is some force in this argument. It is reasonable to expect specialists to concentrate on their chosen periods, and to dig those sites of particular interest to them. Only thus, it is argued, will the peculiar features of barrow or iron-smelting furnace be discovered, since the specialist will know what to look for. Here we have, however, the teleological argument, that people may find what they wish, albeit subconsciously, to find.

The opposite point of view sees the excavator as a technician producing evidence from the ground regardless of its date or function. In an ideal archaeological situation in which excavation was a scientific discipline with the excavator able to choose precisely the material on which to conduct his experiments, specialisation would perhaps be automatic. But this is not the case. With few exceptions our sites consist of a multiplicity of periods, and, more often than not, prove to be entirely different from what we expect. What is the barrow digger to do if he finds he is digging a motte based on a barrow? Or the medievalist if an Iron Age settlement underlies his deserted village? The situation is even more complex in towns. The urban archaeologist must be prepared to find evidence of any date from the palaeolithic onwards immediately under the pavement. It would obviously be ludicrous for a medieval archaeologist to abandon the site and call in a Romanist because he had encountered a Roman building, the Romanist in turn passing on the excavation to a prehistorian when an Iron Age hut circle appears. Under these circumstances, which we cannot avoid, the excavator must be an all-period technician, recording in meticulous detail evidence which he does not necessarily fully understand at the time, but which he can discuss, hopefully while the excavation is open, with his specialist colleagues. If this is not possible, the discussion will have to be based on the recorded evidence, which must therefore be of the highest quality if it is to be properly understood.

I do not believe that sites or monuments of different periods require differing excavation techniques. A Bronze Age hut should be dug with precisely the same techniques as a medieval long-house, a Roman villa with the same methods as a medieval manor house.

Nor do I think that the function of a building or site determines the way in which it is dug. A temple should not be dug differently from a palace; a castle should not be dug differently from a lead mine. It is only when the site is very large that it might have to be sampled. In that case the choice of area or areas to be dug may depend on previous knowledge of similar sites so that the maximum information can be obtained with the resources available. However, when the areas are dug, I believe they should be dug in the same way regardless of the type of site.

The excavation of timber and stone buildings — are different methods required?

The fundamental principle of all excavations should be to remove and record each layer or feature in the reverse order from which it was deposited, over as extensive an area as possible. There will be some occasions on which this ideal must be modified. One of them is the presence of standing walls which may introduce complicating factors into the day-to-day planning and direction of the excavation.

To take a typical example: a large and complicated stone building may lie under continuous or intermittent layers of plough soil, rubble and debris, including the deposits of later timber buildings. These layers should be dug horizontally in the way described in Chapter 5. When the tops of the walls of the underlying building are reached the layers on each side become separated by the walls and the site divides itself into smaller areas which can (in fact, must) be dug separately, in some cases room by room. This introduces a complication, since the site grid

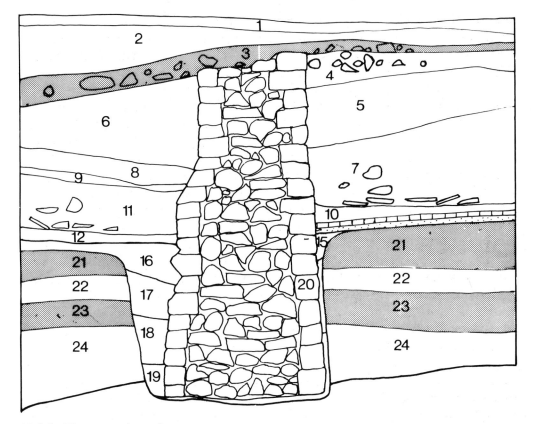

12 *left* Diagrammatic section of wall built in construction trench layers 15-19, cut through earlier layers, 21-24.

is unlikely to coincide with the shape and size of the building's divisions or rooms. If the walls are standing to an appreciable height measuring over them from an external grid point may become tedious and inaccurate. In this case a subsidiary datum point can be established within the walls, or when the walls themselves are accurately plotted they themselves, or points on them, may be used. Excavation within the walls can then proceed like any small-scale area excavation, with cumulative sections taken wherever desired. This excavation of the levels associated with the building should ideally continue downwards until the pre-building layers are reached. However, the situation is unlikely to be as simple as that. If the walls have been built in construction trenches (fig. 12) these trenches should, in theory, be emptied before the layers into which they cut. But the walls themselves are by definition later than the construction trenches and therefore should be removed first. Usually, at this point, non-excavational factors enter. Walls, unlike post-holes, are tangible, emotive fragments of the past, capable of being preserved and displayed to the public. Unless the site is irrevocably to be destroyed, it may well be desirable to keep the walls intact. Under these circumstances it will not be possible to excavate those layers which run under the walls, and the site will have to be dug in smaller areas. This may make interpretation of underlying timber structures exceedingly difficult, if not impossible.

At this point also safety factors must be considered. Foundation trenches, emptied along the lines of the walls, may seriously weaken their stability, and any attempt to dig pre-building layers may leave the walls standing on highly unstable balks. If the walls are to be preserved for eventual display, they must be shored professionally. This further reduces the area archaeologically available.

The situation is even more complicated if the stone walls have been robbed out in antiquity, so that robber trenches as well as foundation trenches have to be dealt with (fig. 13 shows a typical situation in section). Ideally the robber trenches should be emptied in sequence before any earlier layers are removed, but this is not always practicable. If the robber and foundation trenches have been cut through soft or friable layers the risk of collapse will be considerable. In this case it may be necessary to lower the filling of the robber/foundation

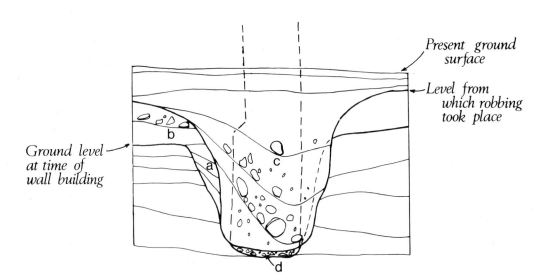

13 *above* This figure shows diagrammatically a section through a robber trench in which it is possible to distinguish: the ground level at the time of building; the construction trench for the wall, a: the accumulations of material with debris during the life of the wall, b: and the robber trench with unwanted debris thrown back into the trench, c; d represents the mortar raft on which the wall originally stood.

trenches a little ahead of the main excavation. This requires strict control of the digging and recording but guards against the loss of evidence which collapse would make inevitable. If resources are available the robber trenches may be emptied completely and then backfilled with sand or sifted earth in order to preserve them intact while the excavation proceeds from the upper levels.

One temptation, which all excavators of stone buildings must have felt, is that when a stone wall or floor is encountered it is very easy to become careless of the fine details of stratification and to follow the wall or expose the floor in a sudden flush of enthusiasm. A subtle form of this aberration shows itself in the outlining of stones or walls by slight over-digging. Establishing the presence of the tops of walls or foundations is almost irresistible, but may destroy important stratigraphical relationships and therefore must be resisted.

The recording and interpretation of standing buildings is beyond the scope of this book. Nevertheless underground archaeology cannot be separated from that which is visible. There have been some notable investigations of standing or ruined buildings together with their underlying archaeology, particularly on the Continent where the opportunities for excavation presented by the bombing of churches were grasped and their interiors excavated before rebuilding took place. Recent examples in England have been the excavation of the interior of All Saints' Church, Oxford, by the Oxford Archaeological Unit (Hassall, 1971), and the excavations of Rivenhall and Hadstock Churches, Essex (Rodwell, 1973 and Rodwell, 1976). Axel Steensberg carried out a classic excavation of a farmstead at Pebringe in Zealand on the occasion of the removal of the standing buildings to the Open Air Museum at Sorgenfri near Copenhagen (Steensberg, 1952) and at Wharram Percy the buried internal and external remains of the church are being fully examined in conjunction with the standing fabric (Hurst, 1969). The Clarendon Hotel in Oxford was an early example, being fully recorded and its underlying deposits excavated before redevelopment (Panton *et al*, 1958) while a highly detailed study of the fabric of Deerhurst Church coupled with sampling excavations has completely revised the long history of this important building (Taylor, Butler and Rahtz, forthcoming). In general though, the opportunities presented by the extensive demolition of buildings with long histories in our towns and cities have only recently been grasped, notably by the units now being established in increasing numbers. A recent example is that of Pride Hill Chambers, Shrewsbury (Carver, Jenks and Toms, in preparation).

The excavation and interpretation of buried walls and foundations appear at first sight to be easier than that of timber buildings. If anything they are more difficult. This is perhaps because the excavated masonry presents more evidence in tangible form than the elusive post-hole or fragment of pebble floor. Post-holes or stake holes which are not understood or which do not fit a pattern can be (and are) conveniently overlooked in the final interpretation. (If this statement is not believed compare almost any field drawing of the excavation of a complex of timber buildings with the final publication.) They can after all be dismissed as

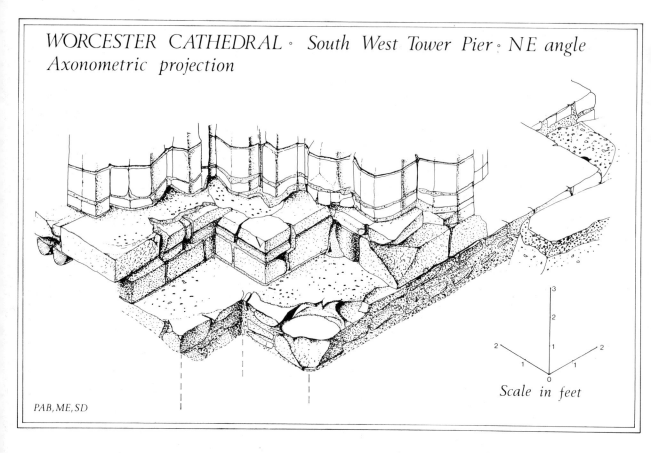

WORCESTER CATHEDRAL · *South West Tower Pier · NE angle Axonometric projection*

Scale in feet

PAB, ME, SD

14a, b   An example of the excavation of a stone building. In 1981 a small excavation was carried out to examine the foundations of one of the piers of the central tower of Worcester Cathedral. The present tower dates from the mid-fourteenth century but it was known that it stood on the foundations of the tower of the Norman cathedral begun by Bishop Wulstan in 1084. However, there is a record in the annals of Worcester that the new tower of Worcester collapsed in 1175 (*nova turris Wignorniae curruit*). Victorian writers were sure that this was the central tower but more recent opinion asserted that it was one of the western towers. The excavation at the base of the pier showed conclusively that there were *three* phases of construction: first, a massive base of uncoursed rubble, clearly, for reasons which there is not space to detail here, the Norman foundations of c.1084. On this stood a foundation which, at first sight, appeared to have a chamfered plinth of Norman date and to be contemporary with the base below. However, closer examination showed that the stones of which it was constructed (*d*) were, in fact, reused *abaci* from capitals or string courses parallelled exactly in the nearby crypt of 1084, but here reused upsidedown. Mortar

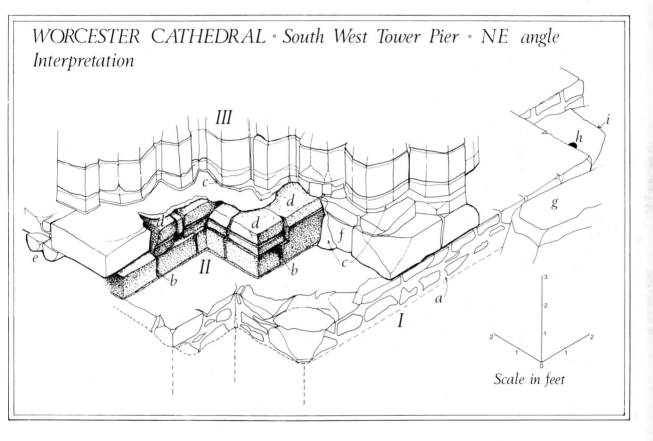

WORCESTER CATHEDRAL · South West Tower Pier · NE angle
Interpretation

Scale in feet

samples were taken from joints at *a* and *b*, examined and compared and shown to be different from one another. Mortar samples from joints in the fourteenth century pier at *c* were also examined and proved to be different again. Clearly there were three phases of construction. However, it was also seen that the fourteenth-century pier, which was a different shape from the underlying bases, had itself been packed with reused Norman architectural fragments, including a column drum, *f*, and a double capital, *e*. *g* is a floor, probably of the first period, which has sunk and tilted, while *h* is a post-hole, perhaps for a scaffold pole, set in a pit, *i*. The probable sequence of events is thus:

the building of the first Norman tower, *I*, after 1084 and perhaps as late as 1150; the collapse of this tower and the building, after 1175, of a second tower, *II*, on foundations derived from the collapsed masonry;

the building of the third tower, *III*, in the late fourteenth century, again reusing Norman masonry, but this time probably from the destruction of the ambulatory of the crypt when the east end of the cathedral was rebuilt in the thirteenth century.

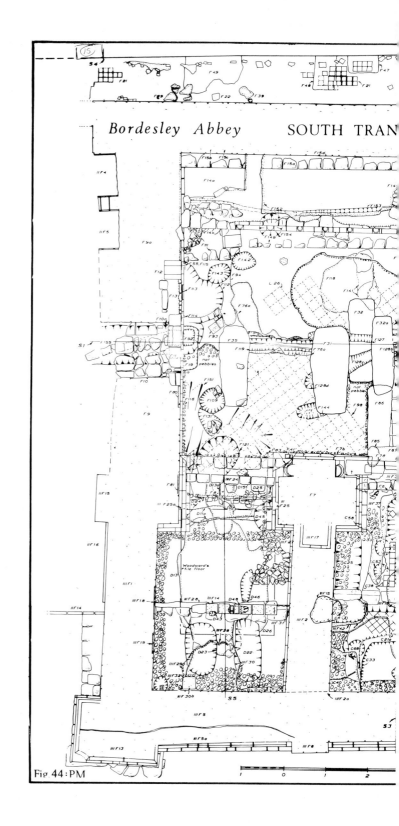

Fig. 44 : PM

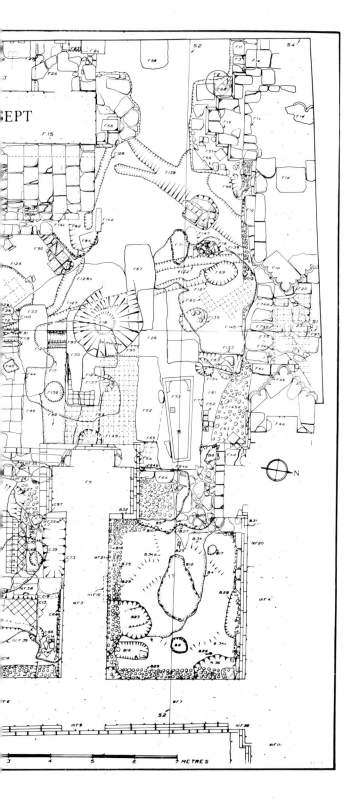

15 Bordesley Abbey: plan of south transept. This illustrates some of the complexities of digging a series of superimposed floors, and overlying builders' levels, all cut by a series of graves. The palimpsest shown illustrates the history of one part of the church over a period of four centuries. The complex evidence represented is not normally recovered on abbey sites, where digging has in the main been done merely to uncover masonry foundations (Rahtz and Hirst, 1975).

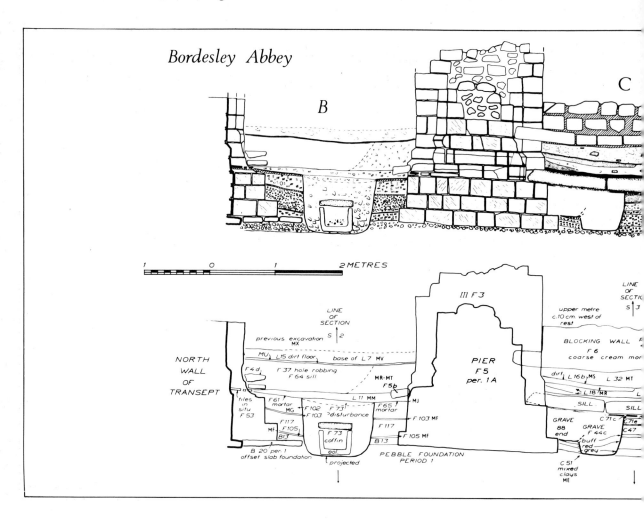

16 Bordesley Abbey: west elevation of piers and section through entrances of Chapels (E5). This illustrates the recording, stone by stone, of the elevations of a complex masonry structure, together with sections of layers and features accumulating between masonry piers on the plane of the elevations. It also illustrates how the 'objective' upper drawing of what is actually seen is supplemented by the 'subjective' naming and interpretation in the lower drawing. Neither part of this drawing would be adequate by itself. Together they supply the information needed; combined in one drawing, however, they would be very confusing (Rahtz and Hirst, 1975).

the remains of ephemeral structures such as scaffolding, or peat stacks, temporary enclosures or whatever the fertile imagination can create. It is not so easy to ignore fragments of masonry, brickwork or concrete foundation, which must represent something large and solid, even if short-lived.

One of the best ways to learn about or to teach the complications and unravelling of the development of a masonry structure is to study a church with a long history, or simply to examine one wall of such a church. Even without a detailed

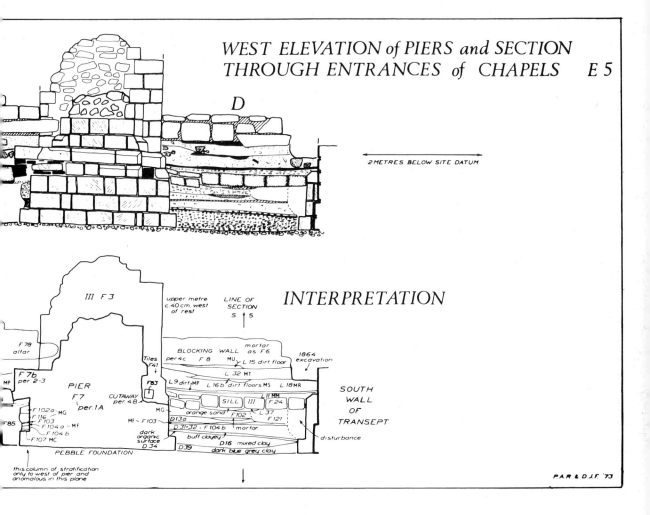

WEST ELEVATION of PIERS and SECTION
THROUGH ENTRANCES of CHAPELS   E 5

D

2 METRES BELOW SITE DATUM

INTERPRETATION

III F 3

upper metre   LINE OF
c 40 cm west   SECTION
of rest   S ↑ S

F 78
altar

                          mortar
          BLOCKING WALL   as F6   1864
Tiles   per 4c   F 8   MU   excavation
F 41   ⌐ L 15 dirt floor
F 7b   L 32 MT
per 2-3
MP   F 83   L 9 dirt MP L 16 b dirt floors MS   L 18 MR
        PIER   L 11 MM
        F 7   CUTAWAY   L 19   F 24
               per 4 B   SOUTH
F 102a   MG   per. 1A   SILL   III   WALL
F 116   MG   orange sand F 102   L 37   OF
F 85   F 103   MF ~ F 103 ⌐ D 13 a   F 121 TRANSEPT
        F 104 a ~ Mf   D 31·32 : F 104 b   mortar
        F 104 b   dark   buff clayey
     F 107 MC   organic   D 16 mixed clay   disturbance
                      surface D 34 D 39 dark blue grey clay
        PEBBLE FOUNDATION

this column of stratification
only to west of pier and
anomalous in this plane   PAR & D.J.F. '73

knowledge of ecclesiastical architecture it is usually possible by a logical dissection of the evidence to determine the sequence of building periods, alterations
and repairs. Add to this an acquaintance with the styles of church architecture
and the relative periods of building can be given dating brackets. As in excavated
buildings and foundations, the interpretation of standing buildings is very often
complicated by repairs, late renovations in earlier styles or reused fragments
of earlier stonework or sculpture.

Differences in types of masonry, of stone, of mortars, of stone dressing, and
the existence of butt or bonded joints must all be looked for and recorded with
the same meticulous detail that is given by the excavator to the recording of a
series of thinly stratified floors or groups of stakeholes. The only satisfactory
way to record and study masonry is by a stone-by-stone drawing annotated
with the types of stone, mortar samples and other relevant detail. In the case
of large expanses of standing masonry or brickwork photogrammetry is a fast
and accurate method of recording the elevations.

If all that is left of a complex of masonry buildings is a series of robber trenches, these must be excavated with the same attention to detail which is given to the rest of the site. It is not enough merely to empty them along their length in order to obtain the outlines of the former buildings.

Close study of the back-filled material and its stratification will give information about the mortar used in the robbed wall, about the direction from which the back-filling was made, about the level and therefore perhaps the date from which the robbing was carried out, and whether the robbing was carried out in two or more stages. It may also yield dating evidence in the form of coins or pottery. Careful trowelling of the bottom of the robber trench may reveal the imprints of the stones, bricks or tiles which formed the structure.

The excavation of the Old and New Minsters at Winchester was a brilliant example of the way in which robber trenches can be made to yield the maximum information (see Biddle and Kjølbye-Biddle, 1969, and interim reports in *The Antiquaries Journal*, 1964-75).

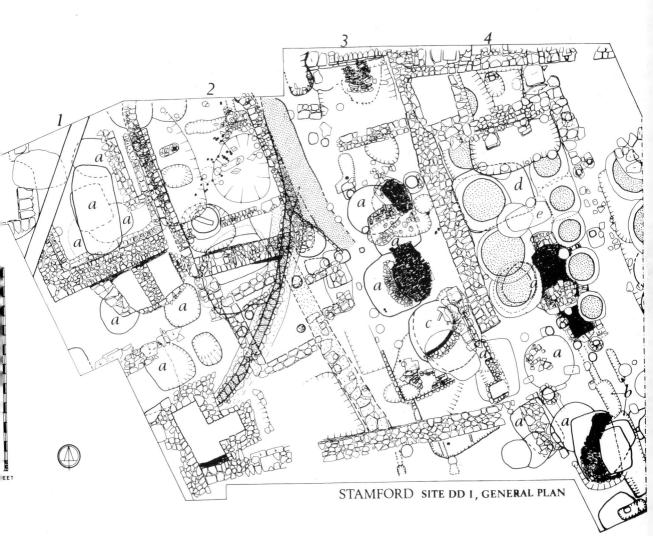

STAMFORD SITE DD I, GENERAL PLAN

17 *left* St Martin's, Stamford, 1968. The drawing shows a typical urban situation in which five rectangular buildings dating from the thirteenth-fourteenth centuries with later cross walls inserted overly Saxo-Norman pits ('a' on plan) and timber slots ('b' on plan). The tile-floored ovens are thirteenth-fourteenth century and the tannery pits ('e') are fifteenth-sixteenth century and are associated with the re-use of Building 4. Other superimposed walls and features are nineteenth-twentieth century.

Although this is not an example of the very complex situations sometimes found on urban sites, which often span two millennia, it illustrates graphically the contrast with rural sites such as Moel y Gaer, fig. 30 and Belle Tout, figs. 58-9, or the sort of timber buildings encountered at York, figs. 80-1 or Wroxeter, figs. 82-5.

5

The Processes of Excavation

This chapter describes the methods and processes of a long-term, highly-detailed excavation. Under present circumstances, when a great proportion of all excavations are carried out under rescue conditions, few of us are fortunate enough to have at our disposal the time and resources to dig at the pace dictated by the nature and complexity of the site, but unless we keep the ideal situation firmly in mind during even the most rushed salvage dig we will lose more information than is necessary. Just as 'all art constantly aspires towards the condition of music', all excavation should aspire towards the condition of total excavation. The excavator's aim should be to explain the origin of every layer and feature he encounters whether it be structural or natural; made by man, animal or insect, accidental or purposeful. It is not enough merely to excavate and explain the structural remains without attempting to understand the processes of accumulation, change and destruction to which they have been continuously subjected. There will always be many aspects of the site which are not fully understood, and others which will be ambiguous in interpretation; but the effort to explain the smallest observed phenomenon will help considerably towards a fuller understanding of the site and its history.

The principle of all excavation, large or small, is to remove the superimposed layers one by one in the reverse order from that in which they were deposited, recording each in as much detail as is necessary to reconstruct, in theory at least, the site layer by layer, complete with its features and finds, long after the actual process of excavation has destroyed it. Only by doing this can we obtain sufficient evidence to begin to understand the evolution of the stratification of the site, let alone interpret its periods and structures.

In any excavation it is a good general rule to regard all observable features as equally significant until they are proved not to be. Only in this way may rubble spreads prove to be building platforms, lines of stones to mark the edges of structures, gaps in the finds plots the sites of buildings, and so on. The alternative is to go for the immediately obvious structures, with the considerable risk of missing equally vital, though more tenuous, evidence (e.g. fig. 18).

The key to all good excavation is the scrupulous cleanliness of the excavated surface. Soil is, regrettably, opaque. A layer of dust or mud only a few millimetres thick will obscure all but the grossest differences in colour and texture. This is why most surfaces are at their best when newly trowelled and why it is useless to use a brush in wet weather. The cleanliness of the surface is so important that site supervisors should require trowellers to go over the surface time and again if necessary until, colloquially, they could eat off it. Sometimes though, stony or rubble layers 'improve with keeping', as they are washed by rain. The improvement in the cleanliness of the extensive rubble layers on the baths basilica site at Wroxeter, currently being excavated (1982), is very marked after a winter's rain, though the individual stones were cleaned as thoroughly as possible during the excavation. Trial hosing of stony surfaces will show if they may be cleaned in this way without damage.

As little spoil as possible should accumulate on the site. It should be the rule, followed wherever possible, that each troweller only accumulates as much spoil as will fill a hand-shovel before it is removed to the bucket, sieve or barrow. In this way the site is kept clean, and the spoil does not get trodden or knelt into the surface. It is sensible to use kneeling mats when trowelling, as they save the knees from becoming sore after long periods of work and, more important, protect them from damp. Rheumatism and arthritis are the occupational diseases of the long-term digger and every precaution should be taken to avoid them.

Tools

The trowel is the fundamental excavation tool. Whatever supplementary tools, such as knives, teaspoons, ladles and the like may be used, the small (3″–4″ long) trowel is the most versatile implement in the hands of the competent digger. The art of trowelling can only be taught in the field, so that if newcomers to archaeology are employed it is a very good idea to use the monitorial system whereby inexperienced trowellers are set to work next to or between experienced ones who will be specifically told to teach them by example. This process considerably lightens the teaching burden of the site supervisors who, nevertheless, keep overall control. The beginner should be taught to use the trowel delicately or strongly, as circumstances dictate, to use the point, either with a scraping motion, or a chopping, digging one, or to clean a horizontal surface with the straight edge with millimetre accuracy.

The basic advantage of the small trowel is that it allows much greater pressure to be put on its point than on that of the 5″ or 6″ trowel, when, for instance the layer to be removed is clayey, or pebbly. It is also capable of much greater delicacy if a new, more vulnerable surface or a fragile find is encountered. On sandy sites, however, the flat edge of a large trowel may be the most useful

hand tool.

The hand-brush is an essential adjunct to the trowel. When it should be used is a matter of constant judgement, controlled by the site supervisor. In dry weather it is easy to brush a soft or dusty surface and produce something that looks like a new layer, or even a floor, especially if the brush removes fine soil or stones from between other stones which are in fact an integral part of the layer. Equally a stiff brush used on a dry clayey surface will often polish it, producing a surface resembling a floor. On the other hand, the brush, whether hard or soft, used at the right time can be a most delicate and subtle instrument. Churn brushes with very stiff bristles which project forward from a wooden handle, softer bristle and plastic brushes of varying degrees of stiffness, and paint brushes, varying in width from ½″ to 2″, all have their uses.

Like many apparently simple operations, brushing is not so easy as it looks and usually has to be taught. The stiff brushes should be used with a motion which rotates them about their long axis, so that the springiness of the bristles flicks the spoil from the surface rather than spreading it across it. It is remarkable how effective this technique is. The brush should be kept clean and once the surface becomes damp enough to clog the bristles with dirt, brushing should be abandoned and the surface cleaned by scraping alone.

In addition to trowels and brushes any implement which will do a job properly may be employed. Teaspoons, dental probes, scalpels and spatulas, all have their uses. Ladles of all sizes and a variety of spoons with the bowls bent at an angle are very efficient post and stake-hole emptiers. A blunt penknife will excavate delicately without damage and for really fragile objects a wooden toothpick might be the most suitable tool.

'The testimony of the spade' is a phrase which has come to be synonymous with archaeology, but in reality the spade is little used on most excavations except perhaps for taking off the turf or trimming baulks. A turf-cutter used in conjunction with a sharp spade will lift turf cleanly and in squares or rectangles of a manageable size. On sites where the turf cover is thin and the underlying layers stony the initial turfing may reveal the latest occupation layer almost immediately. In such cases the turf must be taken off very carefully in order that the archaeological deposits are not disturbed.

18   Tenuous evidence. The photograph shows the north portico of the baths basilica at Wroxeter after the removal of an overlying rubble platform which had supported a timer-framed building. From the angle at which the photograph is taken four equidistant parallel lines defined by pebbles, tiles, mortar, slight hollows and ridges are visible. The most likely interpretation of these traces is that they mark the lines of parallel joists supporting a board-walk which had replaced an earlier portico floor of tiles or pebbles. This view is reinforced by the fact that a number of uncrushed ox skulls were found between the putative joists, suggesting that they lay in the spaces under the floorboards. It will be obvious that only area stripping would have revealed this phase in the site's development. (Photo: Sidney Renow.)

Spades and shovels with D-shaped, rather than T-shaped, handles are more comfortable to use for long periods but this is perhaps a matter of individual choice. Shovels with metal shafts and handles can be obtained and will last a long time, but are cold to use in winter and vibrate uncomfortably when they strike buried stone. Some directors favour the use of a fork for digging in clayey ground, but it has to be used with extreme caution if it is not to do a good deal of damage, not only to the stratification but also to any objects it may encounter. Most people will need to be taught how to use spades and shovels efficiently. An experienced navvy is the best instructor as he will be able to achieve the maximum effect with the minimum of effort, and will work with a rhythm that can

Beckford

Metres

0   10   20   30   40   50   60

19   This drawing shows part of the excavation of a long stretch of intensively occupied river gravels at Beckford on the Avon in Worcestershire. The area illustrated was dug under the direction of William Britnell in 1972-73. The features shown include a Bronze Age linear ditch, early Iron Age settlement sites, Roman field boundaries, enclosures and a scattered inhumation cemetery. A later, medieval, field system has been omitted for clarity.

The bulk of the topsoil was machined off and the underlying features were then dissected by hand, but a small area, that outlined at the northern end of the site, was dug entirely by hand. The drawing shows clearly the increase in the quality and detail of the evidence recovered by hand methods. These methods are inevitably much slower and are therefore not often practicable on the scale demanded by most rescue excavations on sand and gravel sites. If machine methods are chosen for reasons of speed the resulting loss of evidence, demonstrated here, must be accepted.

be maintained for long periods. It must be one of the responsibilities of site supervisors to learn to use tools properly, and to teach their workers to do so too. Both spades and shovels should be kept clean the whole time they are being used, since if they are dirty or rusty the soil will not slide off them, and they will then become very heavy. Needless to say all tools should be cleaned at the end of the day.

Picks of various sizes are sometimes necessary, but heavy picks can only dig 'blind', simply removing soil or clay or shale or whatever in bulk, whereas small hand picks, either of the types used by miners, or those adapted by a blacksmith from coal hammers or other small hand tools, are a necessity when it comes to dissecting a rampart of boulder clay or a mound of chalk. Such small picks are ideally made with one end pointed and one end flattened, for chopping, and used properly, they can be delicate tools. The choice of tool for each job is ultimately the responsibility of the director or his assistants, for while there are undoubtedly great excavators who could dig anything with a 6-inch trowel, the majority of us only achieve the optimum results with the right tools. Coles, 1972, 166-75, contains many useful hints on tools and their uses.

Earth-moving machinery

A great deal of time can be saved by the use of earth-moving machinery, principally in the removal of the over-burden of topsoil or other non-stratified material, but also to speed up an excavation which is being conducted against the clock. Two most useful pamphlets on the use of machinery in archaeology have been published – D.F. Petch, 'Earthmoving Machines and their Employment on Archaeological Excavations', *Journal of the Chester Archaeological Society*, (1965) and Francis Pryor, 'Earthmoving on Open Archaeological sites', *Nene Valley Archaeological Handbook*, I, 1974. In addition, useful accounts of methods used on the Continent will be found in van Es, 1969, and Farrugia, Kuper, Luning, and Stehli, 1973. It is unnecessary to repeat here the information and advice given in these publications.

In addition to the more conventional bulldozers and front-loaders, mini-bulldozers and dumper trucks are now increasingly used to considerable advantage in the small areas left for manoeuvre on many archaeological sites.

The two chief concerns of directors using mechanical equipment on a site must be the safety of the workers and the possible loss of evidence due to the bulk removal of earth. Safety precautions are discussed on p. 105 below. The losses of evidence are not so easily dealt with. Only on those excavations where both mechanical and hand excavation have been used and compared can an assessment of loss of evidence be made. At Beckford in Worcestershire, the Rescue Archaeology Group, led by William Britnell, stripped a large area of prehistoric occupation before gravel working. The bulk of the area had been stripped mechanically, but one area 40m. by 50m. was dug by hand. The results are shown in fig. 19. The losses will be proportionately greater if the mechanical stripping is taken below the immediate topsoil into the junction between the topsoil and the subsoil (the B-C horizon).

In large rescue excavations it is common practice to strip large areas down to the subsoil and to record only those features which have been preserved because they have been cut into the subsoil at its present level. While this undoubtedly gives a swift and broad picture of the occupied landscape the losses here will be at their maximum (see p. 129, below).

Trowelling

It is often difficult to know how best to instruct trowellers in the removal of the uppermost layer. One cannot say 'take this layer down to the clay/pebbles/sand below', since there is no way of knowing in advance what underlies the uppermost layer at any point even if a visibly underlying layer runs under its edge. This layer may peter out, or an intervening layer may start a little way further on. To give an example: A director instructed an experienced troweller to remove a layer of earth 'down to the boulder clay beneath'. The troweller did precisely as he was told, and in doing so removed part of a pebble floor which began some inches from the edge of the earthen layer. The director, not the troweller, was at fault for giving the wrong instructions. It must be impressed on the beginner that one layer only is to be removed at a time. The only general and golden rule which one can give trowellers is to remove the uppermost layer until a change of any kind is encountered, or in other words, 'until you find something different, even if this is only millimetres below'.

It is probably unnecessary to stress that the troweller should move backwards across the site, so that he does not kneel on the freshly trowelled surface and so that he can look at the newly-revealed surface at the optimum time for the distinguishing of soil colour and texture changes. It should be the rule, in fact, that no one may walk on an excavated surface unless they have imperative reasons for so doing. Few archaeological surfaces will stand repeated treading and many will not survive the pressure of even one pair of feet. The necessary encroachments of draughtsmen, finds plotters and photographers should be kept to the minimum, and in some cases paths on to the site can be indicated, by, for instance, using large stones as stepping stones and avoiding fragile pebble surfaces. Back-filled robber trenches (or earlier excavations) are often useful means of traversing the site. If planks or Summerfield tracking are available, pathways supported on sandbags (or fertilizer bags filled with earth) will keep traffic off the site. Control of movement around and over the site is part of the essential site discipline which must be instilled from the beginning.

The direction in which the surfaces are excavated is of fundamental importance. Nothing causes so much confusion among diggers and loss of intellectual grasp of the site by the supervisors as people trowelling in all directions. The ideal situation is that where a line of diggers, stretching the whole width of the site, can trowel downhill. In most cases of course one has to compromise but I am quite certain that a change in the direction of trowelling has to be strictly controlled if layers are not to be destroyed, even if only in part.

Ideally, again, one would choose, if one could, to trowel from a more complicated stratified area into one less complicated, viz:

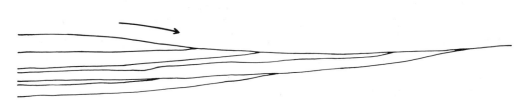

20

In this way the layers 'run out' and there is less danger of digging two layers at once, which may happen if one is trowelling in the opposite direction where layer A is found to run under layer B and so on.

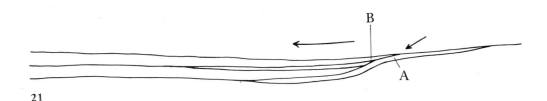

21

Unfortunately the situation illustrated is more likely to happen if one *is* trowelling downhill since there will have been a tendency for layers to accumulate downhill or in hollows. A typically awkward situation is often met with on a defensive site where layers tend to be eroded from the tops of the successive ramparts, to build up in their lee and in the accompanying ditches. If the centre of the site is slightly raised then the following situation may well be found:

22

If we accept the fundamental principle that one layer only at a time should be removed it becomes hard to reconcile this with the sheer practical difficulties of trowelling. If one trowels in the two directions shown in fig. 22 there is likely to be trouble when point X is reached since this means trowelling uphill perhaps steeply. We have so far talked as if layers are neat, homogeneous slices that can be peeled off the surface of the site, but even on more or less level surfaces the situation usually becomes much more complicated and one is often confronted with discontinuous layers interleaved in bewildering variety and, worse, merging imperceptibly into one another so that their edges are impossible to define. In this situation one can only do one's best to determine which layers overlie others, and to do this one may have to explore the junctions of the layers in question, without damaging the site, by miniature trenching. If mistakes are made, and a layer thought to be uppermost is trowelled away and proves to run under one or more adjacent layers, the best action to take is to record the situation by means of a drawing and a detailed note and then proceed to remove the uppermost layers.

Trowelling on a steep slope, such as the sides of a rampart or a motte can be not only arduous but very difficult since the rampart or motte material will almost certainly have slumped or crept down the slope. Under these circumstances, post-holes, timber-slots and other such features will become distorted, so that it is necessary to excavate under an overhang.

The situation is further complicated if the post-hole has been cut into underlying structural layers of similar composition as the filling of the post-hole. viz:

Section   **Section**

23 (left) shows a post set vertically in a sloping surface such as that of a mound or rampart. *a* is an earlier post hole. On the right is such a feature when the post has rotted and the upper wall of the hole has slumped. It illustrates also the possibility of confusing the fill of the post hole with the layers into which it has been cut.

Here it is almost impossible to avoid overdigging in order to establish the slope of the post-hole.

A somewhat similar problem occurs with the excavation of slanting post-holes in level ground, where a typical section might be:

Section   Section

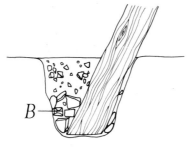
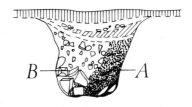

Plan

24   Diagrammatic sections and plan of a raking post showing the tendency of the packing to collapse into the post-void, distorting it. Such a post-hole is difficult to dig sequentially because of the distortion.

It is very difficult to excavate the post-hole, A, as distinct from the post-pit, B, especially if the material is sand or gravel or loose earth. The emptying of A will almost certainly cause the collapse of the backfilled pit into the empty post-hole. In loose soils, moreover, it is probable that the post-pit material will have slumped into the post-hole when the post is withdrawn or has rotted *in situ*. It may then be hard to establish the fact that the post-hole was originally slanting. A classic instance of such a misunderstanding was made in the excavation of the Viking fortresses at Trelleborg (Nørlund, 1948) and Fyrkat where the outer posts of the large bow-sided houses were believed to be vertical, until they were re-excavated between 1961 and 1967 (Olsen, 1968).

Methods of soil colour enhancement, photography with coloured filters and an instrument known as a 'penetrometer' were all used to establish the fact that the outer rows of posts of these buildings were not vertical but sloping inwards.

However, this re-excavation depended on seeing the post-holes in section by cutting a trench across the site of the post-hole and its surrounding post-pit, viz:

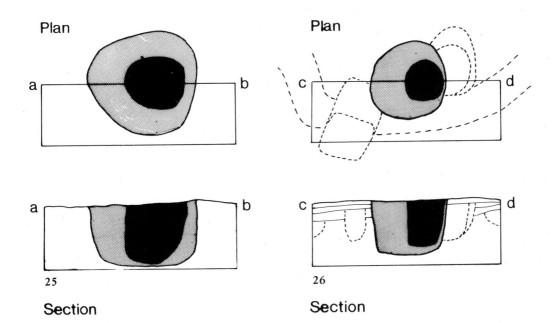

Plan

Section

25

Plan

Section

26

Fig. 25 shows a simple post-hole in a post-pit in plan and section. The situation is, however, much more likely to resemble **26** where the post-pit is cut through a number of earlier features. In such a case, cutting a trench to section the feature will destroy the earlier features unrecorded, and although they will be seen in the section they are not likely to be understood.

It should be a golden rule that every excavational problem should be tackled horizontally, from above. In other words, do not dig in from the side of a feature to determine its limits, but lower the whole surface, if necessary a few millimetres at a time, until the soil differences can be seen. In this way much less damage will be done and far fewer mistakes made.

Natural processes of weathering and leaching, of soil formation and worm action, coupled with the effect of, say, the original occupants of the site treading on the newly cleared surface around buildings under erection, all tend to make the junction between the lowest layers and some subsoils, such as clay and sand, difficult to determine. As a result we probably all over-dig quite considerably in our determination to 'establish the natural'.

On some subsoils, particularly on sands and gravels, and permeable rocks such as chalk and sandstone, confusion is often caused by natural formations which simulate archaeological features. Solution holes look like post-holes, fissures resemble ditches, palisade trenches, or timber slots and ponded hollows can be deceptively like man-made pits (Limbrey, 1975, 281,ff.). On sites where the archaeological features themselves are filled with clean material, and where there are few finds, the help of a geologist or soil scientist is invaluable. Ultimately, experience may be the only guide, and it will almost certainly be necessary to grade the features into all degrees of archaeological validity from positively man-made to positively natural. When the report comes to be written care must be taken not to use too many 'uncertain' features in the interpretation, unless this fact is clearly stated so that the report can be treated with caution.

Care must also be taken in the use of the word 'natural' as a synonym for the undisturbed subsoil, since many layers on archaeological sites are natural in origin. Some may be so thick and free from artefacts that they may be deceptively like the subsoil. Gravel redeposited by flood water, for example, may seal occupation layers under many metres of entirely clean material. Even down-wash from a nearby hill-side can cover archaeological features with 'natural' silt. And, of course, the earlier the periods in which one is interested the more likely it is that the remains of human occupation will be embedded in natural strata, so that most palaeolithic archaeology is carried out in what specialists in later periods would call 'the natural'.

On difficult sites, where the layers are varied in composition and thickness, where, for instance, a very thin floor may lie on a layer of make-up 5-10cm. thick, composed of rubble in earth, it may be necessary to excavate the under-lying layer a centimetre or so at a time, to explore it by means of a miniature *planum* excavation in order not to miss interleaved layers which may be structural. The strictest control must be exercised over this operation as it is only too easy to invent new surfaces (and even new buildings!) halfway down a thick layer.

If timber buildings are founded on rafts of rubble or other material, or their post-holes and slots are packed with stones or tiles and other debris, this sub-structure must be dissected and not merely stripped off until the next putative building layer is reached. It goes without saying that this is a slow process but it is often within these sub-structures that evidence of changes in plan or repairs are to be found.

When a stratified site is being dug it should, whenever possible, be kept 'in phase', that is, all recognizable features of one phase should be exposed at once. This will lead to greater understanding of structures and complexes of structures, since they can be seen and discussed as a whole, rather than as discrete parts reconstructed on paper afterwards. Naturally, there will be many occasions when features of more than one period are visible, or when features, thought at first to be contemporary, will prove, on closer examination, to be of different periods. Nevertheless, the effort to maintain the 'wholeness' of the site is valuable in that it counteracts a tendency to concentrate on the parts, and not to see the wood for the trees. Keeping the excavation, as far as possible, 'in phase' follows naturally from horizontal digging techniques, and is in sharp contrast to the vertical approach, in which the excavator tries to establish the sequence of events from the bottom of the stratification upwards as soon as he can. The temptation to have a look at earlier layers is almost irresistible to some excavators but it is a temptation which should be strongly resisted. We have seen that holes dug into extensive layers can be disastrous for their subsequent interpretation, and anyway the information gained by a 'sondage', however small, relates only to the area of the sondage. One may show that there are ten floor levels at one end of a building, but it does not follow that there will be ten at the other end — there may only be two, and it would clearly be nonsense to dig holes all over the floor to find out where the change in floor makeup occurred. 'Be patient; take it from the top, and all will be revealed' should be the motto.

Needless to say, if later pits, graves, gullies, post-holes or other features have been cut into the earlier layers, examination of their sides once they are emptied, often provides a helpful preview of the layers to come, without further damage to the site. Similarly, backfilled trenches from previous excavations may be emptied for a similar preview. If there is any danger of these emptied features or trenches collapsing they should be backfilled again with sand or sifted earth and lowered progressively as the excavation proceeds.

Sieving

However competent the trowelling on an excavation some small objects such as tiny coins, gems, intaglios, fragments of metal objects and other potentially important finds may be missed. In addition there is no doubt that some excavators, however reliable in other ways, are less sharp-eyed than others. It has been found that dry-sieving with ordinary garden sieves with a mesh of c. 10 mm. recovers a sufficiently large number of otherwise lost finds to make the extra work and time worthwhile. At the excavation directed by the writer at Wroxeter, in spite of very carefull trowelling, some ten percent of all small finds come from sieving. The sieved earth should be kept in a separate spoil heap for winter backfilling or other similar purposes, or even for sale as topsoil, for which there is a considerable demand in some districts.

Finds from the sieve will not be closely stratified, though, if each bucketful of soil is sieved individually, its general context will be known. As far as possible the spoil should be sieved from each layer or feature independently.

Finds from sieving should be marked as such so that the degree of their reliability of stratification is made quite clear. A coin or other datable object found during sieving of a layer from above which a number of layers have been removed can be rightly held to provide a *terminus post quem* for the layers above since it must derive from the underlying layer, even though its precise horizontal position may not be known. Such as assumption depends of course, on the careful and complete excavation of the upper layers.

Sections

Vertical sections

Vertical sections, just as much as horizontal surfaces, must be meticulously clean if they are to yield the maximum information. They should be cleaned from the top downwards (an apparently obvious rule not always observed), with the tip of the trowel and/or with the tip of a stiff brush. With a very loose section a paint brush may be sufficient. It is important to reveal the textures of the various layers by cleaning round stones, tiles and other fragments protruding from the surface. It is not sufficient simply to cut the section vertically with a spade or trowel, when protruding stones will be knocked out of the surface leaving holes, and perhaps causing miniature landslides, or, by being dragged across the surface, produce false patterns or textures. As Limbrey (1975, 271) has pointed out, the nature of the soils which make up a vertical section will best be revealed by using the tip of a sharp trowel in a chopping motion, rather than by scraping, which always tends to smear the junctions of layers. Under some special circumstances, in hard packed gravel, or where there are concrete floors, roads, layers of tile and other rubble in the section, it can be cleaned with a thin high-pressure jet of water, which washes out small particles and leaves a clean section with its textures enhanced. This method should only be used after careful tests on a small area. A soft brush and an air line, if available, can also be used on some loose and dusty surfaces.

Too much insistence has been made in the past on the vertical cutting of sections. If there is any doubt about the stability of the soil there is no reason why the section should not slope at an angle sufficient to reduce the risk of collapse and the resulting loss of evidence. Needless to say, if the cutting is more than 1.5m. (5ft.) deep it should be shored and the Health and Safety at Work Act, 1974 observed (see also Fowler, 1972). A side effect of sloping sections is that in narrow trenches more light is reflected from the surfaces, making them easier to draw and photograph. Equally there is no reason why, under some circumstances, sections should not be stepped. Whether they are sloped or stepped it is important to record them in exactly the way they are cut, and not to make them appear more vertical than they really are, as if in shame at a transgression of one of the cardinal laws of archaeology.

As will be clear from the earlier parts of this chapter, it is my opinion that the cutting of vertical sections should be kept to the minimum. Nevertheless, all sites, however large, have edges, which may ultimately reach considerable depths and provide long sections encircling the excavated area, and on other occasions trenches and sections may be archaeologically unavoidable. A flexible approach is needed, in which no appropriate technique is outlawed on doctrinaire grounds.

The cumulative section
One of the greatest difficulties with horizontal excavation is to reconcile the need for a constant overall view of the excavated surfaces with the need for sections. One of the principal values of drawn sections is for publication, for the visual demonstration of relationships which are otherwise difficult to describe though they may be fully appreciated while the excavation is in progress. (It will be noticed, for instance, that most of the diagrams in this book are sections, though

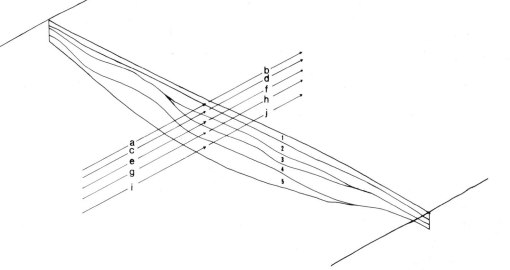

27-28   The   Cumulative
Section. Fig. 27 *above* shows
diagrammatically   a   simple
situation, in which a cumulative section is drawn by
removing Layer 1 up to the
proposed line of the section
(operation a). The section
is then measured and drawn
visually and the remainder of

it removed (operation b).
This   process   is   repeated,
pausing each time after operations c, e, g, and i, to draw
the section before proceeding.
   Fig. 28 *below* shows a
slightly more complex situation where, again, the operations   are   carried   out   in
alphabetical order. Since the

upper layers will have been
removed before the section
of each exposed layer is
drawn it is easier to use a
level and staff than a horizontal string to determine
the upper surface of the new
layer. Needless to say, the
plan of each layer is drawn
before it is removed.

illustrating situations which are often encountered horizontally.) My belief is that if sections are cut, and they reveal relationships not detectable in horizontal excavation, then the excavation is a bad one. The assertion that many layers, easily observed in plan, cannot be seen in section has become a commonplace. It follows therefore that horizontal excavation, so long as it is sensitive enough, is always likely to recover more information than can be seen in a section. The reservation which must be added to this statement is that the section demonstrates the vertical relationships of soils and their development in a way which is not possible by horizontal excavation.

How therefore to reconcile these two requirements: to see the site in plan and in section? The best solution, I believe, is a compromise, using the cumulative section. In this method, the excavation is carried up to a pre-determined line and the section drawn. The excavation then proceeds beyond this line. Each time the excavation reaches that line in the future the section will be drawn (figs. 27 – 28). Needless to say, with this method, accuracy of levelling and surveying are necessary if mistakes are to be avoided; but it has one very considerable advantage over the section cut on a notional line, say along a grid line or at 45° to the grid, in that it can be sited to section particular large-scale features, such as a building, or a rampart, invisible at an earlier stage of the excavation. There is no reason at all why a cumulative section should not be started at any stage of the excavation, based on a line chosen to give the maximum information about an emerging structure. The cumulative section is also very useful for the excavation of large pits or similar structures (figs. 29 and 30), especially if they themselves contain floors or other subsidiary structures.

A slightly different solution, used at Winchester and described in Biddle and Kjølbye-Biddle, 1969, 212-3, is to leave narrow balks which are continuously drawn and removed. This involves working on both sides of a 20cm. balk rather than up to a section line and beyond it, and has the advantage that the whole site can be worked all the time. The height to which a 20cm. balk can be left, i.e. the depth of the excavation on either side, will depend on the nature and stability of the deposits, and on the complexity of the features. For instance, where there is a complicated mass of stake-holes in each layer, the balks will have to be removed at each level if the stake-holes within the balks are to be seen and understood in relation to those around them. On the other hand, in heavy rubble it may be necessary to leave a wider balk. One must adopt a flexible approach which takes into consideration all the special problems posed by the site.

In most cases the edges of the excavation will ultimately form a section round the whole site, and one moreover that can be seen at once and drawn from the vertical face. It should be noted how many layers drawn in plan and cut by the edge of the excavation are not visible in the section seen at the edge of the site. Of course, it may be that some are visible in the section and have not been seen in plan! Here an inquest should be held.

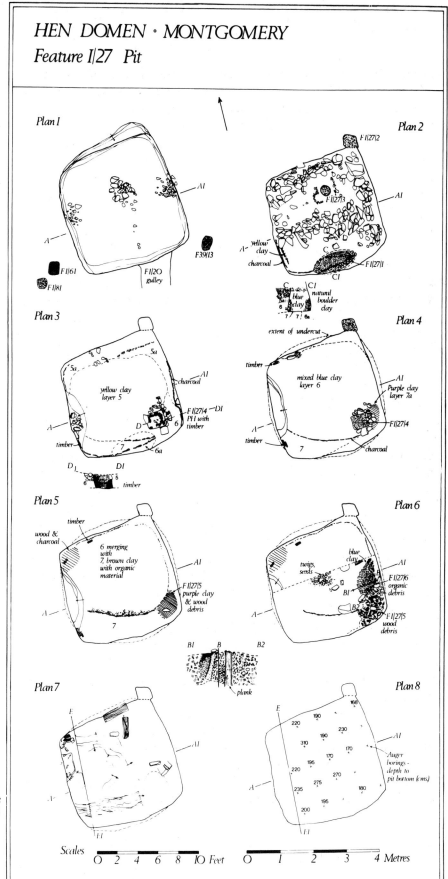

29 Hen Domen, Montgomery, Feature 1/27; Pit Plans at successive levels (see fig. 30)

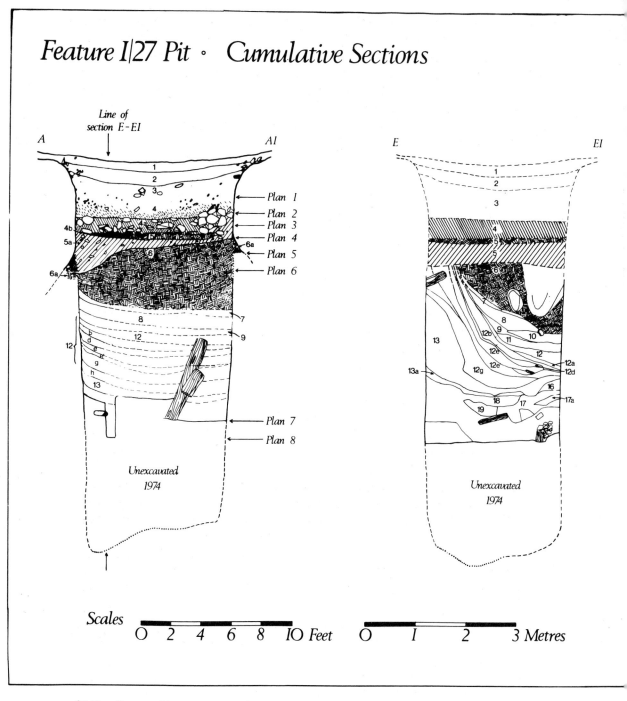

Feature 1/27 Pit · Cumulative Sections

30 Hen Domen, Montgomery, feature 1/27, pit. Cumulative sections on two axes A-AI, E-EI (see fig. 29).

In Scandinavian countries a method of very precise and detailed levelling of all excavated surfaces together with each of their associated finds enables theoretical sections to be drawn at any point and in any direction across the site. Good examples of this technique can be seen in Hatt, 1957. This method is a further step removed from drawing the section visually and I feel that the cumulative section is preferable. However since the site should be close contour surveyed at every stage, profiles and theoretical sections can be reconstructed along any transect if required.

The life history of a post-hole
Posts can be inserted into the ground in a number of ways. The most usual is to dig a hole larger than the diameter of the post, which is then inserted, sometimes against the side wall of a round post-pit, or in the corner of a square one, and sometimes in the centre of the hole. If the subsoil or underlying layers are soft the bottom of the pit may be packed with stones. The post-pit is then backfilled round the standing post either with the spoil taken from it, or with stones or rubble brought from elsewhere to hold it more firmly (fig. 31). The possibility that the post-pit may have been packed with billets of wood must not be excluded. Rarely, the post-pit may be dug the exact size of the post, which is then fitted into it. Occasionally, even quite large posts may be sharpened and driven into the ground like stakes, especially in soft, stone-free soils.

Where timbers are incorporated in ramparts or mounds and are designed to be part of the structure from the first, the rampart material may be piled around the standing timbers which would be either framed or temporarily supported during the operation. There will therefore be no construction pits. Subsequent posts erected on the rampart or mound will have to be set in pits, and by this are distinguishable from the original post holes.

A number of things may happen to a ground-fast post. It may gradually rot *in situ*, principally at the point where it enters the ground. Waterlogged posts, preserved to the present day, may be found to have rotted away at the level at which waterlogging was not permanent. Alternatively if a post is no longer needed it may be extracted or sawn off at ground level. It may be replaced in the same hole, on a slightly different alignment, or replaced in a different spot. If it is allowed to rot in place the rotting wood may be gradually replaced by fine soil, due to the action of wood-consuming insects, and of earthworms passing in and out of the area. Dust and silt will accumulate in the upper parts of the post-hole making its filling different at the top from that at the bottom. Here the action of worms in 'sorting' the earth is debatable (see p. 117 below). Sometimes silt will be prevented from entering to replace the rotting wood, when a void will be left, which may outline precisely the form of the post. If the post is an important one a plaster cast can then be taken. Should the post have been extracted, it may be possible to detect the 'rocking' of the post to loosen it, by observing the displacement of the post-pit filling; or one or more sides of the post-pit may

Section

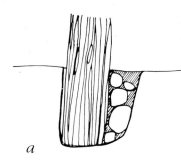

a

Section

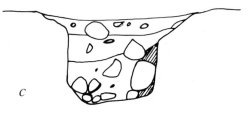

c

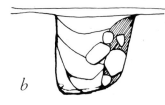

b

d

Section

Plan

Fig. **31** (a) shows a post standing in its post pit supported on one side by the wall of the pit and on the other by boulders, stones and earth packed into the pit. (b) shows a typical section of such a post-hole and pit if the post has been allowed to rot. (c) and (d) show the section and plan of such a post-hole if the post has been dug out, when it is possible that the original post-pit will have been enlarged by the robbing. The material thrown back forms a mixed fill.

have been dug out to make it easier to get at the post. At Yeavering Dr Brian Hope-Taylor postulated the use of sheer-legs to remove very large posts vertically, after part of their packing had been dug out (Doctoral thesis, Cambridge University Library).

When a post has been extracted the post-hole is very often backfilled in order not to leave an open hole in occupied ground. This backfilling should be readily distinguishable from the slow silting described above. However, if posts are being removed from an abandoned site, ragged holes may well be left to fill with water, silt, leaves and other debris.

Alternatively, the post may have been burnt *in situ*. In this case it is probable that the ground immediately surrounding the post will be charred or reddened. If the heat developed was great, the burning may extend to the bottom of the post-hole when, since combustion would have taken place with little oxygen, the post will have turned to charcoal instead of ash. This, if found, must be distinguished from the deliberate charring of the post, before it was inserted, in the hope that its life would be prolonged, in which case the charring will be a thin layer between the post and the side walls of the post-hole, rather than a thicker charcoal layer in the bottom of the hole, usually associated with the charred edges or sides mentioned above.

All the events here described as happening to posts may happen, with modifications, to other features such as timbers lying horizontally in trenches, wattle fences, lined pits, and so on.

Some long-term experiments on the rate of decay of posts set in the ground have been carried out at the Princes Risborough Laboratory of the Building Research Establishment and their results published in Morgan, 1975. The rate at which wood decays depends upon a number of environmental factors, though decay is completely arrested if the organism is deprived of either water or air. If wood is kept dry (i.e. at a moisture content below 20 per cent) there is no danger of fungal attack. Equally, if timber is kept saturated with water, as it may be if submerged or deeply buried, fungal attack will be inhibited through lack of air, though slower bacterial attack may develop under these conditions.

Posts with their bases set in the ground invariably undergo conditions which fall between these two extremes and are therefore subject to differing degrees of rot. Woods vary considerably in their natural durability. The table reproduced below (Morgan, *op. cit.* table 1) is based on the average life of heartwood stakes, 50mm. x 50mm. in cross-section, buried to half their length in the ground. Timber of larger cross-section has a longer life and it is found that the life of buried stakes is roughly proportional to their narrowest dimension. Thus timber with a life of 10 years in 50mm. x 50mm. stakes would be expected to last 15 years in 75mm. x 150mm. size. A massive post 350mm. x 350mm. should, on this reckoning, be expected to last 70 years.*

* These approximations will, of course be affected by the position of the post in the building. Aisle posts, completely enclosed under a roof, and buried in a dry floor, can be expected to last much longer than wall posts exposed, at least on one side, to the elements. Evidence of such differences has been observed, for instance in the West Hall at Cheddar (Rahtz, 1964) where the north wall posts were renewed while the aisle posts were retained.

Table 1 : Natural durability of some home-grown timber species
(based on the time taken for 50mm. x 50mm. stakes to decay in the ground)

Perishable	Non-Durable	Moderately Durable	Durable	Very Durable
Less than 5 years	5 - 10 years	10 - 15 years	15 - 20 years	More than 25 years
	Douglas fir Grand fir Silver fir Lodgepole pine Scots pine Norway spruce Sitka spruce	Larch Lawson cypress Sequoia Western red cedar	Yew	
Alder Ash Beech Birch Horse Chestnut Lime Poplar Sycamore Willow	Elm	Turkey Oak	Spanish Chestnut Oak	

It should be borne in mind that this classification refers only to the heart of wood, and that the sapwood of all species (even the durable ones) has no resistance to decay.

In a further series of experiments at Princes Risborough untreated posts 100mm. x 55mm. were tested under similar conditions against posts treated with various kinds of preservative. The results for untreated posts are tabulated below.

Table 2 : Percentage failure

	18 years	20 years	34 years	36 years
Oak	15	25	45	60
Scots pine	80	95	100	100
Douglas fir	85	100	100	100
Beech	100	100	100	100

It will be seen that the figures for oak are rather better in this experiment than Table 1 would suggest. However the life of a timber building is dependent on all its major timbers, so that if even 15 per cent of its posts have decayed after 18 years (Table 2) drastic repairs or complete rebuilding will be necessary.

Sometimes post holes are found with charcoal around their sides and it has been suggested that attempts have been made to prolong the life of the posts by charring them before they were buried. Experiments with charred posts give the following results (Morgan, Table 3, 24):

Table 3 : Average life of fence posts given in years							
	Oak	Beech	Birch	Corsican Pine	Scots Pine	Douglas Fir	Spruce	Jap Larch
End charred	8	4	3	4	5	8	7	10
Untreated controls	8	4	2	3	5	3	5	6

This table shows that charring increases the life of posts made of softwood, but not of two of the hardwoods tested, including oak, the most commonly used medieval building timber. Although insufficient evidence for the species of timber used in ancient buildings is available, clearly the figures quoted in the tables above should be considered when estimates of the probable life of wooden buildings are being made.

Special problems

The excavation of structural features

Post-holes and pits normally appear as shapes differentiated from the surrounding area by colour or texture or both. However, not every dark patch is a post-hole, and the features must be dissected in order to establish their character. There are a number of ways of doing this. One is to section them either on one or two axes thus:

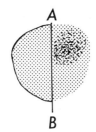

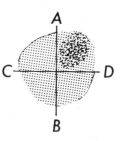

removing either half or two quadrants of the fill to the bottom of the hole when it is possible to draw sections A-B and/or C-D.

Unfortunately it may be that the feature is a post-pit (as the drawings indicate) and that the post-hole may lie completely in either the excavated or the unexcavated portion. In either case no vertical section of the post-hole is seen, which is a disadvantage in rescue excavation, since although removing only half the fill may halve the work, it might recover less than half of the evidence.

If the post-hole can be seen in the post-pit at the surface it may then be sectioned across an axis which cuts both (fig. 000).

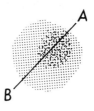

33

Another method, much used in some rescue excavations because it can be applied more mechanically, is to reduce the filling of the feature 5 cm. or so at a time, drawing the series of resultant plans (fig. 34 below).

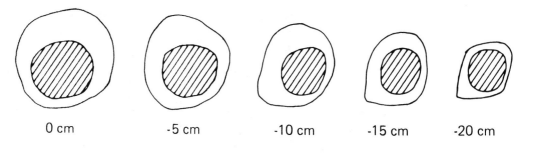

0 cm   -5 cm   -10 cm   -15 cm   -20 cm

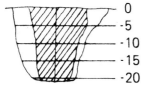

34

35 *right* The cumulative sections showing a stylized gulley with post-holes. It is decided to excavate it so that one longitudinal and two transverse sections can be drawn. Segments 1, 2 and 3 are removed first and the exposed faces of layer 1 are drawn. Segments 4, 5 and 6, are then removed, and the plan is drawn (this stage is not illustrated). Segments 7, 8 and 9 are removed and the process is repeated. When 10, 11, and 12 are removed dark patches, possibly indicative of post-holes, are seen and drawn in plan. The post-holes are themselves quadranted, and drawn in section and plan before 13, 14, 15, 16, and 17 are removed. The process is repeated until the feature is cleared either down to the undisturbed subsoil or until the layers into which it was originally cut have been fully exposed.

The advantage of this method is that the feature can be reconstructed three-dimensionally with some accuracy, especially if the excavated levels are close together. But it requires considerable skill and vigilance on the part of the troweller to ensure that finds from the post-*hole* are not confused with finds from the post-*pit* since they may be crucial in dating, and there may be as much as half a century between the digging of the post-pit and the eventual filling of the post-hole. If the post-hole or pit is large enough the methods can be combined and cumulative sections drawn along any required axes. This method has the added advantage that the line of the section can be changed if circumstances require it; for example, if the post-pit proves to contain two post-holes of different periods. The same principles may be used to excavate the other features cut into the sub-soil or into earlier levels. Gullies may be sectioned lengthwise as well as trans-versely, and cumulative sections drawn at all stages thus:

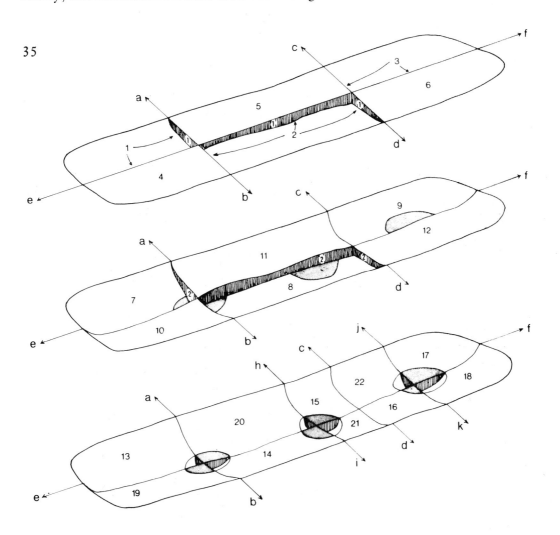

35

Large pits should certainly be excavated in great detail if the maximum evidence is to be extracted from them; and here, presuming that the filling is in detectable layers it is better to excavate them separately, using cumulative sections rather than the planum method (figs. 29-30).

Methods of enhancing soil colour differences

Every excavator of timber structures is aware of the considerable changes in soil colours brought about by the dampening or soaking of the soil with water when colours which are only faintly differentiated in a dry state become much stronger, making features such as post-holes or pits easier to distinguish. This is a different effect from that of the drying-out of the surface after rain or artificial soaking, when pits, post holes and the like may retain the moisture longer and thus appear as damp marks in the drying ground. This is an ephemeral effect which can sometimes, though not always, be repeated by a new shower of rain or a second spraying, followed by a period of drying.

Methods of enhancing the soil differences which are the only means of detecting post-holes and other structural anomalies have been tried with varying success. Olsen (1968) describes some of the methods used in the re-excavation of the Viking fortress at Trelleborg, first excavated between 1934 and 1943 (Nørland, 1948). Doubt had been cast on the validity of the evidence obtained from the earlier excavation and the site was therefore in part re-excavated using a number of methods to enhance differences in the colour of the soil. Use of a blue filter brought one of the post holes up as a darker stain (Olsen, *op. cit.*, plate F) and another post-hole was treated after sectioning with hydrochloric acid and potassium sulphocyanate, which take on a strong red colour when in contact with traces of iron in the soil.

Olsen found that the use of coloured spectacles was not very satisfactory, nor did infra-red photography give very decisive results.

Clearly there is still scope for considerable experiment in the detection of decayed timber structures and related soil disturbances. One of the values of long-term research excavation is that such experiments can be mounted there under something approaching laboratory conditions, usually impossible on an emergency dig. Moreover, the results of such experiments might ultimately speed up the excavation of threatened sites.

The excavation of small finds

The generic term 'small find' tends to be given to almost anything that can be lifted out of the ground, from a Roman *minimissimus*, 2mm. in diameter, to an architectural fragment, so that it is difficult to lay down rules to cover all eventualities. It has been well said by Coles (1972, 185) that every find is important and 'never more so than at the moment of its recognition when its precise relationship with other finds and with its containing deposit can be seen'. Ideally finds should not be removed from their surrounding material by levering or pulling, but should be taken out with the layer itself. Unfortunately this is often impracticable. As a feature or layer is removed finds may be seen protruding from the layer beneath. If these finds are not in any way fragile or vulnerable to exposure they can be left until the layer in which they are embedded is removed; but this might be days, months or even a year or more later, according to the size and nature of the excavation, so that a decision will have to be made on the basis of the lesser of two evils. If the exposed features/layers are given identifying numbers as soon as they are exposed (as they should be) then the finds can be removed from them and labelled as coming from these underlying features. If a find should be deeply embedded and yet vulnerable it may be best to cover it with sand, or polythene and sand, or re-bury it in its own soil until the excavation again reaches that point and the object can be removed with the feature/layer. Only in the last resort should a miniature trench be cut round the find in order to release it from the ground. Doing this destroys its relationship with unseen layers and may well obscure its real function, origin or derivation.

Often a find will first be seen in the loose earth just trowelled from the surface. If the excavation is being kept scrupulously clean, and one layer only removed at a time there should be little doubt from which layer, and, within a few centimetres, from which spot the find came. If, however, finds appear during the demolition of a rampart or the shovelling up of a hastily removed deposit, their provenance should be regarded with considerable suspicion. Sometimes characteristic soils such as clay or sand still clinging to the find may make its provenance more certain, but it would still be unwise to use the discovery of such finds as important interpretative evidence.

Again, finds often appear at the junction between two layers. While it is usual, under these circumstances, to assign such finds to the upper, later layer rather than the one below, a more subtle approach may be necessary. Imagine a pebble surface in use for a century. When it was laid, pottery and small finds contemporary with it and earlier than it become incorporated in it by accident. During its lifetime pottery and small objects and perhaps coins were dropped on it, some of them becoming embedded in its upper surface. When it was abandoned, another layer accumulated or was laid over it. This layer incorporated slightly later material (together, no doubt, with some residual material from earlier deposits). It is useful therefore to distinguish the finds (both pottery and objects) from layer A and layer B and from the junction of the two layers A/B. In practice, it has proved possible in this way to separate out pottery of the medieval period, spanning only a century or so, more critically than if the material from A/B had been labelled simply A. Nevertheless, it must also be borne in mind that potsherds and objects tend to sink through the soil, due to worm action, until they reach a more solid layer (see pp. 118 below), so that some of the material labelled A/B may have moved downwards. Thus the activity of earthworms on the site should be taken into account.

All finds, however indestructible they may seem, should be treated with the greatest respect, and their removal undertaken, as far as possible, without touch-ing them with any tool likely to mark or damage them. Finds which may look most unprepossessing in the ground may prove to be of major importance when they have been cleaned and conserved. Every find, then, should be given equal care in its removal, recording, immediate treatment and storage.

Finds that have been lying in the earth for centuries will have reached a more or less stable chemical and physical state until they are disturbed by the excavator. Immediately they are exposed to the air, to drying, or moisture or any other change of environment, processes which have been halted or slowed to an imper-ceptible rate will begin to affect them, sometimes so rapidly and irreversibly that within minutes irreparable damage may be done to them. In the case of any find which is considered to be vulnerable the golden rule is to keep it in the environ-ment in which it was found. This may mean leaving it embedded in its matrix of earth and lifting it as a block to be dissected under laboratory conditions. If this is impracticable, the find should be kept in conditions approximating in moisture or dryness to its recent environment. For this purpose sealed poly-thene boxes or bags used in conjunction with dessicators or wet wrappings are invaluable. For some exceptionally fragile or vulnerable finds immediate field treatment will be necessary.

An essential handbook, *First Aid for Finds*, has been published by RESCUE (Leigh and others, 1972). This gives short but explicit instructions on the immedi-ate treatment and packing of objects made of all the materials likely to be found during an excavation, emphasising that 'with the majority of metal and organic remains deterioration of some kind is inevitable *unless* positive steps are taken in the field to arrest it'.

The materials and methods of first-aid treatment described in *First Aid for Finds* should be within the budget and competence of even the smallest excava-tion. (If they are not, the excavation should not be taking place.) It must be emphasised, however, that only immediate and essential procedures for arresting deterioration in finds are described. Ideally a trained conservator should be attached to every excavation, but since there are comparatively few conservators in Britain (and probably in the world), and since the annual output of trained conservators does not begin to meet the need, directors have to fall back on their own resources and stabilize their finds at least until they can be drawn, photographed, studied and handed to a museum.

The excavation of fragile finds
An excellent maxim is to treat all finds as fragile until they are proved not to be, although proving that a find is not fragile may damage it irrevocably! This is a problem to which there is no straightforward answer. One can only urge trowellers to be vigilant and to ask for help if there is any doubt about the robustness of a find, preferably at the moment at which it is first seen.

The excavation of finds of potential importance (which will vary according to the site and the circumstances) should be photographed at every stage, and they should be carefully drawn before lifting. Such a record may be crucial to the eventual understanding of their significance, or their relationship with adjacent finds.

If a find is almost completely rotted away and is little more than a stain in the ground the only way to lift it is to cut out the whole block of soil in which it lies. There are difficulties, however. It is seldom easy to see how large the object is, or was; the stain may simply be the tip of the iceberg. Investigation round the object will destroy its relationship with its environment and isolate it from its contiguous layers. Above all one must not become so excited by the presence of an unusual find that the fundamental principles of excavation are temporarily forgotten. Later, when the object comes to be interpreted and its relationship to the site assessed every scrap of evidence will be needed.

Whenever a block of soil has to be taken from the site every effort should be made to record its stratification as it is cut out, and every stage of the operation should be photographed. Here the polaroid camera is most useful. The block may be firm enough to be lifted out on its own, though more often it will need to be supported on all sides with sheets of plywood or hardboard until a sheet of ply, hardboard or metal can be slid underneath it. In extreme cases the block may have to be encased in plaster of paris or polyurethane foam and then in a wooden box in order to get it out intact.

If, to all intents and purposes, the object has disappeared, leaving only an impression of its shape in the ground, a plaster cast can be made of this impression. A recent large-scale example of the use of plaster was in the re-excavation of the Sutton Hoo Ship burial mound (Bruce-Mitford, 1974, 170 ff.).

On other occasions the object may be consolidated in the ground before its removal. Ideally, this should be done by a conservator, who will choose the materials to be used with due regard to the nature of the object, since the consolidating agents may have to be removed in the laboratory before the object can be studied. In general, a 5% polyvinyl acetate solution in toluene for dry objects, and a polyvinyl acetate emulsion for damp or wet objects is recommended. The emulsion can be thinned with water, when it penetrates the object more easily and can be painted on in a number of operations rather than one thick layer. This enables the excavator to judge the effect of the treatment and to use the minimum amount of emulsion necessary to consolidate the object sufficiently to hold it together while it is lifted. It is useful to note that the emulsion hardens without drying so that the object can be kept damp during the operation. If a fairly large find, such as a shattered pot or a mass of metal work, it to be held together, a crêpe bandage may be useful as it has strength combined with gentle elasticity. Needless to say, any fragile object should be taken to the conservation laboratory as soon as possible after lifting so that it can be given skilled treatment. Comprehensive packing instructions for all kinds of objects are given in Leigh and others, 1972.

The excavation of waterlogged finds

In waterlogged deposits organic materials such as wood, leather and fabrics are preserved to a greater or lesser degree due to the fact that their environment is anaerobic, and so does not provide sufficient oxygen for the support of fungi and the bacteria of decay, or for the oxidation of metals. Immediately preserved organic materials (or metallic objects) are exposed to the air they begin to deteriorate, partly due to oxidation but, more quickly, due to drying. This deterioration begins even while they are being uncovered and removed from their layer of deposition; while, for instance, they are being photographed or drawn *in situ*.

Excavation and the subsequent packing of waterlogged finds should therefore be swift and delicate. Sometimes objects such as preserved shoes, or fragments of wood can easily be detached from their matrix, but very often, in cess-pit fillings or the bottoms of moats, the layers may consist almost entirely of preserved organic material: reeds, bracken, twigs, branches, leaves and seeds, together with the remnants of human occupation. If the amount of this solid organic fill is only small it can be saved complete, but in the case of large deposits the logistic problems of lifting and storage and the impossibility of working on tons of preserved material make sampling of the matrix essential. The preserved artefacts then have to be removed from the matrix, an operation which may be quite distinct from environmental sampling. As it is often impossible or highly undesirable to walk on the surface of the deposit, a system of planked cat-walks should be arranged so that they do as little damage as possible to the deposit. The excavators can then lie on the cat-walks in order to dissect and remove the layers. If the deposit is in a deep cutting, such as a ditch section, or in a cess-pit or well, it should not be difficult to erect scaffolding from which a cradle can be suspended. The excavator or excavators can then lie on this cradle (preferably on an air bed if they are to work for long periods).

Where the waterlogged deposit includes extremely fragile objects preserved in quantity the problem of excavating them on the spot becomes almost insuperable, but equally the removal of blocks of the matrix involves the grave risk of damaging unseen objects while the block is being cut out. Obviously under these circumstances the larger the mass of matrix that can be lifted the less damage will be done, and if the deposit is of major importance a civil engineering contractor should be brought in to deal with the problem on a large scale. If sufficient funds are not available, the deposit should be left where it is until it can be dealt with properly. Only under salvage conditions should the matrix be dug out wholesale.

When waterlogged finds have been lifted they should immediately be packed in an environment as close as possible to that from which they came. Polythene bags and polystyrene boxes are the most convenient and efficient means of doing this, and both can be obtained in forms which are self-sealing and water-tight. Self-sealing bags are made with white panels on which details of the find can be written in Pentel or similar pens, but they cannot be opened and resealed more than once or twice without losing their water-tight property. Polythene boxes with air-tight lids can be obtained in many sizes and are useful for more bulky finds.

Large objects can be made into parcels with heavy duty polythene sheet. A waterlogged bridge timber from Hen Domen, Montgomery, a foot square and 14 feet long, was fed into a large-diameter polythene tube and the ends firmly tied, so that it looked rather like an oversize Christmas cracker. It has remained in this tube since 1962 and, when last examined, was still in excellent condition, since the lack of air had inhibited fungal growth and the timber had dried out very slowly.

The lifting and preservation of large timber structures such as dug-out canoes, or complete bridge foundations is not easy but does not always require elaborate museum facilities if one is prepared to be patient. Timber will begin to deteriorate immediately it is exposed. Although the core may be extremely hard, the surface, to a depth of a centimetre or so, is likely to be very soft, and to be bruised even by the pressure of the fingers. While the timber must obviously be handled if it is to be removed from the ground and studied, this handling should be kept to the minimum, and the exposed surfaces kept wet by constant spraying, and covered with saturated sacking or similar materials at night. In the case of especially important remains 24-hour spraying should be maintained if possible. A good account of the large-scale excavation of preserved timber is contained in the Skuldelev Ship report (Olsen and Crumlin-Pedersen, 1968). Except in the most unexpected emergencies, the excavation of large waterlogged finds should be made with the active cooperation of the museum in which they are ultimately to be housed or, in the case of DOE sponsored excavations, with the aid of the Inspectorate's Laboratory. Only thus will the finds be guaranteed professional treatment.

The storage and safe-keeping of portable finds
This is one of the most difficult problems facing the excavator. The rescue excavation explosion of the last five years has added a vast quantity of archaeological material to the crowded and sometimes neglected store-rooms of our museums. As a result a high proportion of all excavated objects is rotting away, most of it unpublished. The training of conservators, the provision of museum or other suitable storage space, and the availability of laboratories are all woefully inadequate. A contributory factor in this crisis in conservation is the apparent reluctance of excavation directors to take an interest in their finds once the more important among them have been drawn and photographed. There is a largely unspoken feeling that from then on they are someone else's responsibility, probably that of a museum, although which one is not often specified. The days are over when excavations could be lightly undertaken, without a great deal of thought about the publication of results or where the finds were to be stabilized and stored. Excavation must be seen as a long and complex process ending only with the

publication and storage of the data, and its interpretation and proper treatment, and the storage and display of the finds. It follows that arrangements of all of these should be made before the excavation begins. If a total lack of facilities in the area prevents this it is the *director's* responsibility to make adequate temporary arrangements. If necessary he must train a conservator in the immediate treatment of the material, and obtain access to a store-room for the finds so that they can be kept under the optimum conditions until disposal arrangements can be made.

Museum directors in general are acutely aware of this hiatus in archaeological provision but lack of funds, space and trained staff make the prospect of an early solution improbable. In the interim, excavators and museums must work closely together to make temporary arrangements, and to agree on their areas of responsibility. One sympathizes with the hard-pressed museum director who blanches at the thought of storing hundredweights of undisplayable pottery, bone, and formless lumps of iron. But it is no solution to keep only selected objects, rim sherds and the like and get rid of the rest, since we do not know what questions we shall be asking of our material in the future. For example, tons of Roman pottery, particularly body sherds, have been dumped from earlier excavations on major sites in the belief that they had told us all we needed to know. However, the study of Roman pottery is constantly changing our views on its dates and places of manufacture. Here quantitative analysis may be as important as qualitative. In addition it is only comparatively recently that it has been realized that a very considerable quantity of pottery was imported into Britain from Gaul, North Africa and the eastern Mediterranean in the late- and post-Roman periods. Very probably a great many sherds from these pots have been dumped unrecognized and as of little interest. Storage of all the finds from very prolific Roman, medieval and post-medieval sites is a daunting task, but inescapable if we are ultimately to extract the maximum information from the material.

Excavating graves and cemeteries

Brothwell (1963) has written the standard text-book on the excavation of human remains and the reader is referred to this. However, he does not pay much attention to the recording of skeletons (and their possible accompanying grave goods) beyond advocating photography *in situ* before lifting. Vertical photography is preferable to oblique if there is only time for one photograph of each grave in a cemetery and ideally a stereoscopic colour pair should be taken of each burial. Very tall tripods with a reversible head enabling the camera to be attached pointing vertically downwards can be obtained and are more convenient to use than the larger structures described in Chapter 8. Since the orientation of graves is crucial in the interpretation of cemeteries it is most important that a north point should be included. Scales should be laid with the skeleton, not on the side of the grave. If grave goods are present the whole complex should be photographed in

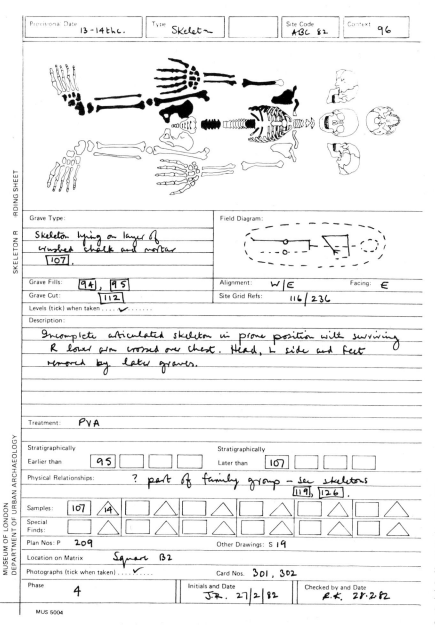

SKELETON R͏ḎING SHEET

MUSEUM OF LONDON
DEPARTMENT OF URBAN ARCHAEOLOGY

Provisional Date 13-14thc.	Type Skeleton		Site Code ABC 82	Context 96

Grave Type:
Skeleton lying on layer of crushed chalk and mortar [107].

Field Diagram:

Grave Fills: [94], [95]

Alignment: W/E   **Facing:** E

Grave Cut: [112]

Site Grid Refs: 116/236

Levels (tick) when taken ....✔......

Description:
Incomplete articulated skeleton in prone position with surviving R lower arm crossed over chest. Head, L side and feet removed by later graves.

Treatment: PVA

Stratigraphically Earlier than 95

Stratigraphically Later than 107

Physical Relationships: ? part of family group - see skeletons [119], [126].

Samples: 107 /14

Special Finds:

Plan Nos: P 209   **Other Drawings:** S 19

Location on Matrix Square B2

Photographs (tick when taken) ....✔....   **Card Nos.** 301, 302

Phase 4   **Initials and Date** J.R. 27/2/82   **Checked by and Date** R.K. 28.2.82

MUS 5004

36 The *pro-forma* for the recording of cemeteries used by the Department of Urban Archaeology of the Museum of London. The surviving bones of the excavated skeleton are filled in with coloured pencil on the outline provided and the position of grave goods can be indicated in relation to the bones.

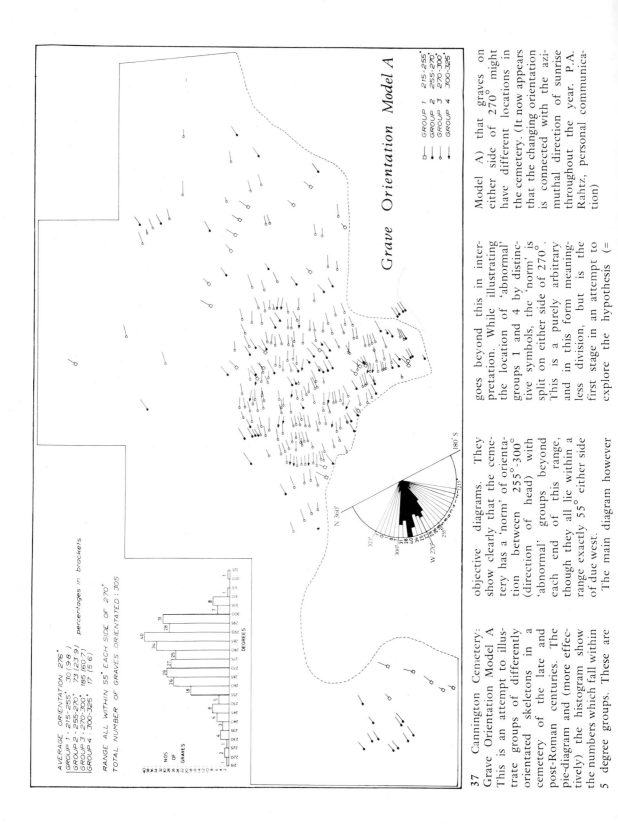

Grave Orientation Model A

AVERAGE ORIENTATION 276°

GROUP 1 - 215°-255°   30 (9.8)
GROUP 2 - 255°-270°   73 (23.9)   percentages in brackets
GROUP 3 - 270°-300°   185 (60.7)
GROUP 4 - 300°-325°   17 (5.6)

RANGE ALL WITHIN 55° EACH SIDE OF 270°

TOTAL NUMBER OF GRAVES ORIENTATED : 305

GROUP 1   215°-255°
GROUP 2   255°-270°
GROUP 3   270°-300°
GROUP 4   300°-325°

37 Cannington Cemetery: Grave Orientation Model A This is an attempt to illustrate groups of differently orientated skeletons in a cemetery of the late and post-Roman centuries. The pie-diagram and (more effectively) the histogram show the numbers which fall within 5 degree groups. These are objective diagrams. They show clearly that the cemetery has a 'norm' of orientation between 255°-300° (direction of head) with 'abnormal' groups beyond each end of this range, though they all lie within a range exactly 55° either side of due west.

The main diagram however goes beyond this in interpretation. While illustrating the location of 'abnormal' groups 1 and 4 by distinctive symbols, the 'norm' is split on either side of 270°. This is a purely arbitrary and in this form meaningless division, but is the first stage in an attempt to explore the hypothesis (= Model A) that graves on either side of 270° might have different locations in the cemetery. (It now appears that the changing orientation is connected with the azimuthal direction of sunrise throughout the year. P.A. Rahtz, personal communication)

black and white, and in colour (to show, for example, verdigris staining on bones where bronze ornaments have been). Here oblique and detail photographs of the positions of ornaments, weapons, dress attachments, and so on will be necessary, if the full implications of the grave-goods are to be understood, or if it is intended to reconstruct the burial for museum display.

Detailed drawing of all the skeletons in a large cemetery may be an impossibly long task, especially if the work is being done under rescue conditions. A most useful form, including a diagrammatic skeleton, has been designed (by S. Hirst, fig. 36), and this is intended to be used in conjunction with photographs, the extant bones being indicated on the diagram by means of coloured pencils. Needless to say, if this method is used it is absolutely necessary to be sure that the photography is satisfactory before lifting the bones. If a dark-room is not available on the site, a polaroid camera will ensure that a photographic record is obtained, though at present polaroid prints are no substitute for large, detailed photographs.

A carefully surveyed plan of the whole cemetery is vital if its growth, use and abandonment are to be fully understood. Changes of orientation (fig. 37) or the size and shape of the graves, or their grouping, can only be studied from a full and accurate plan. This plan will also be the basis for overlays, demonstrating in coloured diagrammatic form, the types and distribution of grave goods, on which much of the interpretation of the cemetery may depend. Further over-lays containing details of the skeletal material, such as age, sex, height and other characteristics can eventually be constructed from the anatomist's reports.

In some cases, where the soil is unsuitable for the preservation of bone, the skeleton may only be revealed as a soil-mark, a series of discolourations in the bottom of the grave (see Jones, 1968, plate Lb.). Here filters of various colours may be needed to give the clearest black and white photographs, or methods of soil colour enhancement may be tried.

If possible, an environmentalist or soil scientist should be present during the excavation in order to sample the soils around and within the skeletons for organic remains, such as clothing or food. If this is impossible, samples, whose origins in relation to the skeletons are carefully noted, should be taken for labora-tory examination.

More information will be obtained from inhumations if an anatomist can be present on the excavation since he will be able to examine the disposition of the bones *in situ* and will also be able to draw attention to the possibility of finding gall-stones, or the remains of food, etc. Chemical analysis of the soils which have replaced the various organs may, under some circumstances, also yield vital information. The evidence to be obtained from human burials will include not only demographic statistics, details of ritual and in some cases a corpus of grave goods, but when closely studied they may also produce data on family groups and other relationships and evidence of disease or skeletal distortions resulting from patterns of work (Wells, 1964).

Berthe Kjølbye-Biddle has published a frank and illuminating account of the excavation of the deeply-stratified cemetery north of the Cathedral at Winchester (1975). Because this cemetery overlay the foundations of the Old Minster, its excavation was accelerated by more summary digging than would be normal on a research excavation. Nevertheless the carefully considered compromise strategy employed recovered a mass of detailed information regarding the medieval population, medieval grave types and graveyard topography 'probably at present unequalled in Britain' (*ibid.* p. 92). The whole article is required reading for excavators of cemeteries, whether under research or rescue conditions.

Vertical stereoscopic colour photography combined with recording on pre-printed forms would speed up the mechanics of planning very considerably and thus leave more time for detailed excavation. The outline plans of the graves must, of course, be plotted on to a master plan as the work proceeds, with the double check of carefully recorded co-ordinates. This is Kjølbye-Biddle's 'approach 2' (*ibid.* p. 97) with the addition of stereoscopic photography to offset the disadvantage of drawing skeletons at the rather small scale of 1:20.

Site organisation

Providing an optimum micro-climate

For most of its existence British archaeology has shared a serious drawback with other major sports in that rain stops play, sometimes for days on end. Even when the rain clears the pitch is seldom fit for hours or even days, and then, in excavation as in cricket, a day's rain can produce a drastically different result from that predicted when the sun was shining.

Apart from the loss of time and temper, relying on the vagaries of the weather is extremely inefficient. We must, especially in these days of increasing emergencies and decreasing resources, use our time and skilled manpower as intensively as possible. I do not believe that the best way to do this is simply to press on regardless through all weathers. Saturated ground is rarely fit for efficient trowelling and often becomes so sticky that it is impossible to work properly. I no longer believe either that 'any information is better than none'. If the information produced under bad weather conditions is only partial, with great loss of detail and possible loss of whole periods of occupation, the evidence is so distorted that it might have been better not to have dug the site at all.

As far as resources permit we must attempt to create over our excavation a micro-climate which will enable us to extract the maximum information from the soil. Anyone who has dug in a temperate, variable climate will know that the changes of humidity in the soil, rain followed by a drying wind, for instance, will reveal soil differences quite invisible when the ground is either dry or soaking wet. What we have to do therefore is not simply to keep the site dry so that we can work in comfort, but vary the humidity (and, if possible, the temperature), thus giving the optimum soil conditions for the area being excavated.

The first necessity is shelter. Ideally a shelter should be waterproof, stable (that is, not so light that it will be blown away by strong winds), and large enough to cover not only the area immediately being excavated, but also to leave room for the removal of spoil behind the excavators. For a comparatively small site, such as a barrow, an inflatable tent of the kind used for temporary exhibitions would be perfectly adequate since these shelters are kept up by a small difference in the interior air pressure. Since this is maintained by a pump (either electric or petrol-driven) it has the advantage that either cold or warm air can be circulated. Air conditioning would be necessary here, as shelters of all kinds become very hot in sunshine, and the type under discussion is, in fact, completely enclosed.

A much less expensive form of shelter is provided by large horticultural tunnels which can be obtained in bays up to 10m. wide and 5m. long. Each bay can be joined to the next forming a tunnel of any required length. Heavy duty polythene sheeting is attached to the supports by means of spring clips. The polythene must be drawn very tightly over the framework so that rain water does not collect in pockets in the roof, and to prevent the wind from turning the whole thing into a highly inefficient sail-plane. In practice it has been found advisable to anchor the shelter along the sides with sand bags, or fertilizer bags filled with spoil. The 'skirt' of polythene on which the sandbags rest also stops water running off the roof from cutting channels in the excavation. The metal framework has proved to be sufficiently flexible to adapt itself to the undulations of the site, as long as these are not too violent.

The surface of the site can be protected from damage by sandbags placed under the edges of the shelter and sandbags can also be used to pack hollows crossed by the edges of the shelter. These shelters, though heavy, can be carried by about six people per unit. They do have a number of disadvantages, however. They produce a feeling of claustrophobia in some workers, they are noisy in rain and in wind, and because they reduce the visible area of the site it may become difficult for trowellers and supervisors alike to see the context of the part being excavated, so that a sense of perspective is lost, and the site cannot be viewed as a whole.

These disadvantages can to some extent be overcome by rolling back the polythene sheeting when the weather clears rather than leaving it on permanently. It is an advantage too if the shelter can be erected so that its back is to the prevailing wind, when the front can be rolled up, lessening the claustrophobic feeling and giving the trowellers a view of the area that has been completed. Shelters, of whatever kind, will keep the site dry, but it is also necessary in almost all cases, to keep it damp. For this purpose hoses with variable jets or lawn-sprinkling attachments are most convenient. The rotating sprinkler should make the droplets as fine as possible so that an evenly soaking 'Scotch mist' falls on the area. On very large sites agricultural sprays of the sort used to water market gardens and race courses would be more appropriate. If mains water or water carriers are not available, hand pumps, such as stirrup pumps or those used for portable showers or for spraying insecticide, are ideal for giving a spray varing from a fine mist to a downpour. For small sites these are preferable to the more indiscriminate lawn sprinkler.

It is important to spray finely and evenly, soaking the site gradually and thoroughly so that false damp marks are not created by the sprayer. Merely dampening the surface is of little use. Great care should also be taken not to flood the site so that hollows become filled with a fine layer of silt, and do not dry out for several days. Spraying is useful, if not essential, on a very dusty site where working conditions can become highly unpleasant, and thus counter-productive. Now that the cost-effectiveness of excavations in both time and money is being more and more studied, it is an economy to spend money on hoses, sprays, pumps and, if necessary, water tanks, in order to provide optimum conditions, where the site can be kept working at maximum capacity. A pleasant aspect of spraying on very hot days is the cooling not only of the surface but of the surrounding air, so that working conditions are improved. The days when it was a test of stamina to dig under the most atrocious conditions are surely on the way out. Efficiency, both in digging and recording, falls off markedly in extreme weather conditions: in rain, ancillary services, such as drawing and photography become difficult, if not impossible, and on a sun-baked surface both the draughtsman and the camera will see less.

If an excavation has to be left open for long periods it is important to protect it from damage by weathering. The surface should, of course, first be recorded as thoroughly as possible. Any vertical face which is left open will be liable to erosion or collapse, taking with it unrecorded evidence. Once useful by-product of area excavation is that, with few balks, there is less risk of this kind of loss. Nevertheless every excavation has edges, and excavated pits, post-holes, gullies and the like will need protection. One way that has proved successful is to fill, or better, over-fill, the pits, post-holes etc. with clean sand, and in the case of especially important or vulnerable features, cover them with polythene sheet, preferably black to exclude the light and inhibit plant growth. The features can then be emptied accurately and swiftly on the resumption of the excavation of that part of the site. If they cut through a number of surrounding layers, these layers can be removed progressively, while lowering the backfilling of the features in parallel. If sand is not readily available sifted earth (derived from the sifted spoil of the site) may be used. If there is any reason to suspect that it might be difficult subsequently to distinguish the backfill the features can be lined with polythene sheet before they are filled. This is in some ways less satisfactory as the free movement of water is impeded and, in the more extensive features, worms are liable to die under the sheet in considerable numbers leaving an un-pleasant layer to be cleaned off. The edges of shallow excavations can be protected by packing sand or sifted earth along them; and horizontal features, such as floors or hearths, can be protected in the same way. Additional protection from frost may also be required, and here straw bales packed on top of the polythene sheet will give adequate insulation. If a ready source is available, expanded polystyrene chips give excellent insulation, are easily removed, and can be re-used. Polythene sheets will need to be anchored against strong winds, by means of large stones, bricks, planks or straw bales.

So long as holes and other features with vertical surfaces are protected in the ways outlined above, extensive areas of varied soils, from soft sands to boulder clays, can be left open for long periods. An area of sandy clay at Wroxeter had to be left open for two years. At the end of this time it was trowelled, and an average depth of some 1-3 cm. was removed. The underlying surface was in good condition and the features of the immediately preceding period of the site's occupation were intact. The same encouraging results have been experienced on boulder clay, and on rubble surfaces. Naturally, some soils weather less well, and all will erode if the site has an appreciable degree of slope.

A site that has to be left for more than a few months will need to be sprayed with weed killer to prevent weed growth, particularly of deep-rooted weeds, as their removal is not only tedious but, more important, will damage the stratification. It is unlikely that a weed killer such as paraquat will alter the chemical balance of the soil for any subsequent soil analysis.

Site logistics
The siting of spoil heaps and the removal of spoil should be given a good deal of thought before the excavation starts. Only too often, spoil heaps prove to lie over crucial areas of the site and have to be moved before excavation can expand, and if this has to be done by hand it can be very dispiriting.

If the site has eventually to be backfilled and the spoil kept for this purpose, the heaps should be as neat as possible with a clear 2 metres between the spoil and the excavation, and if necessary they should be revetted along their bottom edges with sandbags or stones or with planks held upright with pegs. If the excavation is expected to achieve any depth, it must be remembered that spoil is very heavy, especially if it becomes waterlogged, and should therefore be kept as far away from deep excavations as possible; this also considerably reduces the risk of collapse.

If the excavation has to be backfilled and returfed, the turf should be cut carefully and stacked, grass-face to grass-face, well away from the rest of the spoil, and should be kept damp. Topsoil should also be reserved in a separate heap so that it can be replaced on the surface before re-turfing.

If the excavation does not have to be backfilled, skips can be used to remove spoil, and if necessary a number of them can be stood end to end in a line and joined across the top by a plank runway, the furthest away being filled first. Lorries standing waiting are pointlessly expensive, so that if skips are not available it is more economical to employ an earth-moving machine to fill lorries from a spoil heap in one operation, as required.

For barrowing, either on the level or up on to spoil heaps, Summerfield tracking, developed during the war for emergency runways, is preferable to planks, which become slippery and potentially dangerous on steep slopes. This tracking, supported on sandbags, also makes excellent barrow-runs across the site, especially as the separate sections can be wired together to form continuous runs.

Anything that can be done to shorten barrow-runs will save time and labour. It may be more economical of skilled labour to make spoil heaps near the excavated face and employ mechanical or unskilled hand labour to move them rather than to have trowellers barrowing hundreds of yards to a major dump.

Any way of reducing unnecessary work should be used. For instance, it takes less energy to turn an empty barrow to face the way it will be pushed when full, than to turn it after it is full, a simple precept not always observed. Mechanical means of removing spoil include conveyor belts and small cranes driven by electric motors or petrol/diesel engines. Even if such aids are not available it is a simple matter to rig up a system of pulleys over a deep excavation rather than to haul up buckets at their dead weight.

The removal of spoil from the surface of the excavation has always been a tedious and time-consuming task and one has often wished for a series of large vacuum cleaners to do the job quickly and easily. Industrial vacuum cleaners capable of sucking up dirt and stones up to 2in. diameter are available and may be hired. Though it is obviously impracticable to equip each troweller with a vacuum cleaner there are occasions when it might be invaluable, such as in the emptying of a large group of stake holes or the cleaning of a pebble surface. Obviously this would only be feasible in dry weather. On the other hand, excavation inside standing buildings is often a very dry and dusty process which can be made much more efficient with the aid of a vacuum cleaner.

Site logistics are ultimately a matter of practical commonsense, of constantly seeing ways in which work can be made easier and more efficient. However, efficiency in the mechanical sense can be taken too far. On one excavation I suggested that, as it was a very large site divided into its separate areas, each individual area should have its own detached, subsidiary finds-recording box to obviate the necessity for trowellers to leave their area in order to take individual finds to the central finds hut, but the site supervisors pointed out that the average number of objects found per troweller per day was about two, and that the trowellers not only welcomed the break from what was, in effect, a production line, but that they thereby became familiar with the workings of the finds hut and saw finds from other parts of the site. From the other end, the finds assistants welcomed the arrival of trowellers with their finds. The centralised system, though involving more walking and a bit less trowelling, was more efficient psychologically, creating something of a rapport between the trowellers and the finds staff, and giving everyone a brief change of scene and viewpoint.

From another point of view there is an optimum length of day. If an excavation is to work at maximum efficiency it should not go on each day after the point at which enthusiasm and interest wanes. On an emergency or salvage dig this might be at one in the morning, but on a large long-term excavation it is probably counter-productive to work more than eight or nine hours a day as the losses of evidence in the last hour may well be considerable. Loss of efficiency at the end of a long day or after two or three weeks' continuous digging might be monitored by the number of tiny finds missed in the ground but recovered afterwards by sieving. On any large excavation one can almost plot a graph of increasing tiredness as time goes on. It is here that careful consideration of site logistics will save time and energy, and keep morale and enthusiasm high. On permanent or semi-permanent excavations it is clearly necessary for workers to have breaks at week-ends or other agreed times if they are not to become stale and work merely mechanically.

Safety precautions

The Council for British Archaeology has recently produced an essential pamphlet, *Responsibility and Safeguards in Archaeological Excavation*, 1972, edited by P.J. Fowler. This outlines the law regarding excavation current at the time, and describes the C.B.A. insurance scheme for third party and personal accident cover for archaeological societies and groups affiliated to the C.B.A. It has a section on precautions against soil collapse and another on working with machinery. One of its most cogent sections is that on personal safety and medical precautions. The pamphlet as a whole is required reading for all field archaeologists, and as it is cheap and readily available there is no need to reproduce it here.

A facility not mentioned in the pamphlet is the Post Office telephone number Freefone 111 which can be reached via the operator. Through this, information on the position of Post Office telephone cables can be obtained before excavation begins, and expensive accidents avoided. The positions of all other services such as sewers, electricity cables, gas and water pipes should also be accurately ascertained before work begins. This is obviously important in towns and cities, but it must also be remembered that many stretches of open countryside are now criss-crossed with gas or water pipes, electricity cables and drains, the lines of which may only be vaguely known. If in doubt, a geophysical survey should pick them up. In the absence of geophysical equipment dowsing might be tried. Though this technique is regarded by many as suspect, it has been proved to work, in the right hands and given the right conditions.

In 1974 Parliament passed the *Health and Safety at Work etc. Act 1974*. This Act considerably tightens up regulations concerned with duties of employers to their employees in regard to health and safety, and to the general public who may be affected by activities of which they are not a part, such as falling masonry from a demolition close to a public highway, or subsidence of a footpath due to excavation. The Act also includes the self-employed and other persons (not employed by them) who may be affected by their activities. The Act defines an 'employee' as 'an individual who works under a contract of employment'

(Chapter 37 Part I, 53, (1)). There is no doubt, therefore, that archaeologists working under contract to units or other excavating bodies are employees within the meaning of the Act, as are self-employed archaeologists, such as some conservators or other specialists, who will be liable, for example, for the effect of any toxic chemicals or effluents they may use.

The position of volunteers of all grades is less clear. An Inspector of Factories consulted on this point thought that the Act was meant to cover anyone at work and at risk, and that it would be reckless to assume that persons called volunteers and paid subsistence would not be covered by the Act if an accident occurred. He felt that it would need a test case to prove the point. Since the maximum penalities for those convicted under the Act are a fine not exceeding £400 and a term of imprisonment not exceeding two years, it would seem advisable to avoid such a test case!

The parts of the Act particularly relevant to archaeology appear to be Chapter 37, Part I, Sections 1, 2, 3, 4, 7, 8, 9, 33, 36, 37, 40, 52, and 53. Other important regulations include the Construction (General Provisions) Regulations, 1961, (Statutory Instruments 1961 No. 1580); The Construction (Working Places) Regulations, 1966 (Statutory Instrument, 1966 No. 94) and the Construction (Health and Welfare) Regulations 1966 (Statutory Instrument 1966 No. 95). These are all obtainable very cheaply from H.M. Stationery Office and should be used as guidelines even by those directors who do not believe that their fieldwork and excavations are covered by the Act, since it should always be borne in mind that a volunteer, even a totally unpaid one, might bring a civil action for damages against a director in the case of serious accident. Under these circumstances, it would be a powerful defence if the director could show that all the relevant aspects of the excavation conformed with the standards laid down in these regulations, and that every other reasonable precaution had been taken. In spite of a few serious incidents within the last few years, British archaeology has been very fortunate in its accident rate, although safety precautions on some sites are frighteningly non-existent. Now that excavations are larger, and archaeology in general more public, it would not only be potentially tragic for individuals but damaging for the discipline as a whole if it were seen to be amateurish and negligent in its safety precautions.

Site discipline

The best site discipline is a careful balance of that which is self-imposed and that imposed from above; where all the members of the excavation do what they are told or what is required because they understand what they are doing, and the way it fits into the overall development of work rather than through unthinking obedience. This closely parallels the best war-time air-crew discipline where groups of men (most of them the age of the present-day archaeological volunteer) had to learn very quickly to work together under an acknowledged leader, without resentment, and with an understanding of the problems and difficulties under which the other crew members worked, so that unreasonable demands were not made, but above all without bickering or quarrelling, which could, and quite often did, prove fatal. The results of poor site discipline on an excavation are not so drastic, but can be very disruptive, leading to inefficiency, needless mistakes and a resulting loss of evidence.

It is important, if volunteers, site assistants and specialist assistants, such as draughtsmen, surveyors and photographers, are to give of their best, that they should be told the background to the excavation, its aims and progress to date and just where they fit into the team. Sometimes this is best done by means of introductory talks; sometimes, if people are turning up at intervals during the dig, by means of interim reports and other hand-outs. It should be made clear to everyone that they are free to ask why they are doing what they are set to do, to question the need for doing it, or the way in which it is done. If these questions cannot be convincingly answered by the director or site supervisors, they are in the wrong job. The volunteer who works without understanding will work badly.

There should be a clear hierarchy in the organisation, a chain of command known to all, so that each individual knows of whom he should ask questions or to whom make complaints and suggestions. Above all contradictory orders must be avoided. Nothing causes more confusion than an instruction given by a site supervisor reversed by an assistant director minutes later, to be reinstated by the director who turns up demanding to know what is going on in his absence. Situations such as this can be avoided by a meeting of the directing staff before the dig begins so that a broad policy can be agreed upon. Daily site conferences and adequate discussion between all concerned should ensure that this policy is implemented or modified in consultation with the supervisors. Everybody should be aware that the buck stops with the director and that he is available to all for complaints and suggestions. On large excavations and archaeological units he will naturally be sheltered from trivial interruptions by his senior assistants, but the remoter and more inaccessible the director becomes the less sense of unity and cooperation there will be among the body of workers.

No excavation is without its awkward characters, eccentrics or misfits. These must be dealt with sympathetically or firmly as required, and here the patience and skill of the director and his assistants in man-management will sometimes be stretched. A volunteer who disrupts the workers around him by compulsive chattering can be tactfully moved to work on his own; a desperately keen but ham-fisted volunteer who is ineducable as a troweller can be invited to help with something more suited to his talents, or, at worst, placed where he can do least harm.

If paid non-archaeological labourers, prisoners or Borstal boys are used, they too should be given the background and purpose of the excavation if they are to work well and become members of the team. The initial resentment and cynicism of prisoners can be dispersed by careful handling; and if they become interested in the site they will often work with unexpected skill. One of the best trowellers I have known was a 60-year-old window-cleaner serving a prison sentence for petty theft.

This book is not intended to cover the organisation of the domestic side of a large excavation in detail. The welfare of all workers on the site is the director's overall responsibility, though aspects such as catering, first aid, organisation of accommodation and so on should be delegated. There is no doubt that an excavation trowels on its stomach: if the domestic and catering arrangements are not efficient the dig will suffer very considerably. Domestic bursars and cooks should therefore be chosen with great care — they are key personnel.

Cost effectiveness

In these times of economic stress, galloping inflation and the wholesale destruction of sites, cost effectiveness, that is, 'getting', as Philip Rahtz has put it, 'as much history as possible per £', is crucially important. At first sight it seems obvious that the bigger the area you cover and the faster you dig the more you are likely to get for your money, but I believe that this is a fallacy, like driving faster to get to the filling station before your petrol runs out. These thoughts arose from discussions with friends who maintained that very slow, detailed excavations while admittedly producing interesting, even unexpected results were not appropriate to rescue archaeology, where time was of the essence, and the maximum results had to be obtained for the money spent.

It is difficult, if not impossible to quantify the results from excavations on any agreed scale of values, but it is self-evident that some excavations are very fruitful, while others are a waste of time and money, and that many fall somewhere between these two extremes.

It may be argued that on some deeply ploughed sites there is little to find beyond the features dug into the undisturbed subsoil and that therefore the fastest methods of recovering these features will be appropriate and that there will be little chance of recovering a great deal more evidence even if the work is carried out much more slowly and carefully. On stratified sites I do not believe this to be the case. Experience has shown that highly detailed (and therefore necessarily slow) digging can produce a markedly greater quantity of evidence, in the form of buildings and other structures, many of them unsuspected, than fast digging could possibly have recovered.

It is apparent, for example, that the bailey of the timber castle at Hen Domen was packed with timber buildings of which the plans or partial plans of almost 50, spanning some 250 years, have been discovered in one quarter of the bailey's interior. This has taken about 50 weeks' work (spread over 10 years, though under other circumstances the work could have been carried out continuously over one year). However, faster digging would have recovered only the plans of the more obvious structures, of which there are only about a dozen. The recovery rate would have fallen off very sharply as the work was accelerated beyond the point where every thin layer and every pebble surface was cleaned and dissected. It need hardly be added that the recovery rate for finds of all kinds is likely to be higher if the digging is more careful and that the finds will be more securely stratified in closer contexts so that the results adduced from them will be correspondingly more reliable.

Equally at Wroxeter, on a site which had been dug in more summary fashion by a number of previous excavators, the recovery of many periods of unsuspected buildings has only been made possible by slow excavation over a large area. At the same time, the recovery rate of finds of all kinds, including pottery and bones, has been high and should provide information at a level unprecedented for the site. I maintain that more information, and more *reliable* information, is obtained pound for pound by slow, detailed digging than by digging which is faster than the site demands and which produces a 'broad picture' but one that may be grossly distorted.

This, therefore, is another argument for planning a long-term rescue strategy which permits excavation at the optimum speed and not at speeds dictated by the quarryman or developer.

An example of highly detailed excavation under rescue conditions is appended below.

Appendix A. The identification of rectangular timber buildings in the rescue excavation at the hillfort of Moel Y Gaer (Rhosesmor)

Immediately after the turf and thin topsoil are removed the uneroded contours of the final phase occupation deposits are exposed. These consist of a variable layer of stone rubble, nowhere more than 10cm. in thickness, whose continuity is broken by a spread of low humps of pale brown, sandy, stone-free soil. The distribution of these humps is apparently random; equally, their contours and plan would seem to be meaningless. The stone-covered areas are fairly level and it is here that detailed cleaning and recording (i.e. planning stone by stone) has revealed a pattern of stone densities amongst which the former positions of timber buildings can be postulated. Approximately rectangular areas of uniform stone density are recognisable, as in the plan (fig. 38) where a relatively small area, measuring 11.5 x 7.0m. has been selected and all the recorded stones are shown with the humps stippled. A number of these rectangles have been recognised within the 3000 sq. m. of the excavated area. They range from c.10-18 sq. m. in area. The rectangle shown in the drawing is the best example for illustrative purposes, it being rare for all four sides to be this clearly defined. Since these units recur across the site in a relatively standardised size and shape it seems reasonable to interpret them as the floor areas of rectangular timber buildings. There are no associated patterns of post-holes or timber slots and the stones remain the only evidence of the buildings which must have been timber-framed

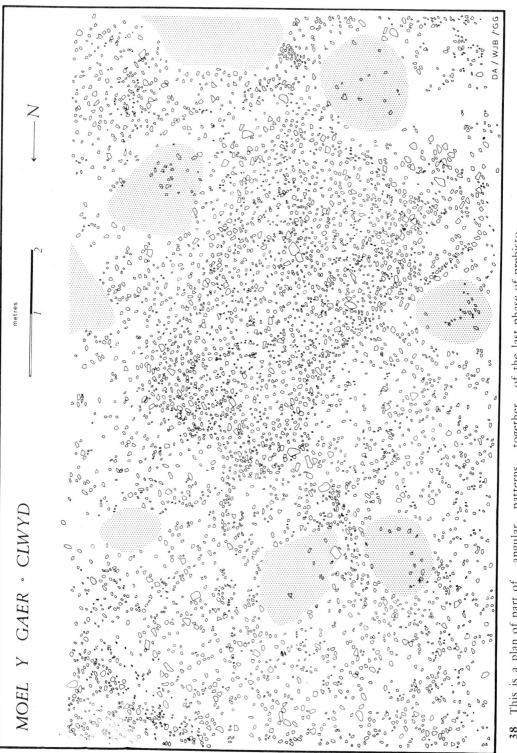

MOEL Y GAER · CLWYD

N

metres

38 This is a plan of part of the latest layers within the hill fort of Moel Y Gaer, Clwyd, showing the distribution of stones within rectangular patterns, together with roughly circular heaps of topsoil. These rectangular patterns are the only evidence for a series of timber buildings of the last phase of prehistoric occupation at this point.

DA / WJB /ˈGG

structures founded on sleeper-beams sitting on the ground surface. The stones themselves seem to have been spread over the occupied areas after the buildings had been constructed, probably for no more reason than to produce a hard-wearing surface upon which matting of, say, straw could be laid, or even as a preparation for timber floor boards. The humps probably represent dumps of turf and humus cleared from the building plots when the occupation was implemented.

It is clear that such evidence as this would only be archaeologically detectable under exceptional circumstances and, in this respect, three factors hold sway at Moel y Gaer.

Firstly, the undamaged condition of the site is an important precursor to the preservation of such tenuous remains. One ploughing, however light, would undoubtedly have totally destroyed all the evidence for this phase of occupation at Moel y Gaer.

Secondly, it will be evident that this must represent the *final* phase of occupation on the site, for had there been a later one the patterns of stone densities must have been disturbed and thus rendered impossible to record adequately, let alone interpret. This must always be the case on this type of site where successive deposits are not cumulative but where later activity tends to erode the evidence of its forerunners; namely, on hilltops and sloping ground where there is nothing to arrest the downhill movement of soil and stones.

Last, but most certainly not least, it should be stressed that the method of excavation effectively controlled the destiny of the evidence. Since the identification of the rectangles depended upon *relative* stone densities it was essential that large areas should be examined at any one time. The truth of this statement was brought home to the excavators by the difficulties of interpretation near the limits of the excavation which covers less than a sixth of the interior of the hill-fort. It was undoubtedly the large scale of open area excavation which allowed the recognition of the rectangles and provided the repeating pattern which prompted their interpretation as buildings. Whilst it should be pointed out that this identification is merely an interpretation of an observed phenomenon (indeed, an interpretation which other archaeologists may choose to challenge), the important thing is that the phenomenon has been systematically recorded in the most objective way that seemed possible under the circumstances of the excavation.

G. C. Guilbert, February 1974

6

The Soil

Timber buildings are by far the most common structures to be found on the majority of our archaeological sites. These sites now consist almost entirely of superimposed layers of soil, or soil and stones, containing the ghosts of structures which themselves have undergone an earth-change into soil. Those of us who excavate these sites often have to interpret soil layers with little more than our intuition and experience to guide us. We say that this feature is a hearth (might it not be a small dump of burnt clay?); this layer was washed down (could it have been wind-blown?); this post-hole filling looks and feels the same as that one (are they therefore contemporary?); does this micropodsol, itself a natural event, reflect a man-made disturbance? – what is the source of this vivianite and what archaeological significance has it? – and so on. An archaeologist who uncovers the substantial remains of stone buildings must have a reasonable knowledge of architecture in order to be able to interpret them. Equally an excavator digging timber structures will need at least a basic understanding of the soils he will encounter if he is to understand fully the medium into which his buildings have been transformed (see Cornwall, 1958, L. Biek and I.W. Cornwall in Brothwell and Higgs, 1963, 108-22, and Limbrey, 1975).

In the process of understanding our excavated structures and their surroundings we must not only be able to recognise and explain structural features such as floors, post-holes, hearths, drains, fences and the rest, but we must also attempt to understand the derivation of every layer that we encounter.

From geological times to the present day the surface of the earth, this very thin series of layers which so preoccupies us, has been subjected to continuous change. Some of these alterations have occurred slowly; the development of the soil, the establishment of vegetation, and centuries of cultivation; some have been much faster. From the moment the site is occupied by man its surface undergoes rapid and drastic changes; and it is principally these changes which we have to excavate and attempt to understand. But the process of change does not stop when the last occupants leave the site and it reverts to pasture or is ploughed or adopted as a car-park. Natural agencies continue to transform it, frost and ice break up exposed surfaces, rain and wind fill its hollows with mud, dust, soil and stones. Water seeps through the underlying layers, leaching out chemicals and redepositing them in new forms. The roots of bushes and trees grow along and into organically rich layers, post-holes and pits, or create their own root-holes. Animals and insects traverse the site with burrows; micro-organisms feed on debris and the remains of timbers, and worms move up and down through the soil, passing, if we are to believe Darwin, millions of tons of our sites through their bodies in the course of a century or so (Darwin, 1881). It is a wonder that we have any understandable archaeology left!

Clearly, we must learn to recognise all the changes that have occurred on the sites we are digging and not merely those which are structural and man-made, attempting, as we do so, to explain or account for every piece of detectable evidence. We shall make mistakes, but these can be minimized by the intensive study of natural, as well as human, factors. We should like to know the subtle but real differences between a number of what we glibly call 'occupation layers' for example, whether a floor has been used by cattle or for corn storage. Experiments in determining comparative amounts of phosphates, lignite and other residual traces have not been uniformly successful; but a comprehensive analysis of soil composition, presented visually and laid over plans of the excavated areas, may prove to be more valuable.

Ultimately, it should be possible to sort apparently un-differentiated post-holes into groups by comparative analysis of their filling. However, observation of the contents of post-holes known to belong to one building often shows that they contain different materials; and it may be that dating techniques such as thermoluminescence will eventually prove to be of more use than physical or chemical analysis. Again, the bottoms of post-holes may contain pollen spectra that will differentiate them into widely separated periods eg. neolithic and Saxon, when superficially they are similar.

At the moment the sampling methods used by soil scientists are often at odds with the excavation techniques advocated here. Soil scientists quite reasonably require to see the whole soil profile, from the surface to the subsoil, in vertical section. Not only is this patently impossible all over the site, unless one dug it by means of a series of thin vertical slices, a sort of *planum* technique (see p. 130-4) tilted through 90° (a method which might be tried on a selected site just to see what happened), but the excavator often does not know that he will require crucial soil information until he has uncovered a layer or feature; by which time, of course, the superimposed layers will have gone; and the very last thing he wants is a column dug through a floor or a buried soil into the underlying layers (about which he knows nothing). It is sometimes possible to reserve columns of soil, leaving them standing until the soil scientist can sample them *in situ*. Again, one would have to know in advance, or predict, what layers lay below the point where the column was to be left.

The only possible solution to this problem is for a soil scientist to work continually on the site, alongside the excavators, taking samples where necessary, and observing the vertical relationships as they are revealed by horizontal methods. This may not be entirely satisfactory for the soil scientist, but test holes or trenches, except on the smallest scale, are unacceptable on an area excavation, especially as they will inevitably be dug into *terra incognita*, and therefore of little value to the excavator who cannot have any idea what the underlying layers may represent when the samples are taken. More important, a dialogue between an excavator and a soil scientist is likely to raise questions that would not have occurred to either individually.

On an excavation where a soil scientist cannot be present, samples may be taken from layers and features. They must be labelled in sufficient detail for a person who has not seen the site to identify them, with the aid of plans, sections and photographs, preferably in colour; and they must be accompanied by specific questions, of a kind which might reasonably be solved by soil analysis. No soil scientist will thank an excavator who sends him 200 polythene bags full of samples divorced from their context and without comment, and the excavator must not expect miraculous solutions to his problems simply because he has collected spoonsful of each layer he has removed.

Soil analysis falls into two main categories: the physical and the chemical examination of the profile or sample. The physical examination will give information about the parent geology of the sample (which may not be that of the underlying subsoil), the particle size, the proportion of humus, the presence of mortar or other building materials, whether the material is wind blown or water-sorted, and so on. Hopefully, this will not only throw light on the derivation of the material, but may also give information about aspects of the site which would be obtainable in no other way. For example, post-holes filled with earth containing flecks of painted plaster may be the only evidence for the former existence of a timber building with rendered or painted walls. Analysis of the back-filling of robber trenches which appear to be the same superficially, may show that the robbed walls were of different materials and therefore perhaps of different dates; or it may be possible to show that a gulley has been filled in its early stages with wind-sorted rather than water-borne silt.

Layers or fillings of features which seem at first to resemble each other may prove, on detailed examination, to be very different. Quite often layers occurring on different parts of a site have been said to be identical simply because they look alike. This in turn has led to generalizations about 'destruction levels' and 'building levels' which may well not be justified.

The chemical analysis of soil provides information of another kind. Sometimes it will go hand in hand with the physical examination to prove the existence or composition of mortars and plasters, or it may be a purely chemical examination which attempts to show, for example, that floors have been occupied by animals;

or determine the existence of industrial processes otherwise undetectable.

At the long-term and very meticulous excavation of the deserted medieval village at Wharram Percy, Yorkshire, it has usually been possible from the house plans to determine their internal sub-divisions and to distinguish the living end from that used for cattle or storage. However, in one area, 6, a house was excavated without any trace of sub-division. The site was left open until the following year, when it was noticed that the vegetation growing within the house was sharply differentiated between the 'upper end', the 'living room area' and the 'cross-passage area' (fig. 39). This clearly indicated that soil differences, hitherto undetected, had operated to provide a different environment in each of the three areas. A highly detailed analysis of the soil would presumably have detected the unseen elements responsible for these differences. While it is not feasible to undertake a total analysis of each layer of our sites it is obvious from this example that much significant information might be obtained from overall examinations, even from one in which specific questions were not asked. Mr

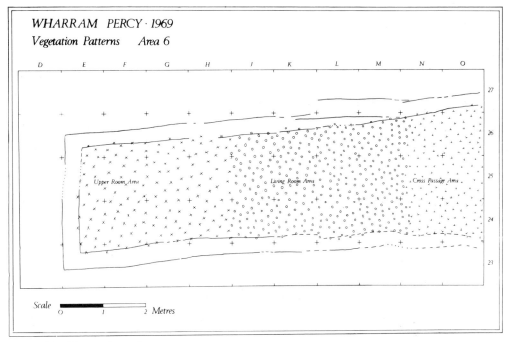

39 This illustration shows the excavation of a house at Wharram Percy, Yorkshire under the direction of J.G. Hurst and Professor Maurice Beresford. Elsewhere in the village such houses were divided into two sections, one the living end, the other the byre end, separated by a cross passage. Here there was no indication of different use for the two halves of the building, but after the excavation had been left open for the winter the plants which began to grow on the house site were different in each half indicating soil differences which were not visible but which were positive enough to affect plant colonisation. Analysis of this phenomenon is not yet completed and I am grateful to Mr. Hurst for permission to mention it in advance of publication.

Norman Bridgwater has been working on the theory that oak beams lying on the ground will leave a deposit of tannin that will show where they have been. While the value of this technique has yet to be verified, it is a good example of the type of experimental approach that may reveal hitherto unsuspected buildings.

It is no longer enough to bag up samples of soil from post-holes, pits and the silting of ditches and despatch them to a soil-scientist, with a list of questions in the hope of solving the outstanding questions of interpretation that are not immediately obvious to inexperienced eyes. On all but the shortest excavations, therefore, a soil-scientist should be a permanent member of the team, available for consultation at every stage about problems of soil interpretation *in situ*. However, this is only part of the solution. For obvious reasons it is vitally important that the soil-scientist and the archaeologist should speak the same language. We must learn to use each other's terms not only in the field, but in publication. At the moment archaeological colloquialisms like 'the natural' (meaning the undisturbed rock or subsoil) have no meaning for soil scientists who rightly point out that a lot of archaeological layers are 'natural'; while the word 'silt' used loosely by archaeologists to describe the soil that has filled a hollow has a much more precise meaning for the soil scientist. A textbook by one of the country's leading authorities on soil-science in archaeology has recently been published (Limbrey, 1975), and it is very much to be hoped that the stimulus this book gives to the archaeological study of soils will convince all directors and would-be directors of excavations to train themselves in soil science; and that this study will be given a greater prominence in all future archaeological training.

There is little point in attempting to summarize Dr Limbrey's book here. It is required reading for all excavators, but it may be useful to re-emphasize some of the points she makes. Soil descriptions should be a normal entry on feature/layer record cards, and the terminology used should be that standardized by soil scientists. Limbrey makes the good point that it is the trowellers themselves, closest to the soils in an excavation, who should be responsible for the soil descriptions, since they will be most sensitive to soil variations, as they are the first to encounter and identify them.

The two chief characteristics of soils are colour and texture. Colours are described using a Munsell Soil Colour Chart, or its cheaper Japanese equivalent. Colour determinations should ideally be made on the soils in both moist and dry conditions. However, the labour, in a damp season, involved in drying a sample of each layer or feature filling encountered on a large site would be enormous and it is probably more reasonable under these circumstances to record all the soil colours when they are damp, since it is obviously much easier to moisten a sample than to dry it. In practice, on very large and complex sites where the colour changes run into thousands it may be necessary to record only those which seem to be significant or anomalous, or different in some way from the general matrix of soil which often covers large areas of a site. These alone may run into many hundreds.

Soil texture, structure and consistence can best be taught in the field, though Limbrey, *op. cit.*, 259-70, is a concise introduction. She makes the point also that the traditional method of using the trowel, by scraping, is not the best way of revealing the nature of the soil since it tends to smear clay soils and obscures the structure of all other soils except sands. Rather the soil should be 'made to part along its structural planes'. This is best achieved by 'a levering or flicking action' with a sharp trowel. In this way also the nature of the boundaries between the layers, often a most difficult problem of identification, is made clearer.

Limbrey's chapter on 'Soils associated with archaeological features' is an essential discussion of the development and composition of soils in pits, post-holes, tree-holes, ditches, mounds and other man-made features. There is little to add to it except to point out that the filling of ditches particularly, but also of pits and post-holes, may be partly deliberate and partly natural. The sleighting of defences on a rampart may lead to a tumble of stones into the adjacent ditch. This may be followed over the next few days or weeks by washed-down soil and small pebbles, which may partly fill the spaces between the stones. If the defences are refurbished, the builders may re-dig the ditch though not deeply enough to remove all the recent tumble and wash-down. The new ditch will immediately begin to silt naturally in the manner described by Limbrey (290 ff), but may again be recut or filled with debris. This process may be repeated a number of times (figs. 8-11).

Worms and weathering

This is the title of a crucial paper by Professor R.J.C. Atkinson (Atkinson, 1957) in which he discusses the role played by earthworms in the modification of archaeological sites, and the weathering of the natural subsoils which lie below the archaeological layers, and which are often considered by archaeologists to have remained sealed and unchanged from time immemorial. It is not my intention to repeat Atkinson's paper here but simply to stress one or two of his most important conclusions.

In favourable soils, the worm population is commonly as much as half a million per acre, and may even be as much as six times this number. Worms passing up and down through the soil and the subsoil below it, transport fine soil, in the form of worm casts, from lower levels to the surface.

Amounts from 2 to 24 tons per acre per annum have been recorded from Britain and amounts up to 36 tons on the Continent. This represents the formation of a surface-layer of fine mould varying in thickness (in Britain) from 1/50 to 1/4 in. per annum, or from 1/5 to 2½in. in ten years.

However, this process clearly cannot go on without modification since at 2½ in. every ten years, there would theoretically be a mould layer 25 in. thick in a century, or 20ft. 10in. in a thousand years. Even at the lowest figure of 1/5in. in ten years the mould layer would be 20in. thick in a thousand years. Observation of worm-rich sites that have remained untouched by the plough since they were abandoned shows that they frequently have only a thin soil cover above the uppermost archaeological levels. At Hen Domen, Montgomery, which is built on boulder clay, and has lain untouched for 750 years, worms have burrowed to a considerable depth, and the layer of fine stone-free humic soil lying on the uppermost archaeological layer is only an average of 3in. (7cm.) in depth. It is possible that the chief activity of the worms was confined to this thin layer of topsoil, except in winter when they burrowed deeper to escape the colder weather and when casting on the surface would be at its minimum. On deeply stratified sites where movement up and down through the layers is easier the movement of fine earth to the surface is likely to be greater. A very important side-effect of this movement of fine soil by earthworms is stressed by Atkinson. This is the burial of small objects, which are continually undermined by the worms' burrows and the deposition of casts on the surface. Small objects left on the surface of a lawn will gradually disappear, moving downwards until they reach a more solid layer. It is a matter of common observation on many archaeological sites that modern objects such as coins, bottle tops, fragments of Victorian teapot and so on lie on the uppermost archaeological surfaces *together with* the objects deposited on those surfaces by the last occupants. This can lead to considerable confusion if the cause, earthworm activity, is not appreciated. As Atkinson summarises:

in many cases significant archaeological finds have been displaced downwards from the position in which they were originally deposited; and in some cases at least the amount of displacement may have been sufficient materially to alter the apparent stratigraphic relationships of the objects concerned (*op. cit.* 222).

He goes on to cite two examples of the way in which the burying activities of worms may affect the interpretation of stratified finds. They are so important that it is worth repeating them here (in slightly shortened form):

In many Romano-British and medieval excavations, for instance, floors are uncovered consisting of *opus signinum* (cement), *tesserae* or tiles. The surface of these floors is often sealed by a layer of fine soil containing sherds, coins and other debris of occupation, which is itself covered by a thicker layer of rubble derived from the decay and collapse of the surrounding walls. Such 'occupation layers' are usually referred to a reoccupation of the building by squatters, after it has been abandoned by the original inhabitants and has perhaps already become partially ruined.

The exact processes by which such 'occupation layers' have been formed is seldom if ever discussed in excavation reports. In fact, such 'occupation earth' is almost certainly the product of earthworms, which penetrate cracks in apparently solid floors and gradually build up a layer of castings on their surface. Meanwhile this layer will itself have been colonized by worms, whose activity will bury coins and other objects dropped on it, and some of these will be displaced downwards so that they eventually come to rest immediately on the surface of the original floor.

Now finds discovered in this latter position will usually be interpreted as belonging either to the very latest stage of the original occupation, or to the initial stages of 'squatting'; in either case they will be held to date approximately the period at which the building was initially abandoned. But in fact, as a result of the processes outlined above, the objects found *on* the floor may be of widely differing dates, and will include not only those dropped just after the abandonment of the building, but also those of much later date which have been displaced from above. Consequently, if the normal practice is adopted of dating a horizon by the *latest* objects contained in it, the date assigned to the initial abandonment of the building may be significantly later than it should be.

Another common case in which the activity of worms may lead to serious misinterpretation of the evidence occurs in the silting of pits and ditches. Such silting usually exhibits four basic divisions. On the bottom, and up to half the depth of the ditch, there is coarse or rapid silting, formed chiefly from the weathering of the sides. Above this is a thin deposit of earthy streaks, due to the undermining and collapse of the surface soil on the lips of the ditch. Both these stages are normally completed within a few years at the most. Thereafter, silt forms much more slowly, and usually contains a far higher proportion of earth, particularly in structures of the second millennium BC, such as barrow-ditches, which collect considerable quantities of wind-blown surface-soil. Finally, at the top, there is the 'turf' layer of virtually stone-free soil which supports the surface vegetation.

Since the first two stages of silting take place rapidly, the formation of the lowest levels of the third stage may be regarded as virtually contemporary with the original excavation; and in the absence of finds from the primary silt (those in the secondary silt, being derived possible from the adjacent surface-soil, are unreliable), objects occurring at the base of the tertiary silt may often be used to date the original excavation. But it is clear that such finds *may* have been displaced vertically through considerable depths of silt particularly where a high proportion of windblown or other soil encourages the activity of worms. Since such vertical displacements may take centuries to achieve, the date ascribed to the structure on such evidence may be grossly in error.

The classic case of the probability of an error of this kind is afforded by the Y and Z Holes at Stonehenge, in which the main part of the silt consists of earth, apparently wind-blown and almost free from stones and rubble. This silt contained Iron Age and Romano-British sherds at quite low depths, which have in the past been held to date the holes to not earlier than the last few centuries BC. But once the possibility of vertical displacement is recognised, it becomes clear that this pottery must have been deposited *on the surface of the silting* many centuries after the digging of the holes; and in fact other evidence suggests a date for the holes as much as a thousand years *earlier* than that of the pottery they contain.

These examples, and particularly the last, may perhaps be regarded as extreme cases; and certainly it would be foolish to deny that in many instances the vertical movement of objects, though it has undoubtedly taken place, has no significant effect on their interpretation. Nonetheless, one may justly say that the excavator who ignores the capacity of worms to displace small objects downwards does so at his peril.

Although there is no doubt that objects can travel downwards through considerable depths of comparatively friable soil* they tend to stop when they reach a harder layer, one that is either resistant to penetration by worms, or at least does not collapse internally if there are worm burrows in it.

Two things should be noted. First of all it is most unlikely that the vertical stratigraphic relationship of objects will be *reversed* by earthworm action; that is, objects will rarely overtake one another so that a later object finishes up below an earlier one in the same series of layers. Secondly, objects will never travel *upwards* due to the action of earthworms. Though it may seem ludicrous to point this out, it should be stressed that the worm cannot be held responsible for every anomalous find in the recorded stratigraphy.

Another effect, not noted by Atkinson, is that one often finds a layer of dark humic soil surrounding buried stones or large architectural fragments. It is easy to assume this to be a pit into which the stone has been set, though it is more likely to be caused by worms coming up underneath the stone and being forced round its sides (fig. 40).

As Atkinson explains, the familiar thin and irregular deposits of pea-sized pebbles, free from admixed soil, found at the bottom of pits, etc., and on the buried surfaces of floors, arise from the long accumulation of the small stones used by worms to line the terminal chambers of their burrows. These layers of tiny pebbles tend to be concentrated at the lowest levels to which worms can penetrate locally (*op. cit.*, 225).

The second part of Atkinson's article concerns weathering and its misleading

---

* At Wroxeter a considerable accumulation of eighteenth- and nineteenth-century sherds was found on the surface of a Roman street on the Baths Basilica site (excavated from 1966 onwards). These sherds had probably been brought onto the site from the mid-eighteenth century when the field was first ploughed. They had travelled between 60cm. and 1m. (2-3ft) downwards through deep layers of top soil before they reached the gravelly surface of the street where they remained. Since the excavation has proved by horizontal stratigraphy that the street is unquestionably late Roman, the eighteenth/nineteenth-century sherds have no dating significance for the street or the layers immediately above it.

effects, particularly on permeable and partially soluble subsoils. The section is too long to summarize satisfactorily here, but, together with the section on worms, is required reading for excavation directors.

Section

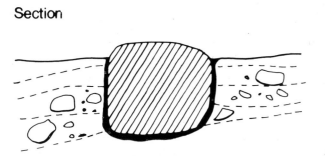

Plan

40 Diagrammatic plan and section of a large stone showing enveloping layer of fine soil (in black) deposited by worms travelling round stone.

7

Rescue and Salvage Excavation

At the time of writing (1982) British archaeology has faced a crisis situation for some years. The implantation of new towns and the enlargement of existing conurbations, with the proliferation of motorways; the extraction of sands and gravels for aggregates; the exploitation of peat bogs containing preserved timber structures and the afforestation of hitherto untouched marginal land, all represent threats to archaeological sites on an unprecedented scale. But the most extensive and insidious threat of all is that of ploughing, particularly deep ploughing, which, though justified on the grounds of increased agricultural yield, levels earthworks and cuts into the underlying structural evidence.

The statistics of damage and destruction have been collated and are published elsewhere (Rahtz, ed., 1974) and they have forced a fundamental debate on archaeological policy. Is there any excuse, in the face of this widespread and inevitable devastation, for the archaeological destruction, in the name of research, of otherwise unthreatened sites; or should field archaeologists devote all their time and energy to rescue and salvage excavation? The crux of the debate is whether sites which are in no danger should be left untouched for future examination and the whole of our archaeological resources, both amateur and professional, used to rescue whatever information can be extracted from those sites which are imminently threatened.

It is often argued that any information rescued from a site about to be destroyed is better than none. But if the documentary analogy, begun in Chapter I, is allowed to continue, one must imagine a newly-discovered manuscript available only for a minute or two before destruction. Under good conditions a few sentences or even whole paragraphs might be rescued before the document vanishes for ever. Some of these sentences might contain information which could revolutionise ideas; other phrases or sentences, perhaps the majority, may be highly ambiguous or positively misleading. A single paragraph, torn from its context, could lead to misconceptions on which a whole series of false assumptions might be based. This is certainly the case with some rescue excavation, which at its worst is done hurriedly and incompletely, often under tremendous pressure, against a background of thunderous machinery or collapsing masonry, when all discussion must be shouted, and when there is no time for the deliberate thought, amounting to contemplation, which is necessary if fundamental errors of interpretation are to be avoided.

Too often we have been led to believe that a sample of a site provides us with a microcosm of its development; but further work, perhaps undertaken many years later, all too often reveals that the earlier interpretation was entirely wrong. If the site had been destroyed during the initial excavation these revisions could never have been made, and the earlier evidence would have been accepted as part of the corpus of archaeological data which we use to build up our picture of the past. If sampling excavations, carefully planned to answer specific questions can be so misleading, how much more so will be those whose course is dictated by the progress of a building schedule or the availability of a bulldozer?

There is also a tendency to believe that a hurriedly carried out total excavation will give a précis or abstract of the site, recovering all its essential information and merely leaving the details to be filled in by further work, if this were possible. Nothing could be more mistaken. Swift excavation by machine or coarse hand-digging is not so much like a photographic negative, which, as it develops, progressively reveals the broad outlines and important masses of light and shade of the subject, but is more like an X-ray, which shows many important elements of the structure but fails to reveal others which are of equal importance in its function.

Here we have the core of the dilemma. If total excavation of most of our sites is patently impossible and partial excavation is known to be potentially misleading, what are we to do? We must, I think, be acutely and continually aware of the situation and its limitations, and attempt as far as possible to reduce these limitations to a minimum. Those sites which are to be completely destroyed by other agencies must claim priority for total excavation, if only we can get at them in time. This will require planning, perhaps years in advance of their destruction, if we are to be able to conduct rescue work in the manner of a research excavation, with the tactics and pace dictated by the archaeologist rather than the developer or gravel extractor.

This desirable situation has already been achieved on a number of sites, and is a policy which is gradually being implemented by the Inspectorate of Ancient Monuments as the limitations of hurried and partial excavation become more generally recognized.

One of the greatest difficulties in assessing the viability and strategy of a rescue excavation is the impossibility of knowing beforehand how complex the site may be and therefore how much time should be spent on each phase of the occupation. This is particularly the case with urban sites. A machine-cut trench may show that there is a complex of Roman and sub-Roman banks and ditches 3m. below the surface, with prehistoric occupation beneath, and many undatable layers above, heavily mutilated by post-medieval pits. It would be easy to strip off the first metre or so by machine and then to deal with the comparatively undisturbed major features below. But by doing so a whole sequence of medieval and post-medieval tenements might be lost.

Alternatively, there is strong argument for the detailed area stripping of the upper layers on the grounds that we should never know what we were losing if they were bulldozed away. Such slow and detailed stripping might produce plans of ten successive backyards and leave us oblivious of the Roman and Dark Age defences below. If there is not time to do everything (and we must work strenuously towards making sure that there is time for everything) then painful decisions must be made. These decisions should be based on an assessment of the nationally considered academic priorities, and not on personal research interests or the ease with which the more obvious features might be excavated. The strategy of any large-scale excavation, whether urban or rural, should be a matter for discussion so that a balanced view can be considered and a consensus of opinion achieved. It is true that a great number of our most spectacular excavations of the past have been the result of individual flair, but the centres of our historic cities and our major rural sites are too precious to be left to arbitrary decisions or personal whims.

Before decisions are taken to sacrifice the uppermost structures, late and comparatively unimportant though they may be, it must be remembered that the attitudes of developers, sand and gravel extractors, farmers, and the Inspectorate of Ancient Monuments itself can be changed in the light of what is discovered. The meticulous demonstration of a group of post-medieval buildings combined with suitable propaganda may convince all those concerned, not only that the excavators are competent, but that they are capable of revealing the whole history of the town in a way quite unexpected by the laymen on the Council who are impatient to add to the town's car parking space, and that they should therefore be given time to do so. Nothing succeeds like success, and it is correspondingly much easier to convince the various interests concerned that they should delay development and even contribute funds to the excavation if the results can be seen and explained, rather than postulated on the grounds of probability.

In an ideal archaeological world all sites would be examined before they were lost or deeply damaged, but the rate of present destruction is far beyond our existing resources. We are forced to choose a course lying between two extremes: to concentrate on a few of the threatened sites, digging them slowly and entirely, and letting the rest go; or trying to salvage something from every site before it vanishes. There is something to be said for both points of view. The total excavation of very large settlement sites such as Warendorf (Wincklemann, 1958) and

Dorestad (van Es, 1969) is enormously impressive, and they yield information far in excess of that given by a hundred smaller excavations. On the other hand, it can be argued that if concentration on a few sites means the abandonment of the rest, the overall picture is bound to suffer; there being no guarantee, for instance, that the sites chosen for full excavation are typical of their kind, or that those left unexcavated were not of even greater importance. Devotees of the distribution map will point out that enough small excavations should eventually provide coverage for the whole country; and that from these maps the broad pattern of invasion, settlement, trade, and social and religious groupings should emerge.

The answer lies somewhere between the two extremes. The selective preservation or long-term digging of carefully chosen sites where optimum conditions for excavation can be arranged, together with the rescue and salvage excavation of as many other sites as can be adequately dealt with, is a policy already being implemented in Britain, and may be thought to achieve the best of both worlds.

What is the relevance of this dilemma for the future of archaeological techniques and attitudes? Clearly, we must keep in mind the limitations and dangers of misinterpretation inherent in the hurried and partial excavation. Beyond the difficulties outlined above there is the much more insidious hazard, unadmitted by most excavators, that, when a site is being totally destroyed, there is an unconscious slackening in the precision with which observations are made; an attitude brought about partly by the necessity for speed, but also by the knowledge that the results can never subsequently be checked, or disputed. For this very reason rescue excavations ought, if anything, to be more rigorously directed than research excavations. They certainly do not require less skill.

Rescue excavations also suffer from the fact that, since layers and features are often only visible for a matter of hours, it is rarely possible for them to be the subject of consultation or second opinion. Thus they represent a particular danger in that the excavator may find, unconsciously, what he wants to find; and, once the evidence has gone, there is no basis for argument. These excavations, therefore, demand the strictest intellectual honesty from the director. This is not to suggest that anyone deliberately falsifies the evidence, since this would be about as satisfying as cheating at Patience, but it is particularly important when digging under pressure, perhaps with the press, the landowner or even one's colleagues expecting instant expositions of work in progress, not to allow subconscious patterns of thought to colour the immediate interpretation of the evidence as it appears in the ground. Attractive hypotheses suggested by the emerging evidence tend to crystallize, especially if apparently supporting evidence goes on accumulating. If at some point a crucial, contradictory piece of evidence emerges it can then become very painful to perform the *volte face* necessary to accept that one's previous theories are wrong and that everything has to be rethought.

In the face of all this destruction is there any justification at all for research excavation? So far as technique is concerned, the calmer pace and controlled strategy of research fieldwork and excavation enable us to evolve and test new techniques and, at the same time, to assess the validity of our rescue work. One discipline illuminates the other. In particular, research excavations warn us how much is likely to be missed under the conditions in which rescue and salvage excavation has to be carried out. To use again the example of Hen Domen, Montgomery, the excavation of a length of 20 metres of the bailey rampart has taken ten seasons' work. The rampart, of boulder clay, has been taken apart entirely by trowel or small hand-pick. A machine-cut section or one dug with pick and shovel would have shown the existence of a number of post-holes but would not have detected the thirteen or so buildings on the rampart's crest and rear slope, nor would it have revealed the sequence of the earliest defences. Beyond this, many features of timber buildings can only be seen under optimum weather conditions, so that one has to be patient and wait for just these conditions if one cannot create them artificially. But during a rescue excavation there may be no chance whatever of obtaining such conditions, and we have to be grateful for what we can salvage.

The recent increases in the scale of rescue excavations, brought about by the need to excavate whole sites and even whole landscapes, have required the development of new techniques of area stripping, principally to speed up the clearance of large areas of topsoil from sand, gravel, chalk, clay and loess sites. There are however no obvious short cuts in the excavation of deeply stratified sites containing stony layers and/or stone buildings.

Under rescue conditions much time may be saved by first examining the site using all the known non-destructive methods. On the collated results of such surveys a reasoned plan of campaign can be based. But it should be remembered that the most important structures on the site might very well escape the various forms of geophysical examination; either because their remains are not anomalously magnetic, or because they are not founded in deep post-holes or on walls which can be detected by the resistivity meter. In such cases, a limited excavation based solely on geophysical anomalies may be seriously misguided; and there are no certain safeguards against such an eventuality.

Under present circumstances a planned sequence of quasi-research excavations may be impossible; but the situation can nevertheless be exploited in two ways. Firstly, even if sites are fully examined in the random sequence in which they are threatened, the accumulating sum of information thus gained can eventually be synthesised. Secondly, if we accept that we cannot dig or even satisfactorily observe all the sites that are being destroyed, we can with sufficient notice select well in advance those sites which we would choose to excavate under ideal conditions; and, if these sites cannot be preserved untouched, try to arrange the most favourable circumstances for their excavation. This will involve the provision not only of much more money for longer and more complex excavations, but of more highly trained personnel, so that an intensive field training scheme will have to go hand in hand with any expanded rescue scheme.

The comparatively recent formation of a number of regional and urban units is an encouraging step towards rationalizing the otherwise *ad hoc* situation which has existed for too long in British archaeology. The even more recent formation of ministerially-appointed regional advisory committees and a national advisory committee may mean that sites will be selected for preservation or excavation on a sounder academic basis than has often been the case, and with a long-term strategy for ensuring that adequate techniques of exploration are readily available for the most important sites.

The rescue excavation of crop-mark sites*

By definition, most crop-mark sites will have been ploughed, and in many cases all, or most, of the vertical stratigraphy of the occupation layers will have been removed, leaving a palimpsest of ditches, pits, post-holes and other features which were dug deep enough to have penetrated the subsoil. The situation may be complicated by non-archaeological features caused by erosion, ice action, solifluction, the filling of hollows with naturally silted material, and the solution of calciferous rocks by leaching water. It is imperative that these natural features should be recognized and separated in the record from the archaeological evidence, since otherwise far-reaching mistakes may be made (Limbrey, 1975, 283).

In sites without vertical stratification, separation of contemporary and related structural features depends very largely on pattern making (what van Es has called the sport of 'granary building', van Es, 1967, 87) and on the intersection of ditches, pits and post-holes where a sequence can be demonstrated. Both problems are illustrated and discussed in a concise article by M.U. Jones (1974) which includes an excellent plan of the excavation of an area of gravel terrace, part of a whole ancient landscape currently being destroyed by quarrying. It is a most useful exercise, for those wishing to understand the principles of interpreting sites of this kind, to take such a plan and attempt to sort it into periods, based on the intersection of features, and into coherent structures, based on pattern making. It is particularly instructive to see how many alternative 'building plans' can be made using the same features kaleidoscoped into different (but mutually exclusive) patterns. The extensive plans included in the Wijster report (van Es, 1967) are ideal for the purpose (see back endpapers). The student's interpretation can then be compared with that of the excavator and discrepancies discussed.

One of the chief difficulties in excavating a crop-mark site lies in locating the crop-marks precisely in the field in which they occur. Very often the photograph shows a field or fields without readily distinguishable landmarks and often, too, the bearing of the aircraft is not precisely recorded. The problem is increased if the photographs are oblique, though it is often only oblique photographs which reveal crop-marks clearly, since in many cases they result from the reflection or

---

* For a concise description of the discovery of sites by aerial photography and of methods of locating sites on the ground see Coles, 1972, 21-45.

absorption of light from the leaves of growing crops, so that a vertical photograph, looking, as it were, straight down the leaf, is least effective.

Two simple methods of transferring oblique aerial photographs on to maps are described by Irwin Scollar in Wilson (ed. 1975, 52). One is the paper-strip method and the other the Mobius network method. Neither requires any apparatus beyond a pencil and a ruler. The degree of accuracy depends on the size and clarity of the photograph, and the corresponding size and detail of the map. Errors are also introduced if the ground is undulating, or, worse, hilly since the method assumes the ground to be flat. If a number of oblique photographs of the site taken from different directions are available they can be plotted together on the map and the mean of the errors taken. Once they are plotted on to the relevant map at the largest feasible scale the best way of locating them on the ground is by geophysical survey, either by magnetometer or resistivity meter. The use of divining rods should not be despised; on some sites remarkably consistent results have been obtained where other, more conventional methods have failed. If there are ditches of clearly defined shapes the identification of these should be aimed at. The problem is greater if the crop-marks consist of a complex of pits and post-holes, or parallel ditches where features may well be confused one with another. If geophysical methods do not locate the features sufficiently accurately, it may be necessary to cut one or more trial trenches across the site in the hope that the features can be related unambiguously to the crop-marks, though it must be borne in mind that all sites prove, on excavation, to contain many features which do not appear on the photographs, so that one must beware of being misled. Such trial trenches also recover significant amounts of pottery, building material and so on which all help in the assessment of the character of the site.

The least damage to the site will be done if the trial trenches are cut down only as far as the uppermost surfaces of the features. In this way their pattern can be recovered without their relationship with surrounding features being destroyed unobserved.

If there is any doubt about the location of the crop-marks on the ground the trial trench or trenches should be wide and sited so that they will certainly cross the crop-marks at some point, preferably where they are densest and have readily identifiable shapes. Trenches narrow enough to pass between pits or post-holes are obviously not satisfactory.

Such wide but shallow trial trenches should pick up recognizable features without damage to the site. The whole area can then be plotted from these as datum points, and the excavation strategy planned on a proper basis.

Where formerly stratified sites have been ploughed it is possible that the latest occupation layers have been destroyed, especially if they were only of timber with pebble or clay floors. In such cases the pottery used by the last occupants will still be there, churned up in the plough soil. If the field has been allowed to revert to pasture, a common occurrence, the latest pottery will drift downward due to worm action until it rests on the undestroyed archaeological layers. It may then be mistakenly considered to relate to these earlier levels instead of the later levels from which it derived.

Inevitably, all fast methods of stripping large areas of topsoil involve the risk of losing not only structural detail and associated finds but also whole periods of occupation. Most, but not all, of the excavators who use these or similar methods are aware of their limitations (eg. Jones, 1968, 229) but are prepared to accept them. The excavator of the Carolingian city of Dorestad has quantified the loss of coin evidence. In the earlier excavations of 1842 Janssen found 11 Carolingian coins in an area of about 400 m.² In the excavations of 1967-8 only ten coins were found in an area of about 55,000 m.² (van Es, 1969). These losses must be weighed against the eventual recovery of the plan of an entire early medieval city.

Where the site has been under the plough (and the fertile nature of the soils mentioned above has usually resulted in a long history of cultivation after the abandonment of settlements), it is usual to strip off the ploughsoil by machine on the assumption that the uppermost structural evidence will be found at the junction of the ploughsoil or humus and the undisturbed subsoil, into which features are cut, or, exceptionally, at some stratified levels below the ploughsoil. However, this assumption has been jolted by the discovery that on some crop-mark sites features seen on aerial photographs have not been discovered when the site has been excavated. Peter Reynolds has suggested that the soil differences which caused the crop-marks were contained within the ploughsoil. A possible explanation of this phenomenon is that ploughing disturbs the soil, but, especially on flat ground, does not move it very far from its original position. The chemical differences that cause crop differentiation, visible in the photographs, may therefore persist in the ploughsoil, which, if the site is to be fully excavated, should be examined archaeologically. This situation is paralleled by soil marks which may be seen on newly-ploughed land. Usually these soil-marks are reflections of features and other changes in the subsoil, but it is quite possible that some of them do not reach the subsoil. Work needs to be done on this problem before we can assess the losses of this sort of evidence due to topsoil stripping.

It is normal to machine-strip topsoil down to within a few centimetres of the subsoil, or, if they exist, of the occupation layers. The subsoil is then cleaned by hand, either with trowels, or dutch hoes (fig. 41) or with spades used horizontally (fig. 42). The latter method is the fastest but the crudest. On stonefree sands, clay, or loess, machine stripping can be refined to produce a surface almost as clean as necessary. The Dutch State archaeological service has developed a dragline cradle with a knife-edge that can strip layers from 5 to 10cm. thick, leaving a relatively clean surface (fig. 43). This sort of machine is ideal for fast excavation of the *planum* kind.

An outstanding example of large-scale rescue excavation both in technique and speed of publication is provided by J. G. Wainwright's work on Durrington Walls (Wainwright, 1971). The reader is urged to study it.

The planum method and the horizontal section

In this method, which can only reasonably be used on sites on stone-free soil and without stone buildings, layers of arbitrary thickness are removed over a whole area. These layers have no relation to vertical stratigraphy, and the method should therefore not be used where there are any preserved occupation layers. Where all the features are cut into the subsoil it can be used more successfully and with considerable speed. As each successive thin layer of the site is removed, the plan of the area with its exposed features is drawn to an appropriate scale. Slowly the pattern of the various features builds up. Some disappear with depth, others emerge, or become clearer. At no stage are the features of one period exposed and dealt with at one time, enabling a view of one building or structure to be seen in its entirety. As small features are not emptied separately and in the order in which they are stratified there is a danger that finds from discrete features will become mixed together, confusing the chronology and perhaps the constituent parts of structures. It is necessary, therefore to plot the finds three-dimensionally, in order that they may be related precisely to the features from which they derive. The method, together with its interpretation can be seen clearly in van Es 1969, figs 7-11. In contrast to the usual methods, in which the subsoil is left unexcavated, this technique involves the removal of enormous quantities of spoil, since slices of the subsoil are removed together with those of the features. It can nevertheless be useful on a smaller scale, for example where the junction of a series of ditches or a complex of post-holes cannot be emptied in sequence, because the soil differentiation is not sufficiently clear. In this case, the attempt to distinguish intercutting features may easily result in overdigging and the loss of evidence, and the planum method used discreetly may be more successful.

It may also be necessary, and valuable, to use arbitrary layers, where, for

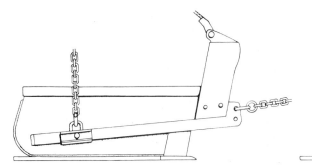

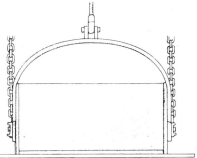

41 *left* Dutch hoes in use in London.

42 *above* Shaving the surface with long-handled spades after removal of top-soil by drag-line Dorestad, Holland.

43 *below* Drag-line bucket as modified by the Dutch State Archaeological Service for large-scale excavation of flat, stone-free sites.

0 ————————————————— 1.5 m

example, the soil or rubble make-up of a timber building is being removed. It may not be at all clear how thick the layer is, or whether it is uniform in thickness and composition. Under these circumstances, rather than taking the risk of over-digging and perhaps destroying or mutilating the evidence for an earlier building, it is better to remove the layer a little at a time. In this way, its composition will be better understood, and interleaved layers less likely to be missed.

Gravel and sand sites are often excavated by bulldozing off the upper layers to the top of the subsoil, the B/C horizon, leaving only the bottoms of the deeper pits and post-holes. The danger here is that much larger buildings, if they have slighter foundations, will be lost. The problem is seen in its classic form on the sites of pagan Saxon villages where sunken-floored huts are the most common structural find. If evidence for larger buildings with shallower post-holes is lost through natural erosion, bulldozing or simply through an inability to recognize the evidence, a completely false concept of these villages may gradually crystallize and become history. Our remoter English ancestors may have lived underground. But we must be acutely aware of the limitations of the excavated evidence and examine it hypercritically before we assert that they did.

In the report of his classic excavation of the Anglo-British complex at Yeavering in Northumberland, Brian Hope-Taylor describes (Hope-Taylor, 1977, pp. 32 and n. 49) what he calls primary and secondary horizontal sections, the first being the surfaces of all the archaeological strata lying immediately under the plough-soil, which had been carefully cleaned off with trowel and brush. His secondary horizontal sections consist of the horizontal dissection of the structures revealed by the first process. He admits, on p. 35 *ibid.*, that if he were to investigate further buildings on the same site he would 'dispense with most of the longitudinal sections and work more directly in terms of successive horizontal sections'.

Salvage excavation and recording

In the ideal long-term excavation every aspect of a site can be dealt with slowly and meticulously; but when only a limited time is available the techniques evolved under research conditions must be streamlined and speeded up and, where necessary, adapted. We must also distinguish between rescue and salvage excavations. By rescue, in this context, I am referring to the excavation of a threatened site conducted under conditions which may approach those of a research excavation to a greater or lesser degree. By a salvage excavation I mean one where the excavator salvages what he can from a site either just before or during its destruction. Salvage excavation requires the greatest skill and experience of all if the questions posed by the site are to be recognized and solved, even if only partially, and if fundamentally disastrous mistakes are to be avoided. This is instant archaeology indeed. When one is cleaning a machine-cut section or a newly scraped surface, both likely to disappear within the hour, a considerable mastery of archaeological technique is essential together with a flexible approach and the ability to interpret the evidence as it appears and to record it quickly and accurately.

Ultimately the value of the evidence from a salvage excavation will depend on the quality of the observations made on the site.

For example, in almost all cases, only positive evidence should be used. Under the sort of circumstances which give rise to salvage work the argument from negative evidence is highly suspect.

A salvage excavation may prove conclusively from a mass of stratified pottery that a site was occupied in medieval times, but it is unlikely to be able to prove that it was just as intensively occupied in the preceding aceramic period, though total detailed excavation may have done so. It may be argued that information at this level is not worth having, but if the pottery comes from an earthwork or crop-mark previously assumed to have been prehistoric or Roman, the evidence may be considered to be worth the day or two spent retrieving it.

As I write, a salvage excavation is being carried out on one of the medieval gates of the city of Worcester, and it provides a good example of the kind of information which can be gained from such smash-and-grab tactics.

A stretch of City ditch and a wide trench behind the wall were being cleared by machine. As the clearance progressed it was realized that it was approaching the site of the Friar's Gate, believed to be a postern in the wall close to the site of the Grey Friars. The machine was digging into the face of the cuttings in the usual way, a method which would have destroyed any remains of the postern without it being seen. Accordingly, the driver was asked to dig the area horizontally in layers. As a result stonework both on and behind the wall and in the ditch was revealed. Rapid cleaning by one person with a trowel and spade, working with the machine, showed that the remains were sufficiently well preserved to justify a salvage excavation. The optimum work force would have been two skilled excavators/recorders plus five or six volunteers/labourers working with the machinery. The results, though much less than total retrieval of all the available evidence, fully justified the time spent. They showed that, far from being a postern gate, the Friars Gate led to a wide bridge with abutments of many periods, the latest of which appeared to be the foundations of a building spanning the whole width of the city ditch. This additional knowledge of Worcester's history certainly justified the comparatively small outlay of time, skilled labour and money spent. A subsequent salvage excavation further along the city wall of Worcester is illustrated in figs. 44 and 45.

The loss of information due to the rushed and partial nature of the work is not so easy to assess, simply because we have not seen it. The excavator himself should qualify all his recorded observations with estimates of their reliability on a scale which ranges from certain to only possible. The dating of structures by means of stratified pottery, coins and other artefacts is particularly difficult under these circumstances, and the excavator must be certain that the datable material really was derived from the significant layer or structure and not introduced by machinery or the soles of boots. The bucket of a drag-line, cutting a section of a ditch, can embed material from the upper layers deep

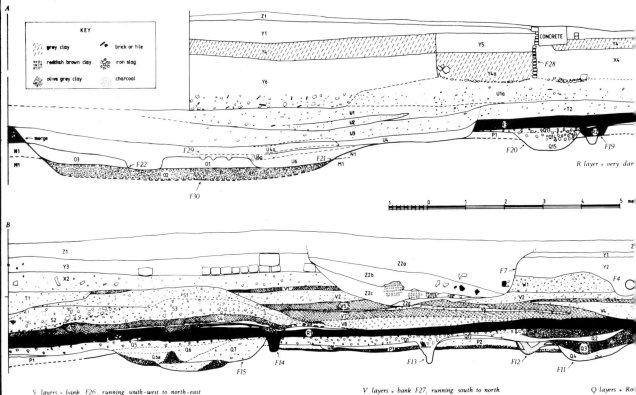

WORCESTER 1975   *Talbot St. South   Section S-N inside, at c. 5° to, the City Wall*

KEY

grey clay		brick or tile	
reddish brown clay		iron slag	
olive grey clay		charcoal	

A

Z1

Y1

CONCRETE

Y5

Y6

Y4a

F28

X4

U1a

T2

V1

V2

V3

U4

P1

Q13

Q12

F19

merge

N1

F29

U4a

N1

F20

Q15

M1

O3

U5a

U6

F21

R layer = very dar

M1

F22

O1

M1

F30

O2

1	0	1	2	3	4	5 me

B

Z1

Y3

Z2a

Y1

X2

Z2b

F7

Y2

F4

T1

KS1

V1

Z2c

W1

V2

S3

V2

Z4

V4

S2

S4

V5

V3

V8

F12

Q5

R1

Q11

P2

Q2

P1

Q6a

Q6

Q7

P3

Q1

F13

Q3

F14

Q4

F11

F15

S layers = bank F26, running south-west to north-east   *V layers = bank F27, running south to north*   Q layers = Ro

into the primary silting, and cover it with a smear of the same material. When the ditch section is cleaned back it is disconcerting to find a half-brick stratified in the bottom of what is quite certainly a Roman ditch of the first century. The half brick can be discarded as contamination and the section cleaned back further until uncontaminated layers are reached, but if instead of a brick a sherd of late Roman pottery or a fourth-century coin had found its way similarly into the early ditch, it would not have been discarded so promptly, thus causing real confusion. For the same reasons, the provenance of finds handed in by workmen or unskilled volunteers must be treated with the greatest reserve unless they can be checked on the spot.

The minimum equipment for a salvage recorder should be two good cameras, 2¼″-square for colour negative film, and 35mm. for transparencies, with two high-level tripods; a quick-set level and staff, if necessary with tripod attachment for single-handed use; a large clipboard mounted with squared polyester film overlaid with drawing film to a predetermined standard size, such as A4, A3 or a square format if this is preferred; coloured pencils to an agreed area (or preferably regional) colour code; record cards, as fully printed as possible, for sites, features, finds and photographs. Thus armed, a salvage recorder or a team of two or three working together can clean features and sections, draw them in outline and photograph them in colour negative and reversal film. The key drawings of both sections and plans must have spot heights inserted, so that they can be related to previous or further work in the area. If the work is in a town or

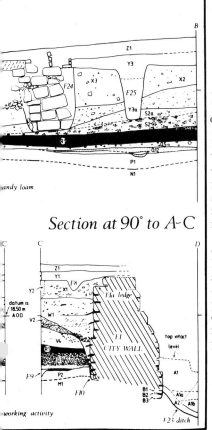

Section at 90° to A-C

44-45 Talbot Street, Worcester, 1975; an example of opportunist salvage archaeology, where a long trench dug by bulldozer behind the City Wall of Worcester (fig. 44) was seen to be densely stratified. An emergency cleaning and recording operation was mounted, and part of the result is shown in fig. 45.

Among a good deal of other detail, evidence of Roman iron-smelting (already attested elsewhere in the city) is shown by layers prefixed with Q; these are overlain by R layer, which represents the immediate post-Roman period; the S layers are a bank of unknown date preceding the medieval wall and running at an acute angle to it; the V layers are a longitudinal section of a pre-wall bank perhaps of the twelfth century; the W layers are the construction trench for the City Wall, while the U layers are the upper fill of an early (perhaps Roman) scoop or gulley (O layers).

This short salvage recording has added much to the evidence for Worcester's defences, though it has also raised a number of problems which only further excavation will solve.

city it should be possible to get the colour negatives processed and printed within 24 hours. If prints (of a section for example) are made to a predetermined scale, they can be pasted together and annotated on the site. This obviates all but the most skeletal drawing. It is also cost-effective. A section 45m. long and 3m. high would take a week to draw and colour in detail. Photographically it can be recorded, printed and fully annotated in 2-3 days, the cost of the prints being offset by the saving of time.

Such recording should be carried out by an archaeologist with considerable experience in research and long-term rescue excavation, experience against which he can assess the significance of features that may only be visible for an hour or two, or even a few minutes. It is not a job for an inexperienced enthusiast. Nevertheless, it is here that local volunteers can be trained and used effectively. A group of eight or ten unskilled but energetic volunteers can enormously increase the amount of information retrieved, by cleaning surfaces, sections and walls, assisting with measuring, surveying and photography, and dealing with pottery and finds on a simple basis. Usually among such a group one or two will rapidly develop skills enabling them to draw plans and sections under supervision, and to adapt previously acquired photographic techniques and so forth.

In the post-excavation work, such a group is of immense value, washing, marking and sorting pottery and other stable finds, assisting with the redrawing of plans and sections, and often going on to more specialised work. In Worcester, between 1965 and 1970, some extremely skilled drawing of finds and pottery, the stabilization of leather shoes and their reconstruction, and the reconstruction of highly decorated pottery were carried out by local volunteers, none of whom had had previous experience. This can, no doubt, be paralleled in rescue and salvage excavations all over the country. It has the added benefit of drawing local people into the archaeology of the town or area, and is a powerful educational stimulus as well as an intensely satisfying recreation for those who take part. Not only that, it also extends and enhances the limited funds available for rescue archaeology since most part-time local volunteers are happy to work on their own town, or on a local site for nothing, except perhaps help with expenses such as petrol. The director of a salvage excavation, however competent and experienced, can increase his potential output tenfold by the recruiting of local volunteers. The maximum number which one person can direct is probably 10-15. Beyond this, a hierarchy of assistant directors or site supervisors will be needed in the proportion of about one to ten.

Needless to say, such local groups should be organised in such a way that they are insured in a scheme such as that of the CBA and, while they may come and go on site at odd times or days according to their other commitments, they must be prepared to accept all the normal site disciplines, and be subject to the same safety precautions as a full-time team. For this reason it is advisable to enrol members by name before they are allowed to take part. The director cannot and must not accept responsibility for casual visitors and small boys who may join in the work uninvited.

Another constraint on excavation techniques is the sheer size of some sites, either in area or in depth. We have seen that unstratified sites of many acres can be stripped progressively by machine and then hand-dug, and in theory, if the money and skilled manpower were available, a site of almost any extent could be dug simply by multiplying the numbers of workers at all levels. This is not the case, however, on sites with very deep deposits where the number of people who can be deployed on the ground is limited by the surface area. If there is a multiplicity of thin but significant layers there will be a maximum speed at which they can be individually stripped and recorded. If, on the other hand, the situation is made more awkward by deep layers of sticky clay or heavy rubble the niceties of sensitive area excavation may be hard to achieve. Here one simply has to excavate with as much precision as is possible. Remembering that our canals and railways were all dug by hand, it should be possible to recruit a gang of navvies who could deal with such a situation, and there is no doubt that hand labour has great flexibility and is less potentially destructive than machinery, although it is far more expensive.

The aim of the director of either a rescue or a salvage excavation must be maximum time and cost-effectiveness; in other words the maximum amount of reliable evidence for the time and money available. Any method of digging and recording that accelerates the excavation process with minimal loss of evidence or accuracy must be tried and exploited.

Assuming ample money, equipment and skilled personnel to be available, the speeding-up of a rescue excavation might be achieved without appreciable loss of detail and accuracy by making the excavation as mechanically-assisted and labour-intensive as possible − a piece of high-priority archaeological civil engineering. As many people (assuming them to be skilled) as could work on the site at once should be employed. It would be necessary, of course, to have a carefully balanced hierarchy of supervisors, recorders, photographers etc., and a very clearly understood chain of command. Adequate shelters, where necessary, and floodlights, using mains electricity or generators, would allow work to continue in two or three shifts of eight or ten hours (with breaks) so that work could go on for 20 or 24 hours a day. Floodlit football is a commonplace. There is no reason why floodlit excavation should not be also.

Shift working would need a considerable degree of organisation and close cooperation between the teams working jointly on the site. Its success would depend on the site supervisors being highly competent, thoroughly briefed, capable of working together, and overlapping with each other in their shifts to ensure continuity. It would be an advantage if some of the excavators and recorders overlapped also to avoid a sharp break in personnel. The director, who clearly cannot be on site continuously, would need to have complete faith in his principal supervisors in such a cooperative scheme and there would be less scope for the brilliant, intuitive individualist. The director would, in fact, chiefly play the role of adviser, organiser and coordinator.

The deployment of a large number of people on a site requires clear thinking and careful coordination if there is not to be chaos. If the work could proceed across the site from one end to another it would be easier for the excavators to be followed by finds-recorders, draughtsmen, surveyors, photographers and so on. In such an excavation the bulk of the recording would be photographic, using polaroid film in large format, and vertical and oblique stereoscopy in colour (see Chapter 8). Nevertheless a minimum of surveying and drawing would still be needed. If it were intended to draw the site photogrammetrically by machine, an accurate prior survey of each run or area would be needed. If the photographs were intended to supplement the plans, outline drawings to the necessary degree of detail rendering the photographs intelligible when related to the skeletal plan would be needed.

The removal of spoil is often a slow and laborious process. Conveyor belts, either with or without buckets, considerably speed up the process, and experiments should be made with vacuum removal of the finer spoil. In either case, it would be possible, with care, to remove the spoil from discrete features or layers separately, so that sieving, either wet or dry, flotation or other sampling could take place outside the excavation area.

Hand in hand with the swift recording of the visual evidence must go streamlined methods of finds recording. Here index cards, bags, boxes, labels and so forth should be printed beforehand, so far as possible, so that the minimum amount of writing is needed. Automatic consecutive numbering and lettering stamps and other such devices would all save valuable time.

The thought of such a high-pressure excavation, with its non-stop activity and continuous noise, will seem a nightmare to many, especially to those of us who enjoy excavation in sylvan surroundings where the silence is broken only by the music of a dozen trowels. And it may be that, however urgent the destruction, noisy work at night would be unacceptable in residential areas. In that case, it may be necessary to do without machinery during the night, and concentrate on those tasks which can be done quietly.

It must be remembered that, whatever accelerating techniques are invented, there is a point beyond which it is impossible, for sheer logistic reasons, to speed up excavation. No technical aids, no amount of money or number of people can strip an acre of thinly stratified deposits in a day. Furthermore, high-speed excavation loses that most essential quality of the slower excavation, the opportunity to think quietly, to contemplate the evidence, to go back to it *on the ground*, and, if necessary, to reassess it drastically. It is useless to achieve speed without understanding.

The sort of intensive excavation outlined here would, it is hoped, only be used as a last resort. We must, therefore, work towards making such extreme measures unnecessary, by means of forward planning coupled with legislation which will permit sufficient time for thorough, less hurried, investigation.

8

Analysis: Recognising and Recording the Evidence

Only what is observed can be recorded; and observation is not an automatic process. It depends entirely on the particular knowledge of the observer. Hanson (1967) deals with just this point:

> There is more to seeing than meets the eyeball, and there is more to scientific observation than merely standing alert with sense organs at the ready . . . . . The visitor (to the laboratory) must learn physics before he can see what the physicist observes. Only then will the context throw into relief those features in the phenomena which the physicist observes as indicating (e.g.) resistance. This obtains in all cases of observation. It is all *interest-directed and context-dependent*. Attention is rarely directed to the space between the leaves of a tree. Still, consider what was involved in Robinson Crusoe's seeing a vacant space in the sand as a footprint. Our attention rests on objects and events which because of our selective interests dominate the visual field. What a blooming, buzzing, undifferentiated confusion visual life would be if we all arose tomorrow morning with our attention capable of dwelling only on what has heretofore been completely overlooked. Indeed our mental institutions are full of poor souls who, despite having normal vision, can observe nothing. Theirs is a rhapsodic, kaleidoscopic, senseless barrage of sense signals-answering to nothing and signifying naught.

However, in scientific investigation there remains a basic and necessary duality of approach. On the one hand the selection of criteria of significance is crucial to the outcome of any investigation. As Alan Gregg, Director of Medical Sciences for the Rockefeller Foundation has said (Medawar, 1969);

> Most of the knowledge and much of the genius of the research worker lie behind his selection of what is worth observing. It is a crucial choice, often

determining the success or failure of months of work, often differentiating the brilliant discoverer from the plodder.

On the other hand it is often the unsuspected fact that turns out to be crucial to understanding. Beveridge (1950) warns:

If when we are experimenting, we confine our attention to only those things which we expect to see, we shall probably miss the unexpected occurrences and these, even though they may at first be disturbing and troublesome, are the most likely to lead to the explanation of the usual. When an irregularity is noticed, look for something with which it might be associated. In order to make original observations the best attitude is not to concentrate exclusively on the main point but to try and keep a lookout for the unexpected, remembering that observation is not passively watching but is an active mental process.

He also adds this corollary:

Effective scientific observation also requires a good background for only by being familiar with the usual can we notice something as being unusual or unexplained.

As Binford (1972) says:

Excavation must be conducted in terms of a running analysis and against a backdrop of the widest possible set of questions to which the data are potentially relevant. This is no technician's job. This is the job of an anthropologist specialised in the collection and analysis (and, I would add, synthesis) of data concerning extinct cultural systems.

All writers of excavation reports will know how difficult it is to keep the excavated evidence separate from its interpretation and this dilemma starts during the excavation itself. It is very easy to slip into the habit of calling dark circular soil marks 'post-holes' before they have been excavated. This not only prejudges the evidence, but can become that habit of mind which is capable of finding what it wants to find. Once a dark area has been presumed to be a post-hole it requires considerable mental discipline to accept, when it is emptied, that it is a root-hole or some other non-structural disturbance, especially if it is in just the place where a post-hole is expected (or even needed!) to complete a structure. On the sites of timber buildings the opportunities for the creative imagination are immense. In the same way, 'timber slots' may turn out to be drainage gullies, or grooves worn by eaves' drip, or intermittent plough furrows, and what at first sight seems to be a dump of broken tile may turn out to be a floor, or vice versa.

One must add the subtle but real pressure from one's colleagues to provide instant interpretations of phenomena as they appear. One has to steer a course between a neutral, non-interpretive approach which will quickly deflate the enthusiasm that buoys an excavation along, and flights of fancy which the evidence finally cannot support. One can occasionally see the fossilised remains of fancies of this kind embedded in excavation reports.

In order to minimize the interpretive element in the record a neutral term such as 'feature' or 'context' is perhaps best used to describe each separately recognizable anomaly, whether it is a layer, a post-hole, a floor, a hearth or whatever. Each anomaly can then be given a serial number either by grids viz: 1/1, 1/2, 1/3, 2/1, 2/2, 2/3, or throughout the whole site. This system has proved to be easier to use than that in which the term 'feature' is used only for anomalies within or cutting through layers. The difficulty arises in marginal cases, for example where a layer may be a hearth, or a hearth may be made up of many layers. 'Context' is an appropriate word to describe a layer or feature from which finds or other specific information are derived; but, being an abstract noun, it lacks reality when used in speech. You cannot section a context, or lower its surface by half a centimetre. There is no reason why the word 'layer' should not be retained for continuous deposits of material. In other words all 'layers' are 'features' (and should be called so in the record) but not all 'features' are 'layers'.

It is difficult to separate in our minds the excavated evidence from its interpretation, which inevitably begins as features are seen, dissected and removed. There are some aspects of the interpretation of features (the word is used in its widest sense) that are at their optimum when they are first revealed, since the site can never again be in that pristine, freshly-cleaned state. Time and weather will immediately begin to alter it. Sometimes weathering produces new information, and sometimes it destroys the uppermost surface entirely; and although subsequent cleaning may reveal new detail, much of the original detail will have disappeared. In addition, however meticulous and accurate the recording, it is impossible to draw every texture of the exposed soil, and record all the nuances of colour in layers which may merge imperceptibly with one another. In addition aspects of the site which cannot be seen or felt are likely to go unnoticed. Differences of chemical composition, for example, may not be visible but may exist and be of considerable significance in the understanding of the site. Some soil colour changes may only be made visible by ultra-violet or infra-red light or when enhanced by chemical treatment (p. 94 above); some important differences of level may only show up under conditions of glancing light; other features may only appear as dry or wet areas, invisible on ordinary days and disappearing when dissected.

To take a wider view there is the necessary contemplation of the excavated area (preferably when work on the site has temporarily stopped, so that there are no distractions), when relationships, unseen before, will become apparent, and when the overall pattern of the evidence will begin to emerge. This, seen three-dimensionally as one walks round or over the site, may be very difficult to record adequately, and virtually impossible to demonstrate in the eventual publication.

Thus at present the adequate and total recording of the evidence is beyond us. It follows that our responsibility for the immediate interpretation, made soon after the structures are uncovered, together with subsequent modifications, made in the light of all the observed evidence, is very great since the interpretive element in the recording can never be completely isolated, nor can drawings, photographs and written records ever be a substitute for the observations which are possible when one is present on the site. In other words, no mechanical process of recording even the nuances of the excavated surfaces will ever replace acute and sensitive observation by minds alive to all the possibilities presented by the evidence.

'Only connect' said E.M. Forster, and I believe that the most important need in archaeological excavation is to establish relationships, to interconnect structural layers and features, to relate them to the finds of all kinds, from sculpture to pollen, embedded in them and to relate the excavated site to its surroundings and to other comparable sites. Contiguous areas of excavation are almost always more illuminating than those separated from one another even by a metre or so, and inter-relationships established across and through large sites by a feature matrix are essential if the site is to be fully understood.

On most sites, except for those in towns, Layer 1 will be humus, topsoil or ploughsoil (though see p. 33). The removal of Layer 1 usually reveals a surface made up of a series of features adjoining, overlapping and running into one another. Even on a small site the number of separately distinguishable features making up the exposed surface may run into hundreds. Each of these has to be identified and recorded. Each distinguishable feature should be labelled as it appears, with a plastic label marked with a waterproof, light-proof 'dry-marker' type pen of Pentel type. It is a good idea to reserve one colour of plastic label for features, keeping other colours for finds or the positions of samples taken and so on. Labels are conveniently pinned to the ground with spring-headed galvanized nails.

Data retrieval

The object of all excavation recording is data retrieval. At the end of the excavation all that remains are the site records, the drawings and photographs, and the finds. Any information which is not contained in one of these is lost for good. If it is there somewhere, but is difficult to find, its retrieval may be as laborious as the excavation itself. All aspects of the site recording system — visual, in the form of drawings, sections, contour surveys, together with photographs, vertical and oblique, in colour and black and white; or written, in the form of record cards, notebooks, punched cards, or tape — should be devised so that they make interpretation, publication and storage as easy as possible. It is not simply a question of data retrieval, but of producing from the data interpretive drawings of the site's phases and periods, buildings and structures; of wresting meaning from thousands of features, hundredweights of pottery and bone, and hundreds of finds, photographs and drawings. All this has ultimately to be distilled into readable prose, museum displays, popular books and reconstructions. Anything, therefore, that shortens this daunting process ought to be considered. What this means in practice is that the end product of the excavation should be borne in mind before the work begins.

There can be no hard and fast rules for excavation recording systems suitable for all types of excavation since sites vary so much in the nature of their structural evidence, and the types and quantities of finds. However, any system must satisfy the following criteria:

1. It must be simple and logical to use and understand.
2. It must be capable of indefinite extension, since the excavation itself may be extended beyond the original intentions or the quantities of finds may be very much greater than anticipated.
3. It must be flexible. For this reason index cards are better than books since they can be sorted into any order, and later interpolations can be inserted in place quickly and comprehensively.
4. The information must be retrievable. To this end, any large excavation should devise its recording system with one eye on computer storage, which, if not immediately available, may become so within the near future.
5. The information should be presented in a form that makes the writing of the final report as easy as possible.

It is maintained by some that none of the data from an excavation is objective; that an excavation produces no *facts*. Nevertheless, a block of sandstone is a fact; mortar is a fact (demonstrable if necessary by chemical and physical analysis); and it is only a slight shift towards subjectivity to call a hundred blocks of sandstone, coursed and mortared together in a line, a wall. Beyond this, however, we become increasingly subjective. The wall's possible or probable function and date, and its relation to other structures must be considered; and ultimately the discussion may, properly, enter the realms of speculation. What is important is that all these stages should be distinguishable one from another.

For this reason, immediate on-site recording, the first stage in the process, should be as objective as it can be. It helps towards objectivity if the written recording is formalised, on cards or sheets, with spaces for answering specific questions and the provision of required categories of information. This is preferable to notebooks which contain paragraphs (sometimes essays) of descriptive prose whose loose format invites the writer to confuse the stages of recording, deduction, interpretation and speculation. The minimum information required on the index card is:

1. The abbreviated name of the site.
2. The area and grid numbers.
3. The feature number.
4. The position of the feature (as a grid reference).
5. Its relation to features above, around and, eventually, below it.

6. A description of the feature, including its composition or filling.
7. Finds directly associated with the feature.
8. A sketch, if this would be helpful, and/or a polaroid photograph.
9. Cross-reference to the measured drawings, sections and photographs.

Provisional Date	Type		Site Code	Context
Medieval : ?14th c.	Wall	110/215	ABC|82	1023

Description of Context

Random uncoursed ragstone (? Kentish) predominantly rough-hewn in large fragments and occasional blocks (eg. 0.23 x 0.38m in elevation) with occasional flints and medium frags of chalk (E side only); also 2 horizontally-laid medium frags of Roman tile. Patches of plaster for 2.6m from S end on E face, with horizontal bottom edge in two parts (see S67) 0.1m above [1067]. Included in fabric, when excavated, was a sculptured stone /39\ and 2 large frags PTO

Site Grid Refs.   112.35 / 216.80

Levels *(tick)* a. when taken ......✓...... b. when transferred to plan(s) ......✓......

Stratigraphically Earlier than

1018									

Stratigraphically Later than

1067									

Method of Excavation   Trowel and gentle picking

Risk of Intrusive Finds *(tick one)*   Low ...✓...   High ....   Unknown ....

Finds

inorganic | organic/biological

	Pot	Glass	T.Pipe	Metal	Brick/Tile	Other B.M.	Leather	Bone	Molluscs	Seeds	Wood/Charcoal
(tick if present)					✓	✓ Plaster					
(collection keyword)					A	S					

Other Finds *(specify & give keyword)* _____

Special Finds   /39\ /\ /\ /\ /\ /\ /\ /\ /\ /\

Samples

	Bulk Sample	Wood/Charcoal	C14	Dendro.	Pollen	Arch.Mag.		
(tick if taken)	Type							
(number of bags)	Multi-context YES/NO							

Plan Nos: P 292	**Initials & Date**
Other Drawings: S 63, 67	Y.W. 25.6.82
Site Book Refs. N/A	
Location on Matrix Square A3	**Checked by & Date**
Photographs *(tick when taken)* ...✓... Card Nos. 135, 140, 169, 232	RK. 26.6.82

Interpretative Notes

N-S wall on foundation [1067]. West wall of Building A. Plaster level at 11.06m OD (see elevation, S67) indicates interior floor level - presumably a wooden floor, see ? joist impressions [1092], [1165], [1166].

Phase	Group	Initials & Date
IV.7	68	RK 31.10.82

SITE RECORDING SHEET

MUSEUM OF LONDON
DEPARTMENT OF URBAN ARCHAEOLOGY

MUS.3477

46

10. Subsequent interpretive notes, e.g. post-hole, part of structure XIII, kitchen, Phase 2.
11. The considered reliability of this interpretation.

(a)

| Site | Area | Grid | Feature | Date Found | Code |
| | | | | Date Dug | |

GRID REFERENCE   GENERAL LOCATION

DESCRIPTION

INTERPRETATION

POST-EXCAVATION RELIABILITY

METHOD OF EXCAVATION..
METHOD OF COLLECTION OF FINDS...
TYPES OF FINDS PRESENT BUT NOT COLLECTED

RISK OF CONTAMINATION   LOW.......... AVERAGE.......... HIGH..........

SAMPLES...
SPECIAL FINDS...

PLAN NOS..

SECTION NOS.....................   OTHER DRAWINGS...............................

PHOTOGRAPHS: B/W NEGS..................   B/W PRINTS...........................

COLOUR SLIDES.............. , PRINTS................   VERTICAL..............

STRATIFICATION   LOCALISED MATRIX
                                                  SHEET NO.
UNDERLIES   □ □ □ □ □ □

OVERLIES   □ □ □ □ □ □   □ □ □ □ □

CUTS   □ □ □ □ □ □   □ □ □ □ □

CUT BY   □ □ □ □ □ □   □ □ □ □ □

ABUTS   □ □ □ □ □ □   □ □ □ □ □

EQUALS   □ □ □ □ □ □   □ □ □ □ □

OTHER

PHOTOGRAPHS AND/OR CONTINUATION

(b)

46 The context (or feature) record sheet used by the Department of Urban Archaeology of the Museum of London.

47 Examples of record cards. (a) and (b) The feature card used at Wroxeter and Hen Domen. (c) The pottery record card used by the Department of Urban Archaeology, Museum of London.

(c)

Publication Ref.		Fabric Code	
E.R. No. of Type Sherd		Common Name	
COLOUR:	ext. margin		ext. surface
	int. margin		int. surface
HARDNESS:			FRACTURE:
FEEL:			
INCLUSIONS: 1	2	3	
Frequency			
Sorting			
Size			
Rounding			
SURFACE TREATMENT(S): ext.		int.	
MANUFACTURE:			
SLIP: extent		colour(s)	
GLAZE: ext. extent	colour(s)		finish
int. extent	colour(s)		finish

Suggested layouts of cards for recording features and layers are illustrated in figs. 46-7. These written records are complementary to the visual records which consist of the site plans and sections and the drawings of individual features, pottery and other finds together with both vertical and oblique photographs. The written records and the drawings and photographs must be cross-indexed so that the complete information about a feature or layer can be readily found. The information relating to an individual feature, for instance, should consist of: a completed feature card; a set of drawings, including plans and sections; photographs; cards for small finds and pottery found within the filling or structure of the feature; and, finally, the drawing of the feature on the main site plan, which relates it to the structures around it. On a site which produces hundreds, perhaps thousands, of features this may seem unnecessarily laborious, but there is no short cut if the excavation is to be properly recorded.

A number of the larger archaeological units are producing their own handbooks on site recording, which lay out the procedures and conventions to be adopted on their sites. A good example is the *Site Manual, Part 1, The Written Record*, published by the Department of Urban Archaeology of the Museum of London and obtainable from them. Figs 46 and 47(c) are taken from this booklet.

It is suggested by some that the feature record cards should be designed so that they can be fed into a computer, either in punched card or tape form. In this way if the necessary three-dimensional measurements are included on the cards the relationships between features can be retrieved in the form of a print-out or visual display. This seems to me to be an unnecessarily abstract way of recording and interpreting the site, except in conditions of extreme urgency where it is impossible to draw or photograph the layers or features in stratigraphical order, and where the only, or principal, records are the cards.

In excavations where there is time to record each layer/feature as it is revealed it is much more economical to use superimposed plans or a matrix or graph of the features, which is built up progressively as they are discovered.

Site notebooks

For reasons mentioned above (p. 147) index cards are preferable to site notebooks for recording of features. However site notebooks should be kept for recording information not to be found on the record cards; a brief day-to-day account of work in progress, observations on areas or clusters of features, speculations and hypotheses. Where a site is full of evidence for buildings and other structures if may be helpful to have a separate card index for buildings each card drawing together the evidence such as post-holes, walls, floors, hearths, finds and so on for the existence, from and function of the building. Such a card index will be of great help when the report comes to be written.

The site grid

The skeleton of any recording system must be the site grid. Under all but emergency conditions this should be laid out before the excavation begins; and it is essential to relate the excavation and its grid to permanent features in the landscape. With the advent of ever larger areas of development in towns, and the wholesale removal of hedgerows and other landmarks in the country, this is becoming increasingly difficult, and the excavator, in these circumstances, may become disorientated and literally may not know where his excavation is. In urban areas it is necessary to obtain the cooperation of the engineers and surveyors concerned with the development in order to locate precisely the excavation areas in the old and new townscapes. In the country, in the middle of a large gravel pit or an area of 'prairie' farming, the situation may not be so easy; rather like fixing one's position in the desert, it may be necessary to do some very accurate surveying. Anticipating the chapter on publication below, it is necessary, where an excavation is taking place in a radically altered landscape, to publish its relationship to the old landscape as well as to locate it in the new.

On any but the briefest excavation a base or datum line should be chosen and its terminal pegs concreted into place at each end. A hooked metal rod is perhaps the most convenient type of peg, so that the ring of a tape will not slip off it when under tension. Needless to say this base line must be measured with great accuracy and in the horizontal plane. A third peg, on an axis at right angles to the base, should be concreted in at a convenient point outside the proposed area of the excavation. From these two lines a coordinate or grid system in the horizontal plane can be established. Other subsidiary pegs should then be fixed on or outside the excavation to form an accurate basis for the rest of the grid. Wherever possible, the intersections of the grid lines should be marked by thin steel rods driven into the ground, thus reducing the inconvenience often caused when nails are used to mark the grid intersections, since they are easily displaced and have to be re-aligned — a tedious and time-wasting job.

Metric units, once adopted, are easier to use than feet and inches. Whether the coordinate system or a system of numbered or lettered grids is used, the corners of the squares should be pegged with accurately placed metal pegs, and it is an advantage to paint these corner pegs a bright colour so that they can be easily seen. The grid can then be sub-divided into as many smaller squares as the site demands, and the corners of these smaller squares pegged.

The problems of planning excavated areas have been dealt with by Atkinson, 1953, 229, Fryer, 1971, Biddle and Biddle, 1969, and Coles, 1972. The Biddles' paper, which the reader is urged to study, advocates the use of a coordinate system based on a metric grid, rather like the National Grid Reference system. This has the advantage that any point on the site can be referred to by a single unique reference given by two coordinates (fig. 48). It is usually convenient to lay out the whole site in a grid of ten metre squares marked out with string (coloured plastic coated varieties are not only easily seen but have the necessary elasticity) so that the excavators can easily orientate themselves on the site. Plastic letters or numbers in the centre or at one corner of each major grid will enable one

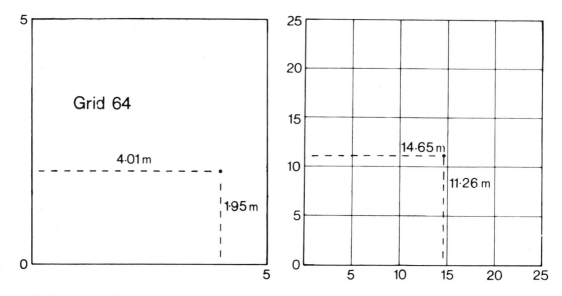

48 *left:* the position would be recorded as G64. 401 195; *right:* as 1465.1126.

to see at a glance in which square one is working.

Site planning
The most usual way of recording features visually is to draw the plan of the surface at a scale large enough for the smallest feature to be accommodated: 24:1
when feet are used, or 20:1 in metric scale are usually sufficient. Since features
and layers will often merge almost imperceptibly into one another, or are distinguishable only by changes of texture rather than of colour, it is sometimes impossible to draw hard lines round the limits of each feature in which case the
drawing should depict the character of the feature as closely as possible, even
though it may be necessary in the interpretation to distinguish the junction more
clearly. In fact the principle of separating the evidence from the interpretation
should be adhered to as far as it can be, though, inevitably, the field drawing will
include many elements of interpretation, at least in part due to the limited
flexibility of drawing techniques. The range of colours and symbols used cannot
be as infinite as the variations in composition of the features and layers, and the
completely pictorial representation of plans (and sections), especially if in colour,
is apt to be overloaded with detail, and 'unreadable'. Some of Professor Bersu's
'impressionist' drawings, attempting to include everything, err in this direction.
Simplification involves selection and is therefore subjective, and this is the strongest argument for photographic recording.
    If more than one draughtsman is used on a site the work should be co-ordinated.
For instance three different draughtsmen drawing the same stony surface will in

all probability produce different results because they will include stones of different minimum sizes. Many surfaces consist of stones of all sizes down to 1mm. across, and therefore a minimum drawn stone size has to be chosen. At 1:20 a 2cm. stone will appear like this:

Stones smaller than this will be dots the size of a pencil point. With further reduction for publication they will all disappear, or will have to be drawn at an artificially enlarged scale. In cases of doubt the director should make a ruling, but usually stones of 1cm. are the smallest that can reasonably be drawn at 1:20 scale. As far as possible all the draughtsmen on the site should draw in the same style; and they must certainly all use the same conventions and methods otherwise the resulting mosaic of drawings will be incoherent.

A considerable problem is posed by hollows and scarps on the excavated surface. Ideally each small hollow, each scarp, each post-hole should be contour surveyed, but lack of time usually prevents this. A compromise which may be used is to contour survey the whole site separately on a transparent overlay on a 20cm. grid for small sites or a 50cm. or 1m. grid for large sites, dependent on the degree of detail required. Minor undulations, small scarps, etc. are then put on the site drawings as form lines with an arrow indicating the downward slope. Other conventions such as hachures or 'tadpoles' can be used; but on complex sites they tend to be more confusing than form lines and tend to obscure detail.

In special cases, where it is required to demonstrate the existence of slight but significant undulations, the contour survey can be made tighter and the contour lines drawn at very close intervals. A fine 'gravel' street was discovered at Wroxeter. On this street differential wear had left only slight humps and platforms like miniature earthworks. Since these were considered to be the sole evidence for a second phase of use of the street, with façades or booths of some sort encroaching on it, the survey was made at 20cm. horizontal intervals, and the resultant contours plotted at 2cm. vertical intervals in order to bring out the subleties of shape of these undulations, which would have been missed in a survey on a coarser grid plotted at a greater vertical interval. For detailed levelling of very uneven surfaces, or rows of post- or stake-holes, structures of rock or rubble and so on a thin staff may be made by attaching a 3m. tape to a metal or wooden rod. If necessary, the rod can be fitted with a long spike for precise positioning in holes or crevices. A more easily read staff of this kind could be made by accurately painting the divisions and lettering them with Letraset or similar stencils which should then be varnished.

Any method of drawing that shortens the steps between the original field drawings made on the site and those eventually published should be tried and developed. If the field drawings are clear and accurate, and are directly and precisely relatable to the site grid it should be possible to trace the final drawings straight from them so that there are only two drawings of the evidence, one made in the field, the other the published figures. To these may be added separate interpretive plans, sections and so on if the amount of detail in the published evidence is considerable.

If plans on translucent plastic film are made of each stage of the excavation, together with subsidiary plans of intermediate stages they can be superimposed on one another so that their relationship can be understood visually. At the same time the inter-relationship between all the features on the site can be recorded and demonstrated schematically by means of a matrix such as that developed by Edward Harris (Harris, 1975); see Chapter 10.

There are four or five principal ways in which the site plan may be drawn:

The drawing frame

One method is to use a frame the size of the grid unit, say a metre square, divided into smaller units such as 20cm., and laid on the excavated surface. Through this the features and details of the surface can be directly related to sectional drawing film on the drawing board, and drawn to the desired scale. The bulk of the drawing can then be made by eye without further measuring. A frame of slotted metal or braced wooden slats is divided either by plastic or nylon string which has sufficient elasticity to stay taut, by wire, or by expanding plastic-covered curtain wires. Frames 2m. square may be found rather large and unwieldy and a 1m. square is often preferable. Snags with the use of a frame arise when the ground is not reasonably level, or more particularly when large stones or other obstructions prevent the frame from being laid horizontally. It is of course important that the frame should be levelled, and not simply laid on the ground if there is a slope. This can be done by propping the corners with stones or wooden blocks and levelling with a builder's level, but more efficiently by making some form of adjustable leg. A simple method of levelling drawing frames is to use long malleable wire pins, like surveyors' arrows, which can easily be bent to any desired shape. They are inserted into the ground and bent to hold the corner of the frame at the height required. If the angle of the pin is placed inside the frame, it will hold it more firmly in place, e.g.:

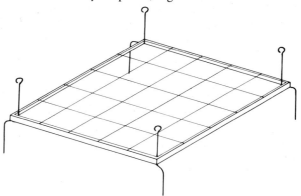

50

Another method, more suitable for stony ground is to make a clamp for each corner of the frame thus:

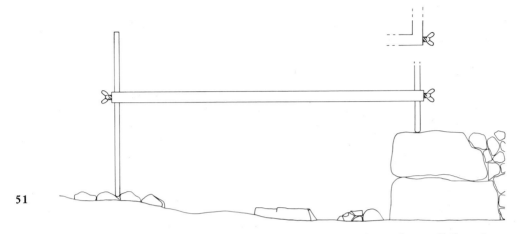

51

with a butterfly nut for quick release. The legs can terminate in small flat plates or rubber balls so that the site is not damaged.

If the frame is divided into 20cm. squares, the draughtsman can usually draw most of the detail (at the suggested scale of 1:20) by eye, taking care to look vertically down on to that part of the surface which he is drawing. If the frame is on sloping ground and has had to be levelled up it will of course be necessary to use a plumb bob on the areas where the frame is more than a few centimetres above the ground.

On steeply sloping ground it may be more convenient to lay out a string grid, using tapes horizontally in conjunction with a plumb-bob, and then draw the detail between the strings by eye, checking by triangulation (fig. 53).

In practice it may be found that the most convenient size for field plan units drawn with a grid is the 5m. square, at a scale of 1:20, which gives units of drawing material 0.25m. square. These are convenient for handling and can be joined together in an infinitely expanding mosaic covering the whole site. If, as the units are drawn, they are taped into place, for instance on a hut wall, the whole site plan can be seen to develop. Interpretation, instruction, and discussion of excavation problems become much easier, and any unit can be removed for completion or emendation. Hard-board is at present sold in units of 8 by 4 ft., and if these are cut into 1ft. squares they make convenient lightweight bases for the 0.25m. drawings, leaving enough overlap for taping the drawing to the board. Larger drawing boards tend to become heavy after some hours of use and are more affected by the wind.

It has been found most convenient to tape sectional paper or plastic film on to the drawing boards, using this as a gridded underlay for the transparent plastic film on which the drawing is made. If the edges of the plastic film are completely taped, the sectional paper is protected from damp. However, if it is felt that this does not eliminate possible inaccuracy due to the stretching and contraction of the sectional paper, plastic film with a printed grid may be used under the drawing film. One important advantage of this method of drawing is that, once the string grid has been laid out on the ground, the draughtsman does not require an assistant to help with measuring.

Offsets

An alternative method of plotting when a grid is not available is by means of co-ordinates set off from a tape stretched across the area to be drawn. In this method a 3m. metal tape or measuring rod is used to measure the distances of features at right angles from the datum tape (fig. 53b). The accuracy of this method depends on the ability of the draughtsman's assistant to judge a right-angle. One of the easiest ways of doing this is to swing the tape with the centre at the point to be plotted until the shortest distance is read off against the datum tape (fig. 53b).

52   The illustration shows a method of drawing on a steep undulating surface. The string grid joins nails located accurately in the horizontal plane by means of a level and plumb-bob. The draughtsman then draws each square as a mosaic to scale (in this case 1:20).

However, since the angle of cut between the arc of the swing tape and the datum tape is minimal at the correct point on the datum tape, it may be thought that this involves an unacceptable degree of inaccuracy and a more accurate method of measuring a right angle such as a wooden or metal frame is to be preferred.

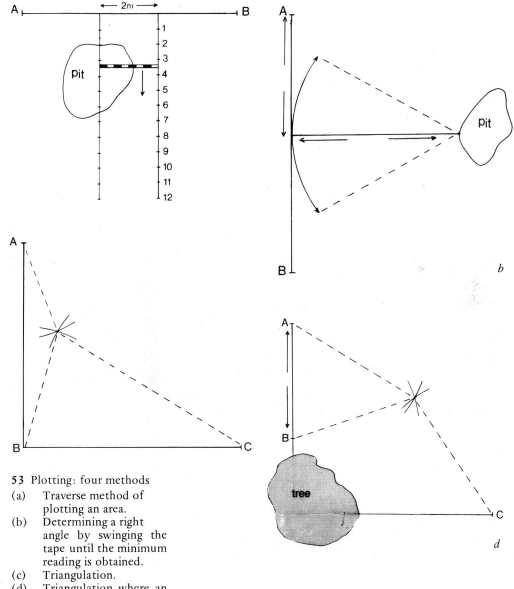

53 Plotting: four methods
(a)   Traverse method of plotting an area.
(b)   Determining a right angle by swinging the tape until the minimum reading is obtained.
(c)   Triangulation.
(d)   Triangulation where an obstruction necessitates the use of a false datum.

Two parallel tapes

A somewhat similar but more accurate method is to lay two parallel tapes across the site a short distance apart. A 3m. metal tape or a measuring rod is then laid across the point to be plotted so that the lengths along the datum tapes are equal, and therefore the cross tape is at right angles, and the distance from the datum 'AB' is read off (fig. 53a).

A variant of this method was used with some success on a training school at Wroxeter when the evidence for the timber buildings on Site 68 was recorded by a team of students none of whom had drawn before, each working across the site in strips 2ft. wide, using the offset method. The site looked rather like a running-track divided into lanes, each student producing a drawing two feet wide and the length of the site. This method was used on this occasion to ensure maximum objectivity, since there was some doubt about the interpretation (or even whether buildings were present at all), and, in a sense, the draughtsmen were working 'blind'. The drawings were finally pasted together and the plan redrawn by tracing (fig. 82). As can be imagined, the quality of draughtsmanship in the strips varied considerably and this method is not one to be highly recommended, though it is swift if time is short, as it can absorb all available manpower.

Co-ordinates

A fourth method is to plot co-ordinates from two axes of the grid. This method using as it does two offsets is, of course, more accurate than the single offset method described above. A variant of this method is triangulation, preferably from two or three corners of the grid (fig. 53c, d).

In order to plot the distances on the site plan, if it is large, it will be necessary to use a trammel and it must be remembered that three measurements will be more accurate than two. If only two are taken a good angle of cut between the arcs must be assured by choosing suitable points of origin on the grid. It is possible to plan single-handed in this way if the tapes are secured to the datum pegs, though able to rotate. The planner can then hold the two tapes in one hand at their junction, using a plumb-bob if necessary with the other hand.

Plastic film

In spite of its cost, plastic film should be used for all drawing. Tracing paper, linen and other similar materials expand and contract under varying conditions of moisture sufficiently to move features as much as half a metre (to scale) according to the weather; and this is clearly unacceptable. In addition, with the use of plastic film, drawing in pencil can continue in wet weather, which may be a crucial factor at the end of an excavation when recording in any other medium may be impossible.

Coated plastic films should be avoided as they are likely to crack with time or the coating may detach itself from the base material. Films based on uncoated Melanex (ICI) are the only suitable materials.

It is suggested that a comparatively soft pencil, HB or F, should be used; partly because these softer varieties give a more flexible line, but also because it is much easier to trace the drawing through the overlay if the field drawings are black in line rather than pale grey. Softer pencils must, of course, be sharpened more often if the line is not to become diffuse, though clutch pencils using very thin leads do not require sharpening. The problem of smudging can be overcome by working from the top of the drawing downwards, by masking the completed part of the drawing, and by the use of aerosol fixatives such as those used for pastel drawings (though these render the surface unsuitable for subsequent colouring with crayon). Better still, the drawing may be made directly in ink using Rapidograph or similar pens, though this precludes drawing in wet weather.

Although costs prohibit the publication of archaeological plans and sections in colour except in the most lavish productions, colour should nevertheless be used on the field drawings, since it considerably extends the range of variety of the recording.

The range of colours to be used throughout the excavation must be decided on at the beginning and a sufficient stock of pencils obtained to avoid unnecessary variations in tint, especially during the course of a long excavation. A number of paler colours, particularly pink, fade within a few days of exposure to light — even during the time taken in drawing the plan! It is therefore advisable to test crayons and coloured pencils for fastness before the excavation begins. Mars-Lumochrom pencils have been tested on site for permanence and can be recommended. Almost all other pinks fade within a week. Colour codes for the varieties of stone, tile, clay, mortar and other building materials anticipated must be decided upon, and adhered to. Other colours may then be used for the plotting of nails, coins, small finds of different sorts and the many other categories of information which may be desired on the plan. In the case of complex sites it is better to avoid confusion by plotting finds and other non-structural information on separate transparent overlays.

Inevitably an element of interpretation will enter the drawing. It is therefore essential that not only the interpretation of the site, but also the drawing (which incorporates, however subtly, some of this interpretation) should be subject to constant discussion and criticism, and not merely left to a lone draughtsman. There is a tendency for some draughtsmen to simplify, and worse, to stylize, the features seen on the ground. Post-holes become more circular on the drawing than they really are; pebble surfaces become more uniform in the size and shape of their pebbles, and courses of stones become stereotyped. Checks on the accuracy and fidelity of the drawing must therefore be frequent, especially towards the end of the day. As an aid to accuracy of the draughtsmanship, it is very useful to have vertical stereoscopic photographs of each sector of the site printed at the same scale as the field drawings and made available to the draughtsmen while they are drawing in the field. This is not very difficult to achieve if a hut can be made into a dark-room, or if a local professional photographer can produce results quickly on demand, and the benefits are considerable. Drawings can then be checked immediately against the photograph and the two used to form an amalgam which is perhaps as near to an accurate record, combining objectivity with a degree of interpretation, as we can hope to achieve at present.

For reasons discussed below (p. 164) there will inevitably be radial distortions in the scale of features recorded by the vertical camera, so that features and detail cannot be traced directly onto the plan from the photographs, except close to the centre of each photograph. However, for practical purposes, and taking into account the eventual scale at which the drawings will be published, errors even towards the edges of photographs carefully enlarged are not totally unacceptable. They can be eliminated by a radial-line plotter if such a machine is available.

Even when a grid, a frame and photographs are being used it is advisable to cross-check the accuracy of the whole plan by triangulating the main features such as walls, major post-holes or timber-slots from the principal fixed datum points, since it is possible for gross errors to occur unnoticed in a mass of detail.

The drawing of sections has been dealt with exhaustively in a number of text books, notably in Wheeler, 1954, Webster, 1963, and 1970, Kenyon, 1964, Alexander, 1970 and Atkinson, 1948. Essentially, section drawing is drawing the plan of a vertical surface: indeed, in Britain such mystique became attached to the importance of the section during the period between the wars and for some years after, that one could have wished that the opposite truth had been realised — that drawing the plan of a site is merely drawing a horizontal section — and that the plan had been given the same precise attention to detail as the highly complicated section drawings which have filled excavation reports for the last 40 years.

The drawing of a straightforward ditch section need not be described here, as the references given above are more than adequate.

However, as Limbrey, 1975, 273-5, points out, sections are often drawn in a stylised way, by joining the dots made on the paper by someone receiving vertical and horizontal co-ordinates and not observing the layers closely while drawing them. Such a section will be meaningless to the soil scientist asked to discuss it later. It is important therefore that generally understood symbols should be used to describe the layers in pedological terms, rather than, or at least as well as, archaeological terms, such as 'destruction layer', 'build-up of foundations' and so on.

Photography

A number of good text-books on archaeological photography is available dealing with the techniques of both site photography and the photography of portable finds. Among the best are, Cookson, 1954, Matthews, 1968, Simmons, 1969, Bracegirdle, 1970 and Conlon, 1973.

In addition there is a multiplicity of books on photography in general, both in black and white and in colour, together with text-books on individual cameras with their related accessories. There is no need therefore to go into the technicalities of photography here, but merely to outline and comment on those aspects which are particularly relevant to the recording of excavations.

Without doubt the larger the negative used the sharper the detail on the photograph. For this reason a 5"x 4"camera is best for photographs which are to be used for publication, or for museum displays; but such a camera is very expensive. The 2¼" x 2¼" or 3¼" x 2¼" format is suitable for most archaeological photography, with 35mm. used for colour transparencies. However, some 35mm. enthusiasts maintain that, properly handled, the miniature camera is capable of producing results that are more than adequate for any archaeological photograph. In these days of relatively cheap 35mm. camera systems with built-in exposure meters and interchangeable lenses there is no excuse for poor pictures. Superb ones are a little more difficult.

The three chief categories of photograph that are required on most excavations are the record photographs, vertical and oblique, both in black and white and in colour, which are specifically taken to supplement the plan and section drawings;

54 G.P.O., Newgate Street, London, 1976. This photograph, of more than 500 post-holes driven into Roman destruction levels, shows the importance of diffused lighting, especially in urban excavations where surrounding buildings cast dark shadows in sunshine. Nevertheless, even with diffused lighting, the modelling of the surfaces is clear. This sense of the contours in enhanced by the angle of the shot. A higher viewpoint would have tended to flatten them. *(Photo - Trevor Hurst)*

colour transparencies designed for lectures and talks; and photographs, both of the site and of finds, which are taken to illustrate the eventual publication of the excavation.

55 *left* New Fresh Wharf, London, 1975: view along the Roman waterfront structure, dated AD 155± 5 years. This photograph is a model of descriptive clarity. The carefully selected viewpoint gives maximum information about and three-dimensionality to the structure, and the use of an exceptional lens combined with a very small stop gives great depth of focus. (*Photo-Trevor Hurst*)

56 *below* Medieval female skeleton with unborn foetus, from G.P.O., Newgate Street, London, 1975. The recording of this long-forgotten tragic incident required very skilful cleaning (in the wind and rain of a winter excavation) which demonstrated the existence of the foetus yet left each bone in place for photography. (*Photo-Trevor Hurst*)

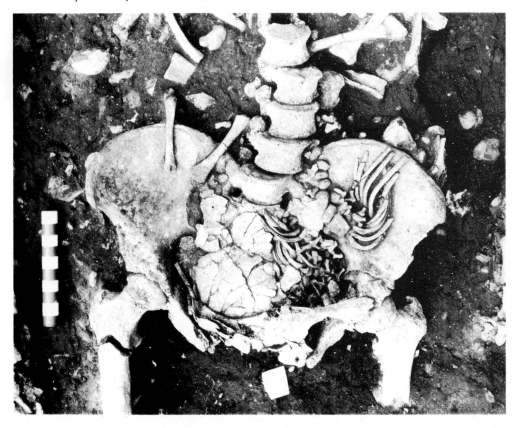

Vertical photographs

Many methods, from ladders to balloons, have been used to suspend a camera vertically over a desired point on the excavation. A number of ordinary folding tripods have a reversible vertical section to which the camera can be attached pointing vertically downward. This method is most useful for photographs of small features, or finds *in situ*, but some large tripods have legs long enough to enable whole graves to be included on one negative. A ladder firmly lashed to two scaffold poles is a cheap and easy way of achieving a tripod up to 4-5m. above the ground. Above this height a scaffolding tower is recommended, though mobility then becomes a problem and the weight of such a tower may damage the excavated surface. Mobile towers such as the Tallescope (made by Access Equipment Ltd., Hemel Hempstead) which extend up to some 10m., can be moved easily about the site but are not very rigid at full height. When the extending ladder is used double, a fairly stable platform is achieved. Any apparatus that lifts the photographer safely above the site may be used, ranging from the bucket of a bulldozer to a fire escape. Such aids are of course equally valuable for high-level oblique photographs.

Kites and tethered meteorological balloons fitted with a cradle from which the camera hangs have been tried, and experiments have also been made with radio-controlled model aircraft. The chief difficulty with all these methods is that of sway due to turbulence of the air which, even if slight, will give considerable angular movement of the lens. But on a perfectly calm day, a kite or a captive balloon carrying a camera triggered by radio has much to recommend it.

It is more difficult to devise a method for making an overlapping mosaic of vertical photographs. Whatever apparatus is used must be easily transportable across the site, and not so heavy that it destroys the excavated surface. Ideally, it ought not to cast shadows over the area being photographed, and it must be as quick and simple as possible to operate if large numbers of photographs are to be taken during the comparatively short time during which the site is at its best, and when the weather, in a country like Britain, is co-operative; and it must support the camera as rigidly as possible. The critical factors are the height to which the camera can conveniently be raised coupled with the focal length of the lens. The greater the height of the apparatus, the heavier it will be, the more unwieldy to move and the more affected by the wind. The longer the focal length of the lens the less radial distortion there will be on the photograph, but the smaller the area covered by each photograph. A compromise between these two factors has to be devised.

The apparatus evolved (principally by Terry Holland and Sidney Renow), for use on the writer's excavations, consists of a quadrupod of square-section aluminium, braced by wooden slats, with an aluminium cradle holding a 2¼" x 2¼" format twin-lens reflex camera. The square-format is preferable to the 35mm. rectangular format because the negative is larger, and the detail therefore clearer, and because the square shape is directly related to the shape of the quadrupod.

Appendix B describes the simple cradle which holds the camera in place. The quadrupod is designed so that the area photographed is bounded by the four feet of the apparatus, so that, once it is set up, the feet show the corners of the photograph on the ground and there is no need to use a viewer. The quadrupod can be put precisely into place by the photographer's assistants, and it is levelled by means of two spirit levels taped to two adjacent horizontal members, and by means of extendable feet inserted into the tubular framework. The feet are fitted with sorbo-rubber balls to stop them from damaging the site. This method has proved to be better than plates mounted on ball-joints.

Various ways of winding-on the film and cocking the shutter without lowering the camera have been tried, but they have been discarded for one reason or another, and now the camera is lowered by means of a simple pulley on nylon cord, and the film wound on by hand. This takes very little time, and eliminates most of the causes of failure in the apparatus. It was found in practice that even with mechanical or electrical cocking of the shutter it was necessary, due to constantly changing English light, to lower the camera quite often in order to change the aperture setting. However, now that automatically metering cameras are becoming increasingly available (though still extremely expensive in the 2¼" x 2¼" format) it is obviously an advantage to have such a camera, and if this is fitted with a motor-drive (or electrically-driven wind-on mechanism, which in some cases is cheaper) the camera can be left aloft and the apparatus moved across the site very much more quickly. In this way a large area can be photographed in a few hours.

The whole apparatus has the virtue of simplicity and cheapness, and is easily transportable by car. Its one major drawback is that in sunshine it is impossible to avoid the shadow of one or more of the legs falling across the area being photographed. In the ordinary way this is no handicap since the photographs would not be taken in sunlight, but there are occasions when, if photography is urgent, it becomes a nuisance. Various methods of screening the ground with semi-opaque polythene sheet have been tried, without success.

One method which may overcome both the problems of cast shadows in sunlight and that of changing light on the surface to be photographed is to mount four electronic flashes (of the type which automatically adjust the length of the flash according to the distance from the subject and its tone) on the legs of the quadrupod. The flashes would have to be mounted at different heights to provide varied light which would model the subject. This method has not yet been tested so far as I know, but, if successful, it would give complete independence of all weather conditions but rain. Among other advantages it would extend the time available for photography into the dusk and even the hours of darkness, given a floodlight by which to work. If mains electricity is available three or four floodlights could be mounted on the legs of the quadrupod for use at dusk or during the night.

An apparatus which does eliminate the problem of shadows is the tripod with a boom extension which projects out over the area to be photographed (Nylen, 1964). This method is satisfactory, but the boom is more susceptible to wind vibration and the apparatus, which has to be built of heavier section tubing, is less easy to transport across the site and its weight may damage delicate surfaces. On the whole, we have preferred a lighter and more stable support than the facility of taking pictures in sunlight.

Vertical photographs are taken with a 60 per cent overlap along the length of the run and a 15 per cent overlap between the runs. This gives adequate stereoscopy, although for accurate contoured photogrammetry of the site the camera would have to be at a constant height above datum, not a constant height above the ground. There is no reason why a line overlap or mosaic of a large excavation should not be taken from an aircraft, though this is an entirely different matter from the highly detailed mosaic required by the site record, in which the smallest stones can be seen in detail. Obviously it is most important that the photographer keeps an accurate plan of the photographs that make up the vertical grid, and that they are labelled so that their precise position on the grid can be quickly found. On many excavations it is unlikely that single photographs will be recognizable from the features in them, so that if the cross indexing fails a great deal of time will be wasted in indentification.

Bipod for vertical and oblique photography

Another method of raising the camera above the ground is a bipod made of wood or tubular metal, which carries a cradle at its apex. The bipod is raised and held in position with the aid of two ropes attached to the cradle, one on each side. In this way heights of up to 10m. have been achieved. The method has considerable advantages on rough or sloping ground or where there are walls or deep rooms. The additional height not only gives greater coverage but also greater depth of focus, necessary if the surface is undulating or if it contains deep holes. Another advantage claimed for this method is that the camera can be tilted, relative to the legs, to take oblique high-level views.

Oblique photography

Oblique photographs of the whole site or large parts of it are very valuable for record as well as publication. In addition oblique photographs should be taken of all but minor features. In many cases groups of small features can be photographed together. All evidence for buildings should be photographed from a variety of angles and with a variety of lighting as sometimes the details of a building will show best in a photograph taken against the light or in sunshine. Normally the best light is strong but diffused, up to pale sunshine. Structures and features can be given more solidity and detail by arranging a large white board or sheet to reflect light into the shadows, or by using flash to fill them in.

A clear but unobtrusive scale should always be used, together with a readable label in the case of features. The scale should be placed in a position which does not distract the eye from the features to be illustrated, and it should not cover or cut across them. Often one or more ranging rods can be placed so that they define the edges of a surface, though they should not be placed on the edge but rather parallel to it so that its character is not obscured. Interchangable plastic figures and letters that fit into slotted wood covered with black baize are a useful form of label, and a small but clear north point should always be included.

Oblique photographs will be needed not only for the site record but also for the eventual publication. In many cases one photograph will serve both purposes but if possible some extensive photographs should be taken, from a neighbouring building or a fire escape or an aircraft, showing the site as a whole as well as its surroundings. Some features or structural details of buildings can be better illustrated by oblique 'three-quarter' views than by plans and sections. It is very helpful to imagine the caption to an illustration while the subject is in the view-finder. In this way the most comprehensive view will be taken. Without this sort of planning it may be found that two views of a vital part of the site have to be published where one would have been adequate.

On most sites a wide-angle lens (35mm. or 28mm. focal length) will be the most generally useful, though it must be remembered that the wider the angle the greater the distortion, since a larger field of view has to be compressed into the same size of negative. With very wide-angle lenses, straight lines become curves, verticals slope and relative sizes are wildly distorted. When taking close-up photographs of features stretching back into the middle distance remember the snaps of father feet-first on the beach at Blackpool, and use a long focal length lens so that distortion is minimised. Rising- and cross-fronts on 3¼" x 2¼" or 5" x 4" cameras will eliminate distortion due to perspective and are especially useful where architecture is involved, or where a section has to be photographed from within the trench.

A cable release and the most solid and stable tripod obtainable should always be used. These, in addition to eliminating camera shake, will enable the lens to be stopped down to give greater depth of field when photographing features or structures which stretch from the foreground into the middle distance.

Experiments should be made with filters to find out which give the best results on the type of soil or other material being excavated. A green filter, for instance, will give more contrast to a hearth of reddened clay surrounded by yellow clay, a yellow filter will enhance dark features in sand, and so on.

When the excavation is within range of electrical power floodlights can be used to give ideal lighting, glancing across textured surfaces or modelling features such as hearths. Three floodlights will give great flexibility so that reflected lights can be used in the shadows to give the maximum detail.

Floodlights or car headlights can be used to photograph faint ridge and furrow or other slight earthworks, or subtle undulations of the excavated surface that would otherwise be difficult to see. Since archaeological photography is rarely concerned with movement, a slow, fine-grain panchromatic film such as Ilford Pan F (50 ASA, 18 DIN) will give maximum definition. Under poor lighting conditions, or if a tripod is not available, Ilford FP4 (125 ASA, 22DIN) or the very much faster HP4 (400-600 ASA, 27-29 DIN) will give satisfactory results if properly developed and printed. However, two new films, Ilford XP1 and Agfa Varia, combine high speed (400 ASA, 27 DIN) with very fine grain and have great exposure latitude (from 200 ASA to 1600 ASA) and this may eventually prove the ideal material for black and white photographs taken under difficult conditions but still producing prints suitable for publication or exhibitions. Meanwhile, nevertheless, under normal lighting conditions, orthodox films, such as those recommended, remain preferable. Perhaps the ideal solution is a true-colour stereoscopic mosaic of photographs of the whole site at each stage of the excavation backed up by interpretive overlay drawings. Trials with the new Kodak Vericolor II film have been most encouraging. Vertical over-lapping colour prints enlarged from 2¼″ x 2¼″ negatives to a scale of 1:20 and printed on glossy paper have proved to show a high degree of detail; for example, pea-grits or 'dried peas' at the bottom of stakeholes are clearly visible as are the divisions and numbers on the 30m. tape included in the print. The colour rendering is exceptional, though dependent, of course, on the colour temperature of the light, which changes according to the altitude of the sun, the amount of blue sky or cloud and the reflection of surrounding trees or buildings. The effect of this is to alter subtle colours continually. Reds become redder towards sunset and purpler or bluer at midday without cloud and the colour of the ground itself changes with the changing light. Moreover this effect is enhanced and exaggerated by colour film. In crucial cases Munsell colour chart numbers should be used. It may be that it will be possible to build an apparatus which will take all photographs by flash, when the colour rendering will be constant and relatively comparable.

There is no reason why sections should not similarly be photographed stereoscopically in colour (if necessary obliquely) when their textures could be viewed in detail.

There is no doubt that such a series of stereoscopic colour photographs is a very adequate, sometimes startlingly naturalistic, record of the site. Further prints from the same negatives can be pasted together to form a mosaic photograph of all or part of the site at any desired scale. If it were not for the necessity of publication the two sets of photographic prints with interpretive overlays might be considered all that was required for site planning. The publication of such photographs with their overlays would, at present, be prohibitively expensive, though not perhaps very much more expensive than a series of highly detailed colour drawings. The distillation of publishable plans and sections from field drawings is discussed in Chapter 13 below. Meanwhile, so far as the primary record of the site is concerned, colour stereoscopic cover is highly desirable since it is comparatively inexpensive. In the trials carried out at Wroxeter in 1975 complete coverage of an area some 200 sq. metres cost less than a group of draughtsmen drawing the same area in comparable detail, over a period of about a week, whereas the photography took only a few hours. The application of colour photographic recording to rescue and salvage excavations therefore is obvious.

It may be argued that vertical stereoscopic photography is only practicable on more or less level sites, but I believe that its value is, if anything, greater on sites where, for archaeological reasons, a number of surfaces at different depths need to be recorded, or the layers slope steeply, or where, under waterlogged conditions, timbers project in all directions from the layer in which they are embedded. Under all these circumstances, drawing itself it difficult, sometimes near impossible. What is needed is an accurate record of the excavated surfaces, features and structures. If photography can provide this record, in colour and three dimensions, it is arguable that detailed site drawing, in the accepted sense, is superfluous, and that the drawing can be confined to outline overlays, which include all the feature/layer numbers. In addition, overlays could incorporate a greater or less degree of interpretation. Such a system would enormously speed up the recording of all kinds of site, but in particular those where the layers consist of stones, tile, tesserae, rubble, pebbles, boulders and so on, where it has become customary to draw the surface in great detail and then to colour each element. Such drawings are often very beautiful, but they cannot, as a rule, ever be published. They simply form part of an archive from which the published drawings are distilled. It may be that we are no longer justified in the expense, in skilled time particularly, of such elaborate drawing but should rely, for the primary record, on photography — which can be equally beautiful. In practice, however, we have found that the attempt to reduce site drawing to a minimum has a number of snags. Permatrace, Ozaflex and other drawing films are translucent, not transparent, and the details of the colour photographs, which have about the same tonal contrast as the site itself, cannot readily be traced through the drawing film, even if a light box is used. There is the added difficulty that, even if the print is enlarged to 1:20 linear, strictly speaking only the centre of the photograph is at the right scale and the distortion increases radially towards the edges. We have, therefore, for the time being, continued to draw in detail and to use the photographs as a check for the post-excavation draughtsman and as an invaluable archive.

There is a danger, however that the excavator will unconsciously let photography take the place of intensive observation. The very act of drawing a plan or section on the ground necessitates close contemplation of the evidence and dependence on photography could weaken this concentrated observation. This is a problem not confined to rescue or salvage work since on any large-scale excavation it is impossible for the director or site-supervisors to do all the drawing. It is important therefore that where detailed drawing is being done by others they should check the drawings carefully with the ground and discuss them and their meaning with the draughtsman.

Photogrammetry
If stereoscopic photographs, either vertical or oblique, are taken of the site the plans or sections can be drawn at a later date. While not ideal, this does provide insurance for loss of drawings or checks on disputed planning. A number of text-books on photogrammetry are available, eg. Williams (1969), so that there is no need to enlarge on the subject here. Radial line plotters such as the Watts SB 100 or Stereosketch are within the reach of the larger archaeological units and arrangements can be made for the hire of time on the bigger machines.

Oblique photogrammetry using two cameras on a sub-tense bar is used by German traffic police for the rapid recording of plans of traffic accidents. Stereoscopic photographs are taken from a number of points of view round the accident and the plan plotted later. This is very quick and obviates the need for policemen to walk about in the road with tape measures (see *Instruments of Photogrammetry and Photo Interpretation*, Zeiss, 1967, U7, and references on U4). Both the speed of the method and the fact that it enables planners to work outside the required area make it ideal for rescue and salvage excavation, as well as in situations where the excavated surface is too vulnerable to be walked on. An example of this use is in the planning of the Skuldelev Ships, five Viking ships sunk in Roskilde Fjord. The wood of the ships and the soft matrix in which they lay was planned by photogrammetry without risk of damaging or losing the evidence (Olsen and Crumlin-Pedersen, 1967). A small bar with a sliding camera mounting equipped with a tripod bush is a simple piece of apparatus which enables oblique stereoscopic photographs to be taken with any available camera. Needless to say the same methods can be used for the recording of architecture.

Infra-red film can be used for the recording of hearths, kilns and other areas of burning or significant colour differences on sites which are notoriously difficult to photograph in black-and-white for publication.

Polaroid film
Polaroid photographs, which have the advantage of instant development, have proved to be invaluable as a supplement to the feature record cards. The photographs can be fixed (with drafting tape rather than paste) to the back of the card and annotated, or may have an explanatory sketch added. Partially excavated features can be recorded in this way without delaying the work and the excavation of a fragile or fragmentary find can be recorded in a rapid series of photographs which may be of great help in the eventual reconstruction. The method has the advantage of comparative cheapness, since it has been found that the simpler, less expensive polaroid cameras are perfectly adequate for the purpose. The rectangular, 110mm. x 85mm., format is preferable to the slightly smaller square format since it gives greater detail and is a more convenient shape for oblique photographs.

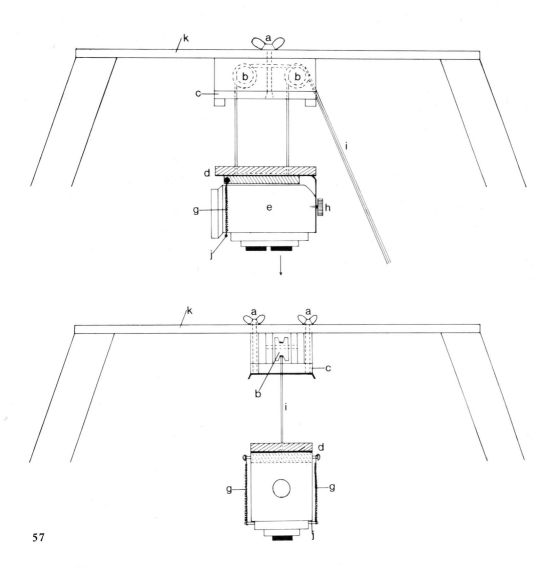

57

Appendix B

Sidney Renow, who was responsible for the development of the quadrupod head writes:

> After a good deal of experimenting it has been found that the most practicable means of suspension of the camera is by attaching it to a cradle which is raised and lowered by a double cord running over pulleys in a head box bolted securely to the top plate of the quadrupod in such a position that the lens of the camera is centrally positioned (fig. 57). Various ways of winding on the film whilst the camera is in the raised position have been tried but have had to be abandoned because of insurmountable difficulties. In practice, lowering and raising the camera cradle after each exposure has not proved to be a nuisance,

and following the principle that the simplest mechanisms are usually the most reliable and trouble-free, the arrangement to be described has been found to work very satisfactorily.

The base of the camera cradle is a plate of aluminium or brass bent at right angles and drilled to take an ever-ready case retaining screw which secures the bottom of the camera to one face. The back of the camera is held against a block of ½" chipboard by a padded rod across the top front which is spring or elastic loaded from screws on either side of the chipboard. Another block of chipboard is secured to the baseplate by bolts passing right through both blocks and the plate. The second block is drilled and suitably recessed to take the doubled nylon or terylene suspension cord.

The head box is made from four similar pieces of chipboard screwed to a chipboard face block the same size as the second block of the camera cradle. The two inner pieces are drilled to take the spindles of two pulleys over which the cord runs. The face block has holes corresponding to those in the camera cradle and it will be obvious that the pulleys have to be suitably positioned to match. The face block is also provided with two strips of aluminium or brass appropriately bent and screwed to it to form mating guides so that when the camera cradle is hauled up it is precisely located against the head box. Long bolts pass through the two outer pieces of the head box to secure it firmly to the top plate of the quadrupod. Butterfly nuts can be used for ease of attachment and removal. It is essential that the camera cradle when in the raised position should be held against the head box under tension, and to achieve this use is made of the natural elasticity of the cord. The free ends of this are knotted together in such a position that the loop so formed can be passed over a bolt on a leg of the quadrupod or to an anchorage specially provided. When the camera is lowered the knot will of course ascend to the head box and it should be arranged that it comes to rest against a stop so that the cradle, which in any case cannot slip to the ground, is suspended at a convenient point for manipulation. The doubled length of cord below the knot can be knotted at intervals to provide grips when hauling on the cord. The most convenient way of operating the shutter is by using a pneumatic remote control release such as the Kagra.

9

The Recording of Pottery and Small Finds

Rare and exotic finds from excavations inevitably attract most attention in the press, and on radio and television, and more significantly in archaeological exhibitions. This high-lighting gives such pieces an exaggerated importance compared with the mass of dull body sherds, animal bones or fragments of wall plaster. Yet, as Pitt Rivers pointed out almost a century ago: ' . . . the value of relics, viewed as evidence, may . . . be said to be in an inverse ratio to their intrinsic value' (Cranborne Chase, Vol III, 1892, ix.). The collection, recording, cleaning, marking and storage of every sherd of pottery, every fragment of bone, every nail, every scrap of painted plaster is tedious, and time- and labour-consuming. But only by the study of large quantities of everyday evidence can we approach an understanding of the site and its occupants as a whole and not simply the more immediately attractive aspects, such as those which lie on the fringes of art or architectural history. An understanding of English medieval life cannot be gained wholly from the study of church architecture, painted missals and *objets d'art* — it is necessary to dig complete villages, including the barns and pigstyes, and collect the whole mass of unaesthetic evidence if we are going to penetrate deeper than the aristocratic crust of medieval society. If this is true of medieval times, where we have considerable documentation to add to the rest of the evidence, how much more true it is of earlier, less literate societies.

The horizontal distribution of pottery and finds is as important as their vertical distribution. It is for this reason that all finds, of whatever material, must be recorded in plan with sufficient precision to make analysis possible. Plots of the distribution of various classes of finds on transparent overlays make it easy to relate the finds to buildings, fences, enclosures and other structures. This distribution may be the only evidence for the use of a building or area. Lines of building nails may give the only clue to the former presence of a building and the quality of the finds from different buildings or areas may be a pointer to the wealth or social position of the occupants. At Wroxeter, sherds of a type of calcite gritted pottery are distributed mainly outside and around the major buildings of the last period, which must, from the evidence, have had wooden floors. This pottery was, therefore, perhaps in use in the last period, being swept off the floors and out on to the grass or trodden areas round the buildings.

Another, more subtle use of the horizontal distribution of finds is demonstrated by the analysis of flints of the beaker period at Belle Tout, East Sussex, by Richard Bradley (Bradley, 1970). This assumes that 'the outline of a building would probably be marked by a break in the horizontal density of finds simply because the material could not pass through a solid barrier. In addition such a barrier might be marked by a build-up of material at its foot' (*ibid*. 317). These effects can be enhanced by using trend mapping, as described by Haggett (1965, 270). In this method the general trend of finds across the site is mapped as a series of contours and the positive and negative residuals where the local density of finds differs from the general trend are mapped separately as contours and compared with the other evidence, of post-holes, lines of stones and etc. (Bradley, 1970, figs 3 and 5, reproduced here as figs 58 and 59). Orton, 1980, 140-155, describes, principally for those of us who are less numerate, the various methods

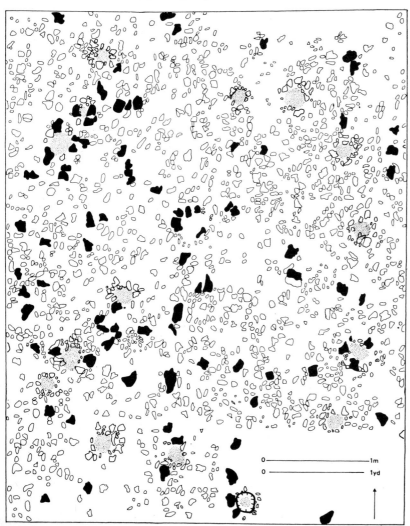

58 *left* Belle Tout, Sussex: Structure I as excavated. Possible post-holes are stippled and intrusive flints lying upon the surface of the natural flint rubble are represented in solid black. The enclosure ditch forms the northern limit of the plan. For interpretation see fig. 59 below.

59 Belle Tout, Sussex: the suggested outline of Structure I in relation to the density of all finds of Beaker date. Possible post-holes are represented in solid black and the inner lip of the enclosure ditch forms the top of the plan. Contours are at intervals of 10 finds to the 5 foot grid square.

which may be used to study the distribution patterns of artefacts from a site.

The study of pottery as archaeological material deserves a book to itself. Because it has a high survival rate, pottery has often been given more evidential weight than it can justifiably carry. The origins, dating and distribution of any pottery are still uncertain. New discoveries change the state of knowledge annually, making it unwise to date sites or phases of sites on the evidence of pottery alone.

The study of prehistoric pottery has had to be drastically revised in the light of recent C14 and dendrochronological dates (Renfrew, ed., 1974) and the dating of Roman and medieval pottery is undergoing similar, though less radical, revision, as more groups, dated by evidence external to the pottery itself, are excavated. In view of these considerations alone, all earlier excavation reports should be revised, where possible, in line with current theories on pottery dating. More than this, they should be kept up to date as present theories themselves are modified. This is a daunting task, especially when the incomplete and ambiguous nature of most pottery reports is considered.

The uses and limitations of pottery as archaeological evidence

Sherds of pottery are by far the most common finds on the majority of excavated Roman and medieval sites. The reason is obvious. Pottery was quickly made and often as quickly broken. The expectation of life of a pot is difficult to assess but it seems likely that jugs, bowls, jars, etc. would have lasted longer than cooking pots, which, by their nature, had to undergo the stresses set up by differential heating, especially if, as is probable, they were embedded in the embers of a hot fire. A pot was virtually useless once it was broken or even cracked since it was very difficult to mend satisfactorily, though riveted repairs

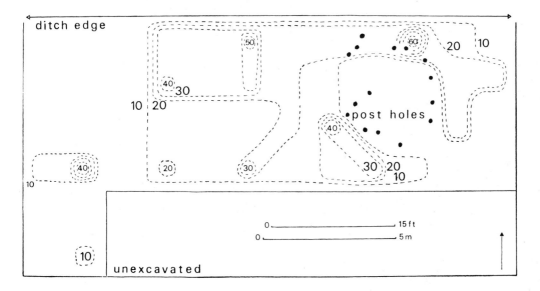

and holes plugged with lead are occasionally found on particularly valuable vessels. Its scrap value, unlike that of a metal object, was small unless it was crushed and used as grog. Since the sherds which remain were virtually indestructible there was little to do with them except bury them in a convenient pit. Here the majority of large sherds and nearly complete pots are found, fragments small enough to be ignored becoming scattered over the site, embedded, and eventually stratified. Complete pots are rarely found except in graves, wells and in abandoned kilns, or occasionally as the containers for hoards or other material. The discontinuance of grave goods with the coming of Christianity, though doubtless a spiritual advance, robbed the archaeologist of his chief source of supply of whole pots, and for each complete or nearly complete vessel the majority of sites yield many hundreds of sherds.

Pottery has the archaeological advantage over most other materials that it is affected comparatively little by most soil conditions. Only if it is grossly underfired will it be soft enough to be weathered away; many prehistoric and most Roman and medieval wares are hard enough to remain unaltered indefinitely under most conditions. Metal objects, on the other hand, with the exception of those of gold, are subject to corrosion in varying degrees, this corrosion tending to obliterate just those decorative features which are likely to be datable.

Factors other than that of mere survival must, however, be taken into account. The objects most susceptible to the close dating so desirable archaeologically are those whose characteristics, whether of form or decoration or both, change most rapidly, and such developments are most likely when details of form and ornament are not dictated by function but by fashion. The design of knives, shears, nails and other common objects, having reached their optimum shape, changed slowly, if at all. Some objects, sheep-shears, cleavers and hand-axes for example, have scarcely altered from medieval times up to the present day (see the *London Museum Medieval Catalogue*, 1954 ed., 153-7). The writer has recovered from the castle site at Hen Domen two figure-of-eight hasps from the thirteenth-century levels which are virtually identical with a hasp at present in use on one of the farm gates leading to the site, and with a hasp found during excavation of the Roman fort at Segontium and now in the site museum there. All these, though interesting from the social and economic points of view, are useless for dating purposes. More personal objects such as brooches, daggers and spurs were not only more highly decorated but changed their forms with changes of fashion and can thus often be grouped typologically and given a relative chronology on the basis of form alone. Coins, on the other hand, whose basic disc shape remains constant, had inscriptions and decorations which were changed frequently, and it is from these that we can date them precisely.

A discussion of the complexities of typological developments in pottery would be out of place here, but it is important for the excavator to be highly sceptical of simplistic schemes which place sherds of pottery in plausible sequences based on appearance alone.

As J.G Hurst has pointed out, in Eastern England Anglo-Saxon pottery is finer and more accomplished than that of the twelfth century, though the reverse is true elsewhere, and 'rim forms in some areas become more developed and complicated, while in others they become more simple' (*Med. Arch.*, vi-viii, 148). In some regions (the West Midlands for example) there seems to have been a tendency for cooking pots to have been made increasingly large during the course of the twelfth century, but in other regions this is not apparent. Coarseness of fabric is by itself no criterion of date, nor is the presence or absence of glaze. Some forms of simple decoration persisted throughout the medieval period, while others reappeared after a temporary eclipse. The thumb-pressed base, for example, so common on thirteenth century jugs, reappears on otherwise quite different jugs of the fifteenth century. It is clear, therefore, in a way which was not fully realised a few years ago, that medieval pottery will only be closely datable on the basis of intensive regional study, and on the study of the composition of fabrics, the shapes of rims, the details of decoration and character of glazes rather than on the general development of types.

The same is true of Roman coarse pottery, which is as regional in character as its medieval counterpart. However, other forms of Roman pottery, in particular samian wares and stamped mortaria, are more closely datable, and, if found stratified in quantity, probably provide the most reliable *termini post* and *ante quem* given by any pottery before the industrial revolution. The absolute dates of prehistoric pottery have been dependent in recent years on the revised radio-carbon dates for the main periods in British prehistory, but there is a very strong regional element also which means that local typologies must be established for most areas.

Any establishment of a typology, even for a restricted area, will have to be based on the study of the more rapidly evolving details of pottery forms rather than of their basic shapes and fabrics, though these may in some cases also show a steady development. Ultimately every characteristic — fabric, shape, size, the treatment of rims, handles, lips and spouts as well as decoration itself — will have to be considered before a pot or sherd can be placed correctly in its local typological sequence. (See Gardin, 1966, for an attempt to categorize all the characteristics of French medieval pottery.) It does not follow that sherds of obviously similar style and superficial characteristics are not by the same potter merely because the composition of fabric or glaze proves to be different. The difference may be due to circumstances: clay from a different bed, or a deliberate change of glaze; but even if the sherds or pots prove to be from different hands, the similarity of style carries its own significance of co-operation or influence between potters. Every scientific aid available should be enlisted to provide as much information as possible on which to base judgements. The composition of fabrics and thus their probable source, the composition of glazes and the temperature to which they have been fired and, with the development of thermo-luminescent and remanent magnetic methods, the possibility of accurate dating independent of both stratification and typology, are all clearly of major importance for determining the relationships of groups of pottery.

It is already apparent that ideally developing typological sequences, in which shapes and decoration proceed logically one from another in the manner relied on by historians of art and architecture may never be established. At Adderley, in Shropshire, for instance, a number of associated thumb-pressed bases seem to exhibit every stage in the development of this form of decoration, yet there is every reason to believe that they are close together in date, and it may well be that all these variations were made at the same time (cf. *Med. Arch.*, vi-viii, 148). Their value as a dating series would therefore be nil. In the face of such difficulties any attempt to establish a precise chronology might seem doomed to failure, but the attempt must be made if we are to date more accurately the sites in which we are interested.

It seems most unlikely that it will ever be possible to date a pottery group more closely than within a bracket of 25 years. Even if we were able to date our pottery closely by archaeometric methods it would still have limitations as dating material. It must be stressed that pottery, like all other dating material, provides only a *terminus post quem* for the layer in which it was found (see below p. 80). Even a coin, whose date of manufacture may be precisely known, gives no more information about its find-layer than this. Too often coins are said to 'date' a layer or building, and a superstructure of dated periods is erected on this basis without regard to the strict logic of the evidence. An example, so extreme that the wrong conclusions could not possibly have been drawn, is provided by the finding in 1774, in the Roman villa at Acton Scott, Shropshire, of Greek coins of the fourth century BC (V.C.H., Shrops., i, 1908, 260-1). These must have been collector's pieces or souvenirs (or were, perhaps, 'planted'), but if they had been Roman souvenirs only 50 years old, might this not have been used, even today, to give a closer date to the structures than would be justified? The danger is as great or greater in the case of pottery. P.A. Rahtz has shown at Cheddar that 2000sq. ft. of levels, dated firmly to the ninth century or later by coins, contained no pottery but Roman (personal communication, publication forthcoming). If a smaller area had been excavated and no coins found, these layers might have been considered to be Roman, whereas within the strict logic of the evidence they should have been dated to the Roman period *or later*. One may wonder how many small excavations producing only Roman pottery have in fact been on post-Roman sites.

These are extreme cases; the danger is more subtle and therefore more likely to mislead when the time-lag is shorter, or when conclusions are drawn from too small a sample, either of the site or of the finds. There is no need to reiterate the misconceptions which may arise from one or two cuttings made into a complex site — examples of the pitfalls which may be encountered are mentioned in Chapter 4. A small sample of pottery may be equally misleading. One or two sherds found in a critical position may be given a significance out of porportion to their real value, unless it can be shown that they were positively sealed and could not have arrived in their position by the action of burrowing animals, rainwash, or other misleading effects. The opposite also holds. A single sherd, positively stratified, which gives an inconveniently late *terminus post quem* for its layer or structure, must not be discarded by the excavator because he cannot bring himself to face the fact that his preconceived theories were wrong. Similarly, among a number of sherds from a sealed layer, it is the latest which gives the *terminus post quem* to the layer, so that a single late sherd among a mass of earlier material must not be discarded — it is the rest of the sherds that must be treated as residual.

By the same reasoning, pottery cannot be dated simply by association, however close, with other datable objects in the same layer. A friend of the writer recently found, on a Roman site, a coin of Edward I of c.1300 positively sealed with a sherd of hard green glazed pot. It is tempting, under these circumstances, to date the pottery, with the layer, to a period after 1300 but, had it not been possible to date the sherd independently, on the evidence of its appearance, it could have been prehistoric, Roman, Saxon, medieval or modern. In other words, the association of coin and sherd tells us *nothing whatever about the date of the sherd*, only that it arrived in the layer after c.1300.

This simple but inexorable logic has so often been ignored or not applied rigorously enough in the past that it is necessary to re-examine critically many excavation reports in which far-reaching conclusions regarding the dating of pottery have been based. Too often, also, the tentative conclusions of the original report have hardened into accepted fact in subsequent references.

Considerations of this kind demand the most careful excavation in layers and the most accurate recording. Without these pottery can be made to prove anything. In addition, the larger the quantity of pottery discovered from each period of a site's occupation, the more valid will be the conclusions which can be drawn. Similarly there is no doubt that the greater the number of sites from which pottery is obtained and the more representative their distribution, the more accurate will be our deductions regarding the pottery's development and economic distribution.

In order to assess the significance of the pottery we find (or do not find) on our sites we must be aware of the general distribution of pottery types in the region and in the country as a whole.

Two examples from the Welsh border will illustrate the point. There is a thin but positive scatter of prehistoric pottery in the region. Neolithic sherds have been found on a number of sites, beaker pottery is very rare but present, Bronze Age pottery is found in some variety, while Iron Age pottery, though not plentiful, has been found on excavated hill-forts and lowland sites dated to the Iron Age by other means. With the Roman occupation comes a flood of pots. All the specifically Roman sites in the area, with the exception of marching camps, produce large quantities of sherds. However, between AD 400+ and 1100 ± 50 there is virtually no pottery in use in the whole region. (See Barker, 1970 for discussion of the problem.) After the beginning of the twelfth century pottery is again in common use and all excavated medieval sites have produced quantities of material.

The first example is taken from the excavations at Hen Domen, Montgomery. Here, sealed under the boulder clay rampart of the eleventh-century castle and under a ploughsoil beneath dated by radio carbon and, more tentatively, historical means to the late Saxon period (Barker and Lawson, 1971) were the post-holes of a rectangular, slightly bow-sided, building with centre posts and with a drainage gulley at the upper end. No pottery or other finds were associated with this building though from the ploughsoil above it came an amulet carved from a sherd of ordinary red Roman pot. The date of the building is uncertain; its form is not easily parallelled in the Bronze or Iron Ages, though rectilinear Iron Age buildings are increasingly being discovered. If it were Roman, it would certainly, in this area, have produced an appreciable number of sherds. The complete absence of pottery suggests a date within the aceramic period outlined above. The Roman sherd, carved into an amulet, speaks of the rarity of pottery at this time, and it is significant that it and the handful of Roman sherds from the overlying castle are all red and abraded. Some have suggested that Hen Domen castle is built on the site of a Roman signal station and have cited the Roman pottery in support of this argument. But there is a massive fort less than a mile away and a more reasonable explanation for the presence of the Roman sherds is that, being red (including samian ware), they were attractive — in an aceramic period, unique — and in the castle period quite unlike the Norman pottery which is mostly black or brown, never bright red. These sherds were probably therefore brought on to the site as curiosities, which would also explain the fragment of Roman tile impressed with a baby's footprint, and more exotically still a late Bronze Age socketed axe-head found lying on a twelfth-century pebble path. We should not underrate the antiquarian interests of the people we dig up.

The second example comes from Wroxeter where excavation revealed the remains of a building whose plan, bow-sided and tripartite with a cross-passage, was that which one would expect from a medieval peasant village, the typical 'long-house'.

The building contained nothing but Roman material, though there was no pottery (smashed round the hearth, for example) which could be shown to have been in use during the occupation of the house. All the pottery which was picked up could have been residual (some of it was samian) used to pack stake-holes. Our building, therefore, could be late Roman (a fourth-century sherd embedded in the clay floor gave a positive *terminus post quem*) or could fall into the aceramic period discussed above. It could not, in spite of all appearances, be medieval since it is inconceivable that there would not be a single sherd of medieval pottery in it at a date when pottery is plentiful. Other methods of dating and the general stratigraphy of the building reinforce the late Roman or 'dark age' date suggested by the lack of medieval pot.

Residual pottery

Mention of the bow-sided 'peasant' building at Wroxeter raises the whole question of residual pottery. The problem is seen in an acute form on deeply stratified Roman, medieval or post-medieval sites where pits, wells and foundations have brought earlier pottery up to later surfaces. The last period layers of such sites may contain a very high proportion of residual pot. Indeed, it is possible that in some Roman towns, whose occupation enters an aceramic period, the latest 'Roman' layers will contain nothing but residual pottery. As one removes the layers of occupation, one by one, the problem will tend to resolve itself.

The situation can be shown diagrammatically thus:

Structural Periods	Layers	Pottery Types
Z	1	g + f + e + d + c + b + a
	2	g + f + e + d + c + b + a
	3	g + f + e + d + c + b + a
Y (ACERAMIC)	4	f + e + d + c + b + a
X	5	f + e + d + c + b + a
	6	e + d + c + b + a
W	7	e + d + c + b + a
	8	d + c + b + a
	9	d + c + b + a
V	10	c + b + a
	11	b + a
U	12	b + a
T	13	a
	14	a

When the pottery eventually comes to be studied as a whole, the points of entry of types b, c, d, e, etc., can be seen. Other types are then shown to be either residual or to go on being used and/or manufactured in parallel with the later types. Resolution of this problem will depend on the relative quantities of the earlier pottery surviving and on its condition, e.g. whether the sherds are large and unabraded, or small and weather-worn.

Some highly regarded pottery, such as samian wares in Roman times and fine jugs in medieval times, may have had a longer life because they were more carefully looked after, and it is common to find examples of the finer Roman wares mended with rivets in order to prolong their life. The date of deposition in an archaeological layer of sherds of one of these more highly prized pots could therefore be a century or two later than its manufacture. It is much less likely that ordinary cooking pots or dishes would have a long life. Once again, the greater the quantity of data, in this case the amounts of pottery, the more reliable will be the conclusions that can be drawn from it.

Because pottery looms so large in the archaeological record of many excavated sites it is easy to overestimate its importance in the lives of the people in whom we are interested.

It is always salutary to keep in mind that there have been long aceramic periods in our history, particularly in the highland zones, or periods during which pottery was scarce and could not have been regarded as an everyday necessity. As far as one can tell the whole Welsh nation managed without pottery from the fifth century until the twelfth, except for small quantities of exotica imported from Gaul and the Mediterranean. But no one would dare suggest that this represents cultural poverty in pre-Norman Wales. And on the other side of Britain, it is illuminating to look at the ugly, badly made flask that is the only pot included in the Sutton-Hoo ship burial. If the splendid objects buried with, or in honour of, this Anglian king had been perishable whatever conclusions should we have drawn about him simply from this pot? Care must be taken not to give too much weight to any surviving evidence as against the evidence which has not survived, but which can reasonably be assumed to have existed.

The recording of pottery and animal bones

Where little pottery is found, its importance is likely to be very great and each sherd should be treated as a small find. Where pottery (and animal bones) are recovered in quantity they must be treated in bulk, to some extent, or the system will be overwhelmed. It is perhaps most convenient to divide the major grids into quarters or sixteenths dependent on the degree of precision required for the subsequent analysis. Each site's pottery and bones recording will have to be assessed on its merits and it may be necessary to modify the system if the quantities recovered are much greater or much less than expected.

Pottery should be stored in polythene bags or boxes, or cardboard boxes. Paper bags are unsuitable as most types disintegrate after a few years. The life of some kinds of polythene bags is uncertain and the storage of pottery, bones and other finds should be checked annually, and the material repacked if the containers are deteriorating. In a number of important cases the re-assessment of excavations carried out only 20-30 years ago has been made impossible because of the complete disintegration of the paper bags in which the pottery was stored. For this reason, also, each sherd of pot should be marked individually with Indian ink. If the fabric of the pottery is friable the marking should be protected with a coating of varnish. The marking of each individual sherd, however tedious on a large site, means that the sherds can be re-sorted into fabrics or shapes without losing a record of the context from which they were derived.

Just as with portable finds, there are three entirely different questions asked of the pottery assemblage. The first is related to the groups of pottery from within a layer, a building or a phase of the site. The second is concerned with the development of the pottery itself, its earliest and latest occurrence, its group or fabric or glaze or form, or its relationships with the pottery of the region or the country as a whole. The third is the function of the various types of pottery found — cooking pots, jugs, dishes, lamps and so forth. It is important therefore to label and store the pottery in a way which makes retrieval as simple as possible; otherwise its subsequent study could become exceedingly laborious, if not impossible.

The quantitative analysis of large groups of potsherds presents a number of difficulties. Counting the numbers of sherds of each recognizable type is not very satisfactory since its validity depends on the sizes of both the original pots and the fragments into which they have been smashed — any number of sherds can be doubled simply by breaking them in half. Similarly, weighing the sherds of each type has its limitations since the results will vary according to the sizes of the original pots and the thickness and density of the fabrics used. A more valid method is to attempt to estimate the number of pots represented by reconstructing each type on paper and estimating the minimum numbers of each type in the assemblage. Orton, 1980, 15ff. describes very lucidly the problems of the analysis of a mass of potsherds and concludes that the idea of estimated vessel equivalents (*ibid*. pp. 164-166), though it has practical difficulties, is at present the most fruitful line of study. The validity of an analysis of pottery (or any other finds including, in particular, animal bones) depends upon the percentage of the total original deposit on the site which is recovered. Clarke, Clarke ed., 1972, 26ff., has demonstrated graphically the considerable distortions in a 60 per cent sample of a series of assemblages (*ibid*., fig. 1:8). As in every other sphere of excavation, therefore, the nearer we approach the total recovery of any category of evidence the more closely our analysis will approach the truth. Our sample must be as large as possible and from all parts of a multi-purpose site, where there may be kitchens, stables, great halls, workshops and many other buildings and areas from which sherds may come not only in varying quantities but in types related to the function of the buildings — glazed jugs from a medieval hall, cooking pots from the kitchen area and so on. Add to this the cleanliness of many communities who swept their floors and disposed of large sherds in rubbish pits often well outside the settlement site, and it will be seen that typological analysis is liable to a series of vagaries not all of which can be quantified or even predicted. It may simply not be worth analysing small groups of pottery (or anything else). However the cumulative assemblages from large long-term excavations or from a series of related excavations, for example, within towns, will provide enough material to set up a flexible analytical framework which will produce increasingly refined and well-founded results.

The division of an assemblage of pottery into types will depend on a qualitative analysis of its fabrics, glazes, and forms. Usually this has been macroscopic and intuitive, depending on a more or less subjective assessment of the colour and texture of the fabrics — 'buff', 'orange', 'red with grey core', 'coarse', 'fine' or 'sandy' — without any clear definition of what these terms mean, together with similar descriptions of glazes as 'apple-green', 'yellowish-brown', or perhaps 'brownish-yellow'. In an attempt to standardize the description of colours, a Pottery Colour Chart has been published by RESCUE (Webster, 1970). This is a simplified version of the sort of charts used for the descriptions of soils, and should remove some of the subjectivity from pottery publication. The standardization of fabric descriptions is a great deal more difficult as anyone who has thought that he has found published parallels for pottery he has excavated will know, when he holds the comparative material in his hand and finds that it bears only a superficial resemblence to his own material.

The Medieval Pottery Research Group has produced a suggested *Key to Identification of Inclusions in Pottery*, which is 'designed to facilitate visual identification of the principal inclusions found in pottery in Britain'. This has not yet been accepted, but something of the kind is urgently needed.

The only really adequate description of fabrics would be based on thin sectioning, when the geology of the fabric can be identified and the origins of inclusions examined by heavy mineral analysis. This would be a formidable, if not impossible, task for all the pottery excavated in Britain every year but anything less must be recognized as being inadequate and potentially misleading.

The comparative study of forms, both of whole pots and of their parts, such as rims and bases, and of their decorative treatment is immensely complicated since the total repertory of forms and decoration is so wide.

Any system must include every form from the smaller globular cooking pot to the most elaborately decorated jug, and since almost all the pottery from excavations is hand-made (as distinct from moulded or machine-turned) the forms will tend to vary slightly from pot to pot. Thus, although broad divisions can and must be made, there will always be a number of examples which shade off into one or another type.

The study of glazes also needs to be more systematized, with analysis of their composition and added colouring agents. By determining the nature and quantities of trace elements in the glazes, it may be possible to sort an assemblage of potsherds into groups distinct from those determined by form and fabric. Since behind the pottery sits the potter, a man making more or less aesthetically pleasing objects for a market, whether local or continental, in the study of pottery we enter the realm of art-history and aesthetics, and must assess the degree of influence which one potter or group of potters has had on another, and whether a potter has moved about the country making his characteristic wares from the available local clays. An example of potters moving across the country is postulated by P. Webster (1975) where the production of Iron Age and Roman tankards is shown to move from the Durotrigian region on the south coast up into the Severn valley. This is a more or less clear-cut example spanning two centuries. Other movements were undoubtedly more complex, and on much shorter time-scales. It will obviously not be sufficient to sort pottery simply by fabric, or by decoration or by form but by a combination of all these characteristics. Pots of a similar form but differing fabrics may well be found to overlap in their distribution with pots of one fabric but differing forms according to whether the potters were influenced by style or by the availability or desirability of local clays and tempering materials. A well-known example of an apparently alien style being imposed on an already well-established technique is the so-called Romano-Saxon pottery found chiefly in Eastern England. This combines the hard, usually grey fabrics of wheel-turned Roman pottery with the forms and decorative slashes and dimples of pagan Saxon pots — a combination which was perhaps an attempt by Roman potters to capture the Saxon market, to make their wares attractive to recent immigrants with different tastes in pottery shapes and decoration.

Very large quantities of pottery must be studied before any generalised observations can be made with confidence about places or origin, distribution and stylistic affinities. The discovery of kilns with their accompanying mass of wasters is of great help, but much pottery was fired above ground in clamps or kilns which have now been destroyed without trace, so that the study of such wares is correspondingly more difficult.

The recording of small finds

Recording systems for small finds must aim primarily to record the find positions sufficiently accurately in three dimensions that they can be 'put back' into the excavation long after it is over. For this purpose two-dimensional grid coordinates for each find are essential. However, it is not necessarily helpful to record the absolute height of the find above Ordnance Datum or its depth below the ground surface or some other site datum except in special cases. What is needed for the reconstruction of the site is to know from which layer (however thin, or discontinuous) the find came; its absolute depth may be misleading unless at the same time the find is tied into the layer from which it derives. A clear example of this is seen in the practice, advocated particularly in the digging of ditch and rampart sections, of projecting find-spots horizontally on to the section. If all layers within the ditch and rampart were themselves horizontal the method might be valid, but they seldom are. More often the situation will be that shown in fig. 60, where a ditch cutting is shown in transverse section, the removed layers being indicated by dotted lines.

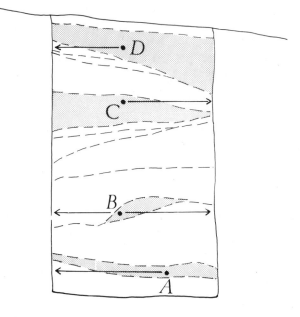

60

If the positions of the four finds are projected on to either of the drawn sections A or B, they will be transferred to a layer above or below the one to which they really belong, with consequent distortion of the interpretation. This is a simple example, but it is not difficult to visualize its extension into more complicated situations. Only if the find comes from a thick layer will a vertical measurement be necessary. This should be taken as a spot height which can be plotted on the site plan so that it is directly related to the contour survey of the layers. Since the upper surfaces of all layers should be levelled (and ideally contour surveyed), the absolute depth of the find spot can, if necessary, be recovered. However, the really important information is the position of the find relative not only to its own layer or feature but to those above and below it. If the procedures advocated in Chapter 9 are followed, the position and dimension of each feature/ layer are recorded on its layer record card and visually on the series of site plans. All that is necessary therefore is to refer the find to its feature/layer without further elaboration on its vertical position.

The essence of a finds recording system should be simplicity. The position of the find must be marked in the ground, so that it can be recorded three-dimensionally, and the point plotted on the site plan or overlay, to ensure that, subsequently, the find can be married to its find-spot, long after the site has gone. Each find should be given a serial number, which is attached both to the find and the recorded spot on the plan and it should have its own record card on which the grid reference, feature (or layer) number and, if necessary, depth or spot height, are recorded. On large sites, when finds are pouring out, the system should be streamlined as far as possible to avoid time wasting in recording. A system of double numbering is useful, in which cards, each with a serial number printed twice, or ordinary raffle or cloakroom tickets, are used. One of the pair is pinned to the ground in the find spot while the other is put in the bag with the find to identify it with its find spot. As a double check a finds book should be kept with the finds listed serially by date and by the signature of the finder. The find spots can then be plotted by the triangulation or the use of grids on to the plans or overlays at a convenient time, such as the end of each day. If both horseshoe and building nails are plotted, each ancient nail can be replaced by a modern large-headed nail, if necessary with the head painted to distinguish one type from another. These are plotted in the same way on the plans and overlays and each find should be given a record card, conveniently printed as a pro forma.

A description of the find when it was first discovered is required and this description will be expanded when further details are revealed by cleaning, X-rays, or other scientific examination. Details of cleaning and conservation treatment should be added to the card as work proceeds so that the history of the find as it passes through the excavation and post-excavation processes is recorded. Only in this way can either specialists in the type of object, or laboratory technicians, properly assess degrees of wear, corrosion and loss due to chemical action (either before or after discovery!). Preliminary identifications may have to be modified in the light of subsequent treatment. In cases of doubt the first attribution may be pencilled in or given a question mark so that second thoughts are not inhibited.

Ultimately, there are three principal ways in which the data regarding the finds will need to be retrieved. One is the relationship of the finds to structures and to important structural, occupation or dating layers. The second is the classification of finds into types or into groups according to their function and the third is according to the material from which they are made.

The first category will throw light on the evolving occupation of the site; the uses to which buildings or areas have been put; the changing economy of occupants; the extent and nature of imports and so forth. The second will be used to demonstrate the development of particular categories of object, both in relation to the site and in relation to comparable objects from other excavations and museum collections. The third will demonstrate the ways in which particular materials such as bronze, or shale, or ivory have been worked and the types of object which have been made from them.

On excavations producing large quantities of finds, computer storage is the most efficient means of handling them, since the computer is not only able to produce lists of required categories of information but can also provide distribution plots either printed or on visual display. Where the quantities of finds do not justify the use of a computer, edge-punched or light-hole cards are perfectly adequate.

Sophisticated techniques of statistical analysis are being developed to deal with artefacts of all kinds recovered from excavations. These techniques and their origins are described in Binford and Binford (1968), Binford (1972), Clarke (1968) and Orton (1980). No statistical analysis, however, can be better than the quality of its raw data, the true reflection of the nature and distribution of the samples used in the analysis. This is not the place to discuss analyses based on such disparate data as the location of Roman towns or the chance finds of a distinctive type of medieval pottery. But so far as evidence from excavations is concerned it will be obvious that only securely stratified, correctly identified and closely recorded evidence; whether of portable artefacts or of bones or other environmental material, will give a basis secure enough to justify conclusions based on an analysis which otherwise may be far more sophisticated than the digging on which it is based. Statistical analysis of material derived from partial and inadequately recorded excavations will inevitably be misleading though unprovably so. It is, therefore, incumbent on those of us who dig to provide the most reliable data possible and this can only be done, on the one hand, by large and strictly controlled excavations, and, on the other, by the adoption of agreed scales of reliability for those excavations, such as salvage digs, which by their nature, cannot provide the necessary degree of precision.

The value of coins as archaeological evidence

Coins, together with seals, tokens and specifically datable inscriptions, are probably the most closely datable of all archaeological finds. As a result, they are welcomed in excavations as providing positive dating evidence. But it must never be forgotten that they provide only a *terminus post quem* for the deposit in which they are found (see p. 193 below). Nevertheless, it is helpful to try to estimate the date at which the coin was lost as distinct from the date at which it was minted, by considering its condition, that is how much wear it seems to have suffered during circulation, and to translate this into years. Before the introduction of decimal currency in Britain it was highly instructive to look at a handful of coins taken from a pocket at random and to see how different the amounts of wear were on coins of similar date. Pennies dating from the beginning of this century would range in wear from crisply readable to almost smooth discs. The writer was with P.A. Rahtz one day when he took from his pocket four old pennies in order to make a telephone call from a pre-STD phone box. This was in the early 1960s. None of these pennies was later than 1914. If Rahtz had been buried at that time in the clothes he stood up in, his interment would almost certainly have been dated half a century too early. One could only hope that his excavator would apply the *terminus post quem* rule as rigorously as he does himself.

Another factor affecting the estimates of wear on coins is the nature of the soil in which they have lain, so that it is important to attempt to distinguish between wear and corrosion, and to record the nature of the surrounding soil. For this reason, it is especially important not to overclean coins, and in fact they should, ideally, be cleaned by a trained conservator. However, sometimes it is desirable to know the date of a coin immediately (though whatever the date the coin proves to be, the *strategy* of the excavation should not be altered, since the relative chronologies will remain unchanged, the coin merely providing a *terminus post quem* — see p. 193). If light cleaning with a stiff brush or glass bristle brush (not a metal bristle brush) does not render the inscription legible under a magnifying glass or binocular microscope, a scalpel can be used for careful mechanical cleaning. Harder corrosion products can be removed by vibratool. Careful mechanical cleaning is to be preferred to chemical stripping but is comparatively time-consuming. If mechanical methods fail, the following chemical methods may be used:

Acids
30—40% formic acid or 5% citric acid made up in fresh distilled water. Action is rapid, and the solution should be changed when it becomes deeply coloured (either dark green or blue). The coins should be kept under observation and removed before the metal becomes etched. Formic acid is to be preferred as it is less likely to do harm.

Alkaline Glycerol
    120g NaOH
    40ml glycerine
    1 litre distilled water
Coins should be soaked in the solution in glass or polythene containers. This method is rapid and the coin should be removed for observation periodically. The solution should be changed when it becomes deeply coloured.

Calgon
    15% solution
This method takes longer than the methods described above but it is less likely to cause damage. This method can be used for the removal of calcium and magnesium salts. It may etch the coin if it is left in for too long.

Sodium Sesquicarbonate
    5% solution
Not a very good method. The solution should be changed every week or when it gets too blue. After stripping, coins should be brushed with a glass bristle brush to remove any powdery deposits.

All treatments should be followed by impregnation in a 3% solution of Benzotriazole preferably under vacuum. The coins should then be dipped in alcohol to remove any Benzotriazole from the surface. When dry, they should be lacquered using Incralac or other chloride-free cellulose nitrate lacquer. This treatment prevents further deterioration.

It should be stressed that chemical stripping should only be used when absolutely necessary.

The assessment of the archaeological and historical significance of coins depends on factors other than mere dating, especially where whole coin series are discovered. An understanding of the economic conditions in which the coins were issued is of vital importance if gross errors in interpretation are not to be made, since the recovery rate of coins from sites will have to be measured against the known profusion or paucity of the issues. The subject has been concisely dealt with by Casey (1974). His paper deals with Romano-British coins but the principles apply to all coin finds.

It is tempting to equate richness of coin finds with periods of economic prosperity or growth, but histograms of coin recovery plotted against known economic conditions show considerable anomalies. For example, far more Anglo-Saxon than medieval coins have been recovered from Worcester, a city which was of great importance in the twelfth and thirteenth centuries, especially as a place of pilgrimage, where one would expect coin loss to be high and varied in content (Barker et al, 1970). There is no ready explanation for this, but obviously an assessment of Worcester's prosperity based simply on the coins discovered there over the last century would be wildly misleading. In Russia, the long sequence of coins from Novgorod exhibits a similar hiatus (Thompson, 1967, XVI, 7 and fig. 18). The excavations at Novgorod, which were almost entirely carried out on the preserved wooden levels of streets and house foundations, are also instructive on the relationship between the presumed dates of coin losses and the dates of the streets and buildings provided by dendrochronology (Thompson, op. cit. 30-4). In general, dating from the coin and seal evidence tended to be too early; in other words, it was assumed that the coins had a shorter life than they had in fact.

Over and above their value as dating evidence, coins often tell us, obliquely or directly, a good deal about the aspirations and intentions of the rulers who issued them. The propaganda uses of Roman coinage are well known, and the inscriptions on these coins are documentary sources of considerable importance. The size of coins together with the progressive debasement of the metal from which they are struck reflects inflation, while the restoration of the currency will be reflected in improvement in the composition of the metals and usually in the quality of the dies from which the coins are struck. Similarly the study of forgeries and spurious issues can throw considerable light on economic conditions in the regions where they circulate.

No less important than the study of coinage is the appreciation of the significance of lack of coins. At Hen Domen, a castle of some importance from the Norman Conquest to the late thirteenth century, only one half silver penny has been found in sixteen years of excavation. Clearly the soldiery were either not being paid in coin, or they were exceptionally careful. It seems probable, in this case, that payment was almost entirely in kind, castle guard being an imposed service for which payment would not be made, though one wonders how many mercenaries, if any, were employed on the Welsh border in these violent centuries.

Any assessment of the significance of coins, or lack of them, from excavations should be made with the help of an historian who is familiar with the economy of the periods being examined.

10

The Interpretation of the Evidence

The detailed dissection of a site and the elaborate recording of all its observable phenomena are simply the preludes to an attempt to give meaning to the evidence: to decide how layers were formed; to recognize and interpret patterns in the excavated surfaces which show the former presence of buildings, fences, ditches, ramparts, fields and all the other traces which human occupation leaves in the ground; to explain, as far as possible, the complete sequence of events on the site.

This mass of evidence must then be set into a pair of chronological frames, one relative, one absolute.

The relative framework is based on the study of the superimposition of layers and features, or the intersection of walls, post-holes, slots, ditches, gullies and other similar features. Such a framework gives only a 'floating chronology' which can be moved up and down, or extended or contracted according to datable finds securely stratified within the sequence. Such finds may be coins, seals or tokens, datable pottery or other artefacts, or architectural or sculptural fragments; or they may be samples taken from the layers and dated by scientific methods.

The relative chronology of a site is likely to be more certain than the absolutely dated chronology, since there is usually little doubt about the broad sequence of events, even if the details are not unequivocal, or the horizontal relationships cannot be demonstrated. However, the absolute, or calendar, dating may be subject to considerable fluctuations, as the evidence of coins is supplemented by that, say, of dendrochronology (eg. Novgorod, Thompson, 1967) or radio-carbon dating; or if the dating of a pottery group is reassessed in the light of research elsewhere; or the excavation, as it proceeds, uncovers further dating evidence which modifies that already used.

The establishment of structural patterns and chronological frameworks is itself only the first stage towards the economic, cultural and, in the widest sense, historical interpretation which should follow. Obviously, if the earlier stages of the interpretation are mistaken, the subsequent stages will be further removed from the truth about the site as it was in the period under investigation. If we add to this Coles's reminder of the law of diminishing returns: that the evidence which we understand from an excavation is less than we record, which, even in the best excavations, is less than has survived, which in turn is less than the total evidence once existing on the site, we shall see that our understanding of an ancient site or settlement or landscape will, at best, be severely limited. We must strive, therefore, to minimize these limitations. For example, there is little doubt that the larger and more complete the excavation, the more valid will be the interpretations which we can draw from it. Though this is particularly the case with the excavation of timber buildings, even stone structures are more certainly and completely understood in large areas.

It is not possible to give detailed advice on all the problems of the interpretation of evidence that will occur in a complex excavation. The best general advice that can be given is to keep an open mind, expect the unexpected, and then, when a provisional interpretation has been made, stop, and take the opposite view or views of its meaning. By thus initiating a dialectic, false assumptions are not so likely to be perpetuated and built upon by the addition of subsequent plausible, though mistaken, evidence. For example, if a pebble surface, bordered by stake-holes, is assumed to be an internal floor, it is likely that further emerging evidence will be adduced to support this theory. But if someone then says 'Let us assume it is an outside yard', the matter can be debated in detail, and either resolved on the balance of the evidence, or, if no positive conclusion can be reached, alternative explanations published. This is a simple, perhaps simplistic, example, but it should be extended to cover everything found on the excavation.

It follows that it is a great advantage to have supervisors or assistants on the site who are capable of taking and expressing a constructively critical view of every stage of the work. Conversely the interpretation of an excavation by a forceful individual with inexperienced volunteers or labourers can easily go awry simply because he is not obliged to consider all the alternatives. Under these circumstances, he should, if he is wise, dispute with himself over the meaning of each piece of evidence.

It is often valuable to think 'laterally' when considering the meaning of what we have dug up. In 'lateral' thinking we discard our preconceptions of the solution to a problem and look at it from a new viewpoint, perhaps one that at first sight appears ludicrous or at least highly improbable, but which may be ultimately seen to fit the evidence better than any other of the postulated solutions. Lateral thinking has been described in a number of books by E. de Bono (e.g. 1970).

A valuable aid in the interpretation of excavated evidence (and a check on flights of fancy) is to attempt to explain the origin, derivation and purpose of every recognizable feature in the light of commonsense and practicability. This involves imagining the process by which a structure might have been built, the actual work of barrowing, shovelling, and spreading rubble, digging post-holes, laying foundations and so on. For instance, in determining whether a bank has

61   This photograph shows the very worn threshold stone of one of the west doorways of the baths basilica at Wroxeter. Earlier excavations have destroyed the stratification above and beside the threshold and a considerable area in the background of the photograph has also been dug in earlier times. However, the rubble beyond the threshold in the centre of the picture can be seen to be of two sorts — a light coloured area of worn stone, bounded by an area of darker, unworn stone. The area of light, worn stone leads diagonally towards the site of the door of the basilica, and is clearly a path leading into the interior of the former basilican area long after the threshold was buried by rubble (removed by the earlier excavators). It follows that the west wall of the building was still standing to an effective height at this time, otherwise there would have been no need to have entered at this point. It can be further deduced, therefore, that robbing of the end wall took place after this. Since the worn rubble surface is of the last period occupation, the robbing is likely to have taken place after the site was deserted. This contrasts with the robbing of many of the other walls of the building which can be shown to have been robbed as early as perhaps the third century. (*Photo-Sidney Renow*)

been piled against a wall, or whether the wall has been built against a vertical face cut into the bank, an examination of the character of wall where it met the bank will usually show whether the joints of the wall were pointed, or whether mortar had been merely poured down behind the stones as the wall-building proceeded up the face of the cut-back bank, since it would be impossible to point the joints if the bank was there first, unless there was a construction trench wide enough to take a man. Often explanations of excavated phenomena can be tested by trial and error, or by observation of similar situations on present-day demolition and construction sites. A simple example of the information which may reasonably be deducted from the observed evidence is shown in fig. 61.

The understanding of a series of robber trenches, for example, is helped by taking the practical view and imagining a group of labourers faced with the job of digging out the walls, or perhaps only the facing stones, of a ruined building. Were the walls visible? If not, how did they find them? Trial trenching? Stone robbers will work as economically as possible, digging the narrowest possible trenches, and usually backfilling them afterwards. If the walls have been completely robbed out, the unwanted stone and mortar debris thrown back will give a great deal of information about the walls as they were when they stood. Biddle and Biddle (1969) have discussed the interpretation of robber trench excavations in some detail. To their suggestions can be added the analysis of the mortars thrown back into the trench, which may differentiate walls of more than one period.

However, the commonsense, practical approach to interpretation does not always work, partly because our habits, modes of thought, and our view of what is practical may be very different from that of the people we are digging up. Robson Bonnichsen (1972) describes an illuminating exercise in the interpretation of a recently deserted Indian camp site, Millie's Camp, where the debris, litter and other evidence of occupation were recorded as carefully as in an area excavation, and their interpretation subsequently checked by reference to the recent occupants. The mistakes made showed the fallibility of some 'commonsense' reasoning. The behaviour patterns which produced the anomalous, misunderstood evidence were unfamiliar to the archaeologists and the reasons behind these behaviour patterns could not have been deduced from the available evidence, so that we must be careful not to project back into the past our own habits and ways of thinking except into situations where they can reasonably be assumed to be valid, either because we have lived and worked in comparable situations, or because we know of living communities who do so now.

Another limitation of the 'practical' approach is that we may be reluctant to accept the evidence in the ground for what it is, if it seems impractical or unlikely. An example is the discovery on a number of sites of very shallow post-holes and circles of small stones which in many cases form definite structural patterns, thus implying a style of building in which posts are set on, not in, the ground. At first sight, this seems a highly impractical, if not impossible, manner of construc-

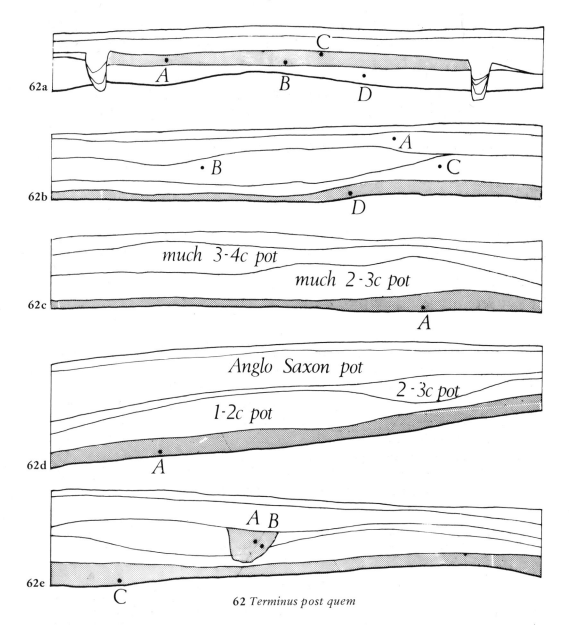

62a

62b

62c

much 3-4c pot

much 2-3c pot

A

Anglo Saxon pot

2-3c pot

1-2c pot

62d

A

A B

62e

C

62 *Terminus post quem*

62a A clay floor is bounded by post-holes. The floor contains three coins of the second century AD. Coin D is of the first century. The floor was therefore laid *during* or after the second century AD.

On the basis of this evidence alone, the floor could be twentieth century. It certainly might be fifth century or Anglo-Saxon. However, if coin D was third century, coins A, B, and C are all negated as dating evidence, and the floor which seals coin D must be third century or later.

62b Coin D is first century AD. Coin C second century; coin B third century and coin A fourth century. Here is a fairly common situation, somewhat simplified, in which we have a superficially plausible sequence of dating evidence which suggests that the four layers span the

tion, but as the evidence has accumulated from a number of excavations, the former presence of such buildings has become undeniable. Accordingly instead of working from our preconceptions of what the evidence for a timber building ought to look like, we should explore methods of construction that would fit the evidence. This has resulted, among other things, in the full-scale simulation of such a structure, Building I from the Baths Basilica excavation at Wroxeter which, though not yet complete, has already proved that post-built structures will stand even if their posts are not embedded in the ground.

Dating

The understanding and strict application of the concepts of the *terminus post quem* and *terminus ante quem* are of fundamental importance in the relative dating of layers and features. Unless these concepts are applied in all cases with the most rigorous logic far-reaching mistakes in dating and interpretation will be made. The rules can be set out simply as follows:

The terminus post quem

A datable object, such as a coin, or other datable find, such as a radio-carbon sample from a layer or feature, only gives the date *on or after which the layer or feature was deposited*, that is, the so-called *terminus post quem*. It follows that in any continuous sealed layer in which there is a number of finds of varying date, the find of latest date is the one which provided the *terminus post quem*. It must be established that the object is not intrusive, that it has not been taken down an animal hole, or slipped down the interstices between the stones of a wall. If there is any doubt about this the object should be rejected for dating purposes. The argument is most easily demonstrated graphically (figs. 62-3).

whole Roman period in sequence. However, if we apply the *terminus post quem* rule strictly, as we must, the whole lot could be post Roman, even modern. Other dating factors would have to be discovered and assessed before a Roman sequence could be maintained.

62c In this figure there is increased probability that the layers above A were laid down in the second-third century and the third-fourth century *but no certainty*.

Again A is crucial. If it is a ninth century coin or thirteenth century pot, all of the material above it must be considered residual.

62d In this similarly plausible sequence, if A is an otherwise undatable sherd or object one must be careful not to use a false *terminus ante quem* reasoning and maintain that A must be earlier than first-second century. It may ultimately prove to be, say, fourth century, when the two layers above take

their *terminus post quem* from it.

62e The two objects A and B, though found together in a pit, tell us *nothing* about each other except that they were buried in the pit together at some time *at or later than* the date of the later of the two objects. However, if object C can be shown to be of later date than either A or B then the whole sequence takes its *terminus post quem* from C.

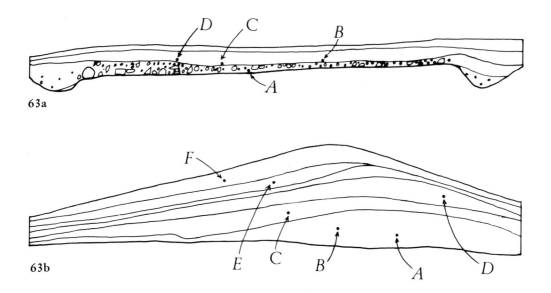

63a

63b

63a A is a Roman coin or sherd, B is a medieval spur.

It is tempting to see this as a Roman road still in use in medieval times. However, the road could be of any date, from the Roman period onward. (It cannot be prehistoric if the sherd is thoroughly sealed). It is even possible that the spur was an antique dropped recently.

63b This illustration is based on an actual example (at Quatford in Shropshire, Mason and Barker, 1961).

F — 19th-century sherd
E — medieval sherd
D — medieval bronze object
C — Roman sherd
B — neolithic flint
A — 1881 halfpenny

The presumed medieval rampart was shown to be dated to 1881 or later by the presence of the Victorian halfpenny.

The danger here is that the halfpenny might not have been dropped, or that it would not have been found if the cutting had been made elsewhere along the 'rampart'. In fact, the bank was formed by ploughing during the 1939-45 war, so that the 1881 coin gives a *terminus post quem* some 60 years too early.

The terminus ante quem

The *terminus ante quem* argument arises when features or layers are sealed by or are cut through by later, datable features. The later features give a *terminus ante quem* (that is a date *before* which the earlier features must have been deposited) to all those features which can be demonstrated to be earlier. For example, if a series of layers is sealed by a mosaic floor of unquestioned fourth-century date then all the layers below will be fourth century *or earlier*. Similarly, if a wall itself can be dated, say by architectural features, then the layers which are cut by its foundation are given a *terminus ante quem* by the wall. Thus, if the wall can be shown to be Norman, the cut layers are Norman or earlier. They may be Saxon — or palaeolithic.

However, we must be careful not to be led into a circular argument. A *terminus ante quem* cannot be given by a layer which is dated by an object embedded in it which merely gives it a *terminus post quem*. For example, if a floor in a house contains a coin of AD 267 firmly stratified in it, the floor must have been laid

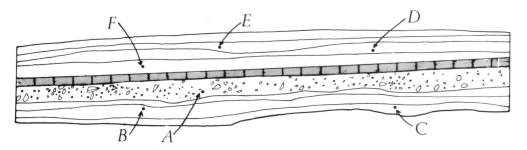

64 *above* All the layers under the tiled floor including finds A, B and C in the illustration are given a *terminus ante quem* by the floor. If the floor is made of, say, fourteenth century tiles then all the layers beneath must be fourteenth century or earlier. They might be prehistoric. Be sure that the floor has not been taken up and relaid in later times, perhaps in a nineteenth century restoration.

65 *below* This again is a diagrammatic representation of an actual situation. The walls are those of an early Norman passage leading to the cloisters in Worcester Cathedral. The steps lead down into a Norman undercroft.

Both these buildings are firmly datable by their styles of architecture. The two graves *a* and *b* are therefore clearly given a *terminus ante*

quem by the early Norman passage since they must have been dug from the contemporary floor level. They are therefore late Saxon or earlier. Similarly the underlying pit *c* is given a *terminus ante quem* by the graves. The pit produced a large sherd of pottery of a type not readily paralleled in the region. However, it must be late Saxon or earlier. It is very possibly Iron Age.

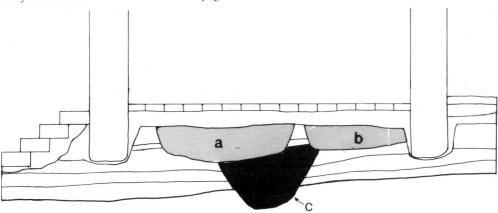

in *267 or after*. It does not follow that the layers below the floor were deposited in *267 or earlier*. Subsequent excavation of another floor many layers below the first might produce a stratified coin of, say, AD 370. In that case all the layers above take a new *terminus post quem* of 370 or later. The whole complex might ultimately turn out to be tenth century. Unless the limitations of stratified datable objects are fully appreciated there is a danger that serious dating errors will occur in interpretation, to be perpetuated in the literature.

It must also be re-emphasised that a number of objects retrieved from one layer or feature are 'associated' only in the sense that they have a common context in the excavation. Their 'association' implies nothing about their relative or absolute dates, or ultimate provenance. In the past, a great deal of weight, has been placed on the argument that objects are 'associated', and quite unjustifiable conclusions drawn from this. (See the example cited on p. 175 above.) Pottery cannot be dated by 'association' with a coin. It is only too easy for a stray Roman coin to get into a medieval rubbish pit. No one would redate a group of glazed jugs to the Roman period on that evidence alone. But how many times have we seen objects and pottery dated by association with coins when the dates look more plausible?

Nevertheless, under some circumstances the association of objects can be accepted as of considerable importance. Objects found together in a grave, for instance, though they may not all be of one date or even of one style or culture, are associated in the sense that they were deposited either on or with the body for specific reasons — as heirlooms, trophies, equipment for the after-life or perhaps even as sentimental keepsakes. Similarly, objects found strewn on the floor of a house, particularly one that has been burnt down, when it can be supposed that the occupants fled without stopping to collect all their belongings, may be assumed to have been in use by, or at least in the possession of, the occupants when the house was abandoned. The greater the quantities of material in association the more reliance can be placed on conclusions drawn from them. The objects in a single grave may be a unique assemblage. If similar objects are found in a majority of graves in a large cemetery, it can reasonably be assumed that the finds were a normal part of the belongings or equipment of the people interred. Similarly, if great quantities of pottery and coins are found in a stratified sequence, as they are on many Roman sites, it strengthens the argument for assigning in broad terms the assemblages of pottery in the layers to the dates of the coins in those layers. For example, if there is a military presence on the site which is followed by a civil development, clearly marked off in the stratification, and the earliest civil phase is followed by a period of demolition and rebuilding, the associated groups of sealed pottery, coins and finds can reasonably be assumed to be broadly contemporary, though increasingly contaminated by residual material.

Relative chronology

The principle of stratification is fundamental to archaeological excavation. This principle states that if one layer can be shown to lie upon another, the lower layer must have been deposited before the upper. The interval between the deposition of the two layers may be a millennium, or the time it takes to tip two separate barrow-loads of rubble, but the relative chronology remains the same. On a simply stratified site, the layers may be stripped off one at a time, in the reverse order to that in which they were deposited, and the result shown as a straightforward table — which amounts to a diagrammatic section of the site:

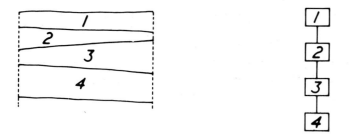

However, things are not usually so simple. Much more often layers are discontinuous so that a theoretical section across the site might look like this:

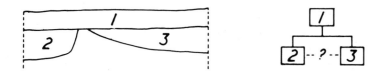

It will be apparent that the relationship between layers 2 and 3 cannot be demonstrated directly — but that they have a common relationship with I — they are both earlier.

In more complicated cases the stratification can be shown diagrammatically thus:

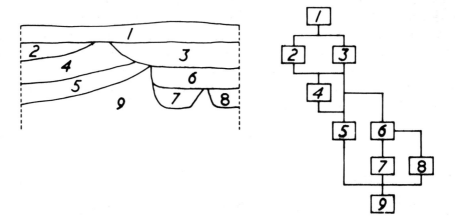

The problem of stratigraphic relationships and their demonstration has been discussed at length by Harris (1975) with illustrations of a number of theoretical situations. His figures 26 and 27 (reproduced here figs. 67 and 68) deserve close study, since they show a typical, though very small, excavation analysed by means of a matrix or graph of layer numbers. Most excavations are far more extensive than this example and are thus likely to produce many more discrete

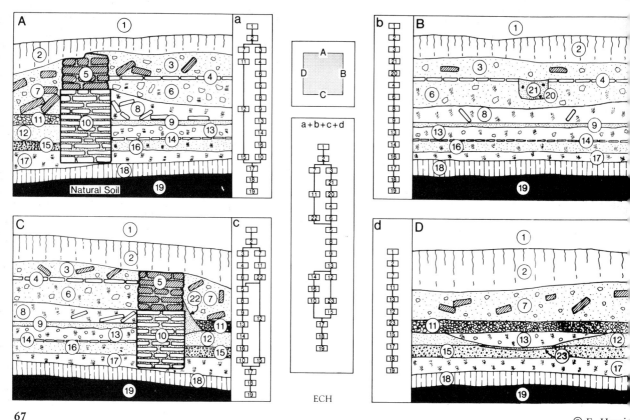

© E. Harris

layers and features. One advantage of stripping the largest possible area of a site is that in this way the layers are removed progressively over the whole area and recorded on the plans and photographs in the order in which they were removed. If the plans are drawn on plastic film the whole relative sequence can be seen and understood as a series of transparent overlays. These are supplemented by detail drawings, photographs and the record cards for each layer, feature or context. From all this information a graph of feature numbers such as that described by Harris can be produced. The chief use of such a graph is to help to clarify thinking in the understanding of the site. The exercise of including each layer or feature somewhere in the graph ensures that every piece of evidence is taken into consideration, and that inconvenient or apparently insignificant features are not ignored. It is also a convenient way of displaying the stratification of a large and complex site on one page, though in an abstract form which must either be taken by the reader at its face value, or referred back to the mass of feature cards and site plans, which will not normally be publishable in the necessary detail.

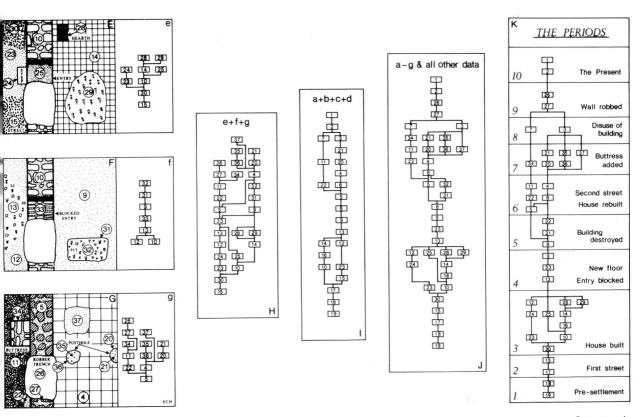

68

© E. Harris

Two modifications of the matrix form as printed by Harris are suggested as a result of use in the field. If the boxes for feature/context numbers were square the forms would be more flexible, since large horizontal excavations need many numbers written across the page but comparatively few downwards. In practice also, it is common to construct the matrix in rough before transferring it to the printed form, a process which often involves much crossing out and rearrangement. A board, fitted with rows of slots, made either of bands of cloth or metal, so that numbered cards could be slotted into them, or, alternatively, a peg-board with a series of movable numbers, would save time and aid clear thinking. Needless to say, the numbers could be used repeatedly.

Such a graph can be made more informative by inserting in the appropriate places the structures represented by the features listed, and the principal dating evidence relating both to these structures and to the whole sequence.

Where, in my experience, such a graph of feature numbers has been used it has not altered the interpretation arrived at from the study of the ground and the plans and sections. It is more an instrument for aiding clear thinking and coherent publication than for primary interpretation.

The limitations of archaeological evidence

In every excavation we must expect aspects which are beyond interpretation from the material evidence alone. A reed pipe will tell us its range of notes but not the tunes played on it.

If we can temporarily forget all that we know of the last two thousand years, we can play a salutary archaeological game. What would we make of the archaeological remains of Christianity if we knew nothing of it except what evidence could be recovered by excavation? Recurring fragments both sculptured and painted of a crucified man, of a gentle mother and her child, of other figures, male and female, some of them being tortured and killed, others surrounded by singing winged figures; flagons and dishes included with selected male burials; temples varying in size from tiny to gigantic, many of them cruciform, perhaps significantly, perhaps not; palatial buildings set round courtyards, often in remote and beautiful settings. What reconstruction of this religion would we attempt from such remains? A cult of human sacrifice connected with worship of a mother goddess? Should we equate the child with the crucified man? Could we make the connexion between the oratory of Gallerus and the ruins of Rievaulx?

It is a sobering reflection that we can never excavate the upper room in which the Last Supper was held, and would not recognize it if we could, and that the site of the Crucifixion would be merely three large post-holes.

In spite of the clear limitations of excavated evidence, some deductions can be made about the spiritual aspirations, the pretensions, hopes and fears of the people whose house foundations we dissect and whose rubbish we reverently collect. Two examples must suffice here. The fact that very many burials from the earliest times onwards are furnished with grave goods or other evidence of posthumous provision suggest that man has always hoped for continuation of life after death. If the provisions which are made include the equipment, furniture, food and weapons of the dead man's everyday life, it is a reasonable assumption that the after-life, in that case, was considered to be a continuation or resumption in some form of the life he had just left, and not a spiritual Nirvana, or a Dantean paradise.

Another example is furnished by the petty king (if that is what he was) who rebuilt the centre of Viroconium sometime in the late fourth or fifth century (Barker, 1975). He had pretensions to former grandeur; his buildings, though all in timber, are symmetrically planned on classical lines, with colonnaded porticoes and a private alley or arcade (*ibid*). They are quite unlike the aisled halls of the immediately following Arthurian period or the Saxon palaces of Yeavering. We can see in his mind a conscious attempt to revive (or keep alive) the rapidly fading past, the last flicker of the classical tradition in Britain until Inigo Jones and Wren.

The importance of negative evidence

Negative evidence should be 'that which can be shown to have been absent from

the site in antiquity'. It may, however (for instance in the case of organic materials), be 'that which is absent from the site now'. Unfortunately it may also be
'that which was not found' or alternatively 'not recognized'. In order to use
negative evidence, one has to be aware of what is missing, which implies being
aware of its presence in a similar context elsewhere. A gap in the distribution of
a type of pottery or a class of bronze object only becomes apparent when the
positive evidence is plotted. Similarly a gap in the distribution of a type of pottery
over an excavated area only becomes apparent if the rest of the pottery is recorded and plotted accurately enough to reveal the gap. The recognition of the
absence of structural evidence will depend on similar evidence having been found
on another similar site, or on a comparable part of the same site, for example, in
a stretch of defensive rampart in another part of the circuit. Clearly the distinction must be made between negative evidence which is adduced from the absence,
at present, of the class of information concerned, and that which can positively
be said not to be there. If one is certain that, had the evidence been there, it
would have been found, then one can reasonably, if paradoxically, speak of
positively negative evidence. If arguing from the mere absence of evidence, it
may be safer to enclose the term 'negative' in inverted commas. An example from
Wroxeter will illustrate the point. A number of fragments of human skull were
found in the upper rubble layers of the site. If the excavation had been partial,
confined to trenches or boxes, like those on the same site in the 1850s and the
1930s, the skull fragments would have been construed as the remains of disturbed
burials (especially since Professor Donald Atkinson had found complete burials in
the gutters and elsewhere in his excavations of the Forum nearby in 1923-27).
When the vast collection of animal bones from the same layers was searched for
human long-bones, none was found. Since our excavation was total, we were able
to say with confidence that there were only skull fragments present, and that they
were therefore not from disturbed burials of the sort found by Atkinson. Further
examination of the skulls showed that they had been soaked in or anointed with a
yellowish oil containing linoleic acid, perhaps sunflower or linseed oil. Some of
the skulls also had post-mortem knife or sword cuts on them. The inescapable
conclusion is that we have here evidence of a cult involving skulls either as trophies
or relics. Without the negative evidence of the lack of long bones, vertebrae, and
etc, it would not have been possible to make this assertion. It is also extremely
probable that the earlier excavators found skull fragments in their excavations,
but discarded them, since under the circumstances, they could not have recognized
or proved their significance.

Alternative explanations of excavated phenomena

Whether interpreting single features, or whole structures, or periods of occupation,
it is satisfying to be able to offer clear-cut explanations. As a result, doubts
expressed in the field about whether a post-hole might not be a root-hole; a

hearth, a dump of burnt clay; or a floor, a mere random scatter of pebbles, tend to dissipate themselves as the field drawings are converted into final definitive plans, and when the interim report, necessarily concise, comes to be written. The process may be accelerated by radio or television interviews (who wants to sound doubtful about almost every aspect of his site in front of six million viewers?), or by lectures even to learned societies. When the final report comes to be written all the doubts and uncertainties should be retained in it, but even here this makes for such dull reading and gives such an impression of vagueness and lack of conviction that it is tempting to opt for positive, even dramatic, assertions rather than pedantic fumblings after the truth. When we also bear in mind that the reservations and alternative explanations we express in our reports will very probably be removed before the results of our work reach the specialist text-books and history books, we must take the greatest care to record them from the start and find some way of preserving them throughout the distorting processes our work will subsequently undergo.

It is helpful to adopt in the field a series of grades of probability, from certain, through probable and possible, to very uncertain. (But see cautionary notes by Rahtz, 'How Likely is Likely?' 1975.) These, which should be incorporated in the record card, can either be expressed in words, or in a series of numbers, say 1 to 5, with 1 the most certain and 5 very dubious. If this system is also reflected in the field and published drawings by a colour code (which may be complicated if colour is being used already for other purposes, such as identification of materials) or by the number code written next to the feature, or by means of dotted outlines or hatching, the written record is reinforced. If the drawings appear to give all features equal status, reference will continually have to be made to the record cards. Not only is this time-consuming but the picture given by the drawings will be unnecessarily misleading.

It is only reasonable, however, to offer the reader our carefully argued opinion as to which of the alternative interpretations we favour, and why. If two or more interpretations carry equal weight we must say so, even if this does mean an inconclusive final chapter in the report. What we must not do is to favour one interpretation before another because it furthers our research interests, or tends to prove a theory we expounded a year or two before.

An excellent example of the way in which evidence, unequivocal in itself, may be interpreted in a series of alternatives is provided by C.R. Musson's study of building forms at Durrington Walls, Woodhenge and the Sanctuary, in Wiltshire (Musson, 1971). He analyses, from the point of view of an architect, the possible structures which could be represented by the excavated circles of post-settings, and while reaching no firm conclusion, frees the reader from stereotyped interpretations not only of these but of other similar monuments.

11

Scientific Aids

Compared with the situation as it was only fifteen years ago, the amount of information which can be added to and deduced from excavated evidence by scientific means is enormous and increases annually. It is instructive to compare the descriptions of techniques in Brothwell and Higgs, 1969, and in Sherratt. ed., 1980, 416-432.

One of the most important advances is in the development of dating techniques. These include radio-carbon dating, which is based on the assumption that upon the death of a living organism, whether animal or vegetable, carbon 14 atoms present in the organism decay at a measurable rate (Brothwell and Higgs, 1969, 46 ff.). While the early theories postulated by Libby in the years immediately following the second world war have undergone modification, particularly in methods of calibration, and while tree-ring analysis of the same samples has achieved greater precision, the method remains of supreme importance for the dating of organic material (Sherratt, ed., 1980, 417). Another important though less widely applicable technique is that of thermo-remanent magnetism, in which the directions of the magnetic fields induced in hearths, ovens, kilns and the like while they are being fired, are compared with the earth's magnetic field at the present day (Brothwell and Higgs, 1969, 76 ff.). Though the method is still being developed it provides dating evidence from material not susceptible to other forms of analysis. Thermo-luminescence, in which pottery is heated until visible, measurable light is emitted by released electrons, is a method of dating the pottery, since for reasons explained in Brothwell and Higgs, 1969, 106 ff., the greater the age of the pot, the greater the thermo-luminescence. Though at present the method is liable to errors up to ± 10%-15% it is a most important technique, offering, for the first time, a method of pottery dating independent of stylistic or typological criteria. Other scientific dating methods include the dating of obsidian artefacts based on the fact that the surface of obsidian absorbs water from its surroundings at a known rate from the moment it is chipped or flaked until the present day (Brothwell and Higgs, 1969, 62 ff.) and the determination of relative dating by means of the fluorine, nitrogen and uranium contents of ancient bones (Brothwell and Higgs, 1969, 35 ff.). These techniques are independent of the usual stylistic or typological criteria, the studies of which were tending to become bogged down due, very often, to lack of independent dating criteria, so that there had been a tendency for circular arguments to develop between excavators and finds specialists.

In the environmental field, examination of the contents of pits, ditches, wells, cess-pits and other deposits in which organic materials are preserved has revolutionised the understanding of the ecology of our sites and their environs. The study of animal bones on a much increased scale is beginning to build up more reliable pictures of the development of domestication and of food habits, while more sophisticated examination of human bones is shedding light not only on the incidence of diseases, but on the relationships of blood groups among populations, information which, if extended, may solve many problems of invasion, diffusion, immigration and integration. In addition, analysis of metals, pottery clays with their inclusions, glazes, and other manufacturing materials throws light, often unexpected, on methods of manufacture and on patterns of trade.

Two indispensable conspectuses of archaeologically-orientated scientific techniques will be found in Brothwell and Higgs (1969) and Sherratt, ed. 1980. To these must be added the Council for British Archaeology's *Handbook of Scientific Aids and Evidence for Archaeologists*, 1970. This is a handlist in loose leaf form which deals with 'artefacts and other material providing evidence' together with 'instrumental techniques (analytical, dating and geophysical)' and which contains bibliographical references for each technique. Recent work and technical advances are described in the journal *Archaeometry* and the *Journal of Archaeological Science*. To these should be added more specialised text-books such as Dimbleby, 1967 and Fleming, 1976.

Since these publications are readily accessible there is no need to repeat here the information given in them, but rather to urge that they, and the other more specialized text-books referred to, be studied by all directors of excavations.

There are two chief problems in the use of scientific aids. One is the necessity for the excavator to comprehend the processes involved, some of which are highly technical. Unless he understands at least the basic theory behind each process it will be impossible for him to use the results with the necessary degrees of caution and flexibility, or even to discuss the method intelligently with the scientist concerned. It is certainly not enough to accept a bare statement about the origin of pottery inclusions, or a thermo-luminescent date, and use it blindly in a report. Even if we are not capable of carrying out the techniques involved ourselves, we must appreciate their possibilities and limitations or we are likely to compound errors of all kinds. There is no doubt that the present-day excavation director is required to have an increasingly wide understanding of disciplines ranging from nuclear physics to the history of painting. He cannot simply be a technician who digs competently, takes samples, and then receives a mass of information from a battery of experts which he welds into a conglomerate of unrelated facts embedded in archaeological jargon.

The other problem facing the excavator who seeks scientific help is the cost of such help and, more particularly, the comparative rarity of scientists able and willing to provide *ad hoc* services. State-financed excavations are in the strongest position, being serviced by the Inspectorate of Ancient Monuments Laboratory which can arrange for a great variety of scientific help. This service is being strengthened by a series of research fellowships in a range of specialised disciplines sponsored by the Department of the Environment throughout the country. In some cases these fellowships will be able to offer help on a national basis. In addition, some of the major units now being developed have their own environmental and scientific staff.

For the director of non-State-aided excavations scientific help may be difficult to obtain, often being dependent on local personnel and facilities in museums and universities. The larger museums may have at their disposal a comprehensive range of techniques; others will be only able to offer a minimal service with access to other facilities in urgent and important cases. Universities offer a wide but variable range of scientific aids to the excavations which they run or with which they are associated. It is, at the moment, largely up to the director to arrange what facilities he can within the comparatively restricted network of specialists, an unsatisfactory situation, but one unlikely to be improved in the immediate future. As a result, many excavations suffer from a partial or total lack of scientific and specialist help and as a result the full potential of the excavated evidence is not realized. Sometimes the aid of scientific amateurs can be enlisted. They will obviously vary in the quality and accuracy of their techniques, and considerable tact may be needed, first to persuade them to allow their work to be assessed by a professional, and then, perhaps, to dissuade them from carrying on. A veterinary surgeon may not be a zoological anatomist, and an industrial chemist may not be the man to ask to analyse your soil samples. In addition, they may not use techniques and criteria which are compatible with those used by the leading specialists in the field, so that their work cannot be readily assessed and compared with data from other excavations. It should be added that such difficulties also exist between professional specialists, though moves are being made to establish common criteria and methods in a number of the more widely used techniques of analysis, such as that of animal bones and the characteristics of pottery.

The battery of scientific information potentially available to the excavator is formidable, but, if it is to be fully exploited, requires a greater understanding of and sympathy with scientific method than has often been the case in the past.

Relationships between excavators and scientific specialists have often been bedevilled by difficulties arising from the lack of mutual understanding of each other's problems, and from the essentially part-time nature of much scientific involvement in archaeology. The problems have been succinctly described by

Mrs D. S.Wilson in an open letter to archaeologists (Wilson, 1973) which incorporates many valuable suggestions to archaeologists on the ways in which scientists should be treated. Equally, any scientist who is anxious to make the fullest contribution to an excavation should learn the scope and limitations of the techniques involved, ideally by taking part himself. It is far more satisfactory if a scientist can take his own samples, rather than receive them in a laboratory, even if they are accompanied by drawings and photographs of their contexts. The more understanding each has of the other's techniques, problems, and limitations, the greater will be the value of the joint work which they produce.

The use of scientific evidence

Excavators have tended either to seize on pieces of scientific evidence and give them undue weight in the support of their theories, or to relegate them to appendices, printed in the report beyond the acknowledgements, as if they bore little relevance to what was dug up. Pressure from the more forward-looking archaeologists and from scientists themselves, who see the potential of the information they can extract, has now made it *de rigueur* to send samples of all kinds for analysis, often without great thought of the relevance of the information which is likely to come from them. For instance, identification of a scatter of charcoal samples from the occupation layers of a medieval site is unlikely to add much to our knowledge of the arboreal flora of medieval Britain, and will only give a broad and diffuse picture of the trees growing in the vicinity and used for firewood. The information from these scraps of charcoal is, in most circumstances, not worth the considerable labour involved in identifying them. A large quantity of charcoal, clearly part of the structure of a burnt building, will be of more interest, especially if it can be shown that the sample comes from floor planking or weather-boarding, since the types of wood used for subsidiary structural elements are not well known.

The identification and analysis of a scatter of unstratified or poorly stratified mollusc shells, animal bones, mortar fragments or lumps of slag may simply not be worth the time it will undoubtedly take. Under these circumstances it is wise to ask the specialist to assess the probable importance of the material in the context of the excavation, rather than to collect it and send it, regardless, for analysis. This necessitates the specialist visiting the site, or at least being kept fully informed about the nature of the excavation and the contexts of any samples. This in itself would be a step forward from the situation in which the specialist never sees the site and perhaps does not even know it is being dug until the samples land on his desk. Only if the scientist, whether an environmentalist, a soil scientist, or an expert in mortars, slags, window glass or other materials, can discuss on the site the problems raised by the samples can he be expected to give a full appraisal of their significance rather than a mere identification and tentative interpretation. This is asking a lot. Since there are many excavations, all bristling with problems spanning the whole spectrum of scientific expertise, and few archaeological scientists, it is imperative that excavators help scientists to give the most effective service by prior consultation and by pruning requests for identification and analysis to those subjects and samples which are most relevant to the excavation, or the archaeology of the region, or which the scientist himself wants as comparative material.

It may be argued that an accumulation of small samples of apparently irrelevant material might eventually be synthesised in the manner of a large sample, but this is a decision to be made by the specialist in the discipline concerned. It is always possible, too, that a small sample may provide unequivocal evidence of something quite unexpected; the bones of an exotic animal, a vital fragment of a wall-painting or proof of an otherwise undetectable industrial process. But, in general, it is the large well-stratified samples that are likely to be the most useful, and to yield the most valid results.

If scientific reports on excavated material are to be comparable with one another it is important that the same criteria are used in the assessment and measurement of the samples. This again, is ultimately a matter for the specialists concerned, but archaeologists should be aware of the problems, and should perhaps initiate discussions aimed at solving them.

Excavators are as prone to simplifying scientific evidence as historians are to simplifying archaeological evidence. A prime example is in the use of radio-carbon dates, where too often the central date of what is, in fact, a bell-curve stretching over maybe two centuries, is taken as the most probable date for the sample, and a historical argument built on this assumption. There is no doubt that a long series of determinations can be the basis for revolutionary reassessments of conventional dating (see Renfrew (ed.), 1974) but a single radio-carbon date is beset by too many uncertainties to justify its use as more than a suggestion of the range within which the true date falls (see Mackie *et al.*, 1971). If the central radio-carbon date happens to coincide with the excavator's nascent theories, it is tempting not to point out in the report that the real date might be far from the central one.

Many other scientific dating techniques such as thermo-luminescence and remanent magnetism share the same lack of precision, and they should not be made to carry a greater weight of argument than they can bear. Dendrochronology can, under optimum conditions, give a fairly precise date for the felling of a tree for timber. But it would be unwise to date a whole building on the evidence of one of its beams, which might have been reused from an earlier building. Here again, the larger the number of samples the more reliable the conclusions which can be drawn from them.

The arts and sciences which converge in an excavation are all imprecise in varying degrees. The wider the areas from which we draw our evidence, the more detailed our digging and recording, the more samples we take, the more techniques we deploy, the nearer we shall get to the truth about the site in the periods which concern us.

Excavation and environment

In the past the study of the environment relating to archaeological sites has often been peripheral to the excavation of structures, the recovery of a dating sequence or a series of pottery types. In many cases the environment in which the site developed was completely ignored. These attitudes are now changing and with techniques for recovering and interpreting environmental evidence being rapidly developed and multiplied ancient environments are seen to be crucial for the full understanding of the siting, the food economy, the exploitation of the surrounding countryside and in some cases the uses to which the site has been put.

Most excavated sites contain a wealth of biological evidence which, properly interpreted, can add another dimension to the understanding of the site and its region by producing otherwise unobtainable information about the contemporary flora and fauna, pests, diseases, climate and weather. Seeds, mollusca, insects, and the elusive bones of the smaller mammals, birds and fishes, are not so easily recovered as potsherds and food bones, but techniques of sieving, both wet and dry, can produce significant quantities of material from the majority of sites. The extraction of pollen is a more specialized technique which supplements the information given by seeds and other preserved plant remains.

A number of wet-sieving and froth-flotation methods for the recovery of organic remains have been developed recently. Some are quite simple; others, for use on large-scale excavations, are designed for the continual processing of large quantities of soil.

The simplest method is the use of sieves of various meshes through which the soil, made into a slurry, is passed. An even more basic method of recovering the larger fragments is to agitate a sieve full of the deposit in a barrow filled with water. Various more sophisticated mechanical flotation and sieving machines have been developed. Their chief attribute is cheapness achieved by the ingenious use of scrap machinery. A number of plans have been published, among them the machine used by David Williams at Siraf (Williams, 1973), a mechanical sieve developed in Italy (Guerreschi, 1973) and the machine developed by the Marc 3 Unit in Hampshire (Lapinskas, 1975). To these must be added the Ankara and Cambridge machines described in Renfrew, Monk, and Murphy, 1976.

Some environmentalists believe that flotation machines should be used with reservation, since they are apt to distort the sample due to some of the specimens floating while others of the same species do not. Tiny snail shells full of silt, for example, may sink, while those that happen to be empty float. There is a case for recovering the complete evidence from some large samples of the material by washing and sieving everything, including the sediments in which the organic remains are embedded. Only in this way will control samples be recovered, samples which will monitor the recovery rate from the flotation of very large quantities of deposits.

As in all other sampling techniques the larger and more representative the samples the more valid the results are likely to be. If possible, the samples should be taken by the specialist himself. They should not simply be derived from the pits, ditches, floors, or other structures in which we are particularly interested, but from a wide variety of contexts (if not the whole site), in order to provide controls and comparanda.

The nature of the soil, as well as its degree of waterlogging will affect the survival of bones, or seeds, or pollen. Any assessment of environmental evidence must take this into account, and no doubt the specialist consulted will do so, but it is important that the precise nature of the soil and the conditions under which samples were taken should be made clear so that valid comparisons can be made with other sites.

The analysis of preserved organic materials, of pollen, seeds, insects, snails and the microscopic remains of plants has implications which are only just beginning to be realized. As an example, work on the silt from a Roman sewer system in York has provided a spectacular demonstration of the information to be inferred from microscopic remains. The presence of sewerage flies, human intestinal parasites, and sponge spicules (derived from toilet sponges imported from the Mediterranean) in some of the channels contrasted with entirely different assemblages from other channels. One of the other systems contained grain beetles and grain weevils, derived in all probability from a grain storage building, while another series contained mollusca, water beetles, pollen, and other evidence which suggests that it drained a closed, artificially heated baths building. Thus the presence of long-destroyed buildings can be postulated on the microscopic evidence alone (Buckland, 1974).

Recent work on past climates has shown that there is now sufficient evidence from glaciology, environmental archaeology, and historical records to justify postulating climatic reasons for some of the major changes in agriculture and population movements over the last 10-15,000 years (Lamb, 1972, esp. 170-95). For example the well-attested increase in ploughland in the twelfth—thirteenth centuries AD with its corresponding increase in population and the expansion and creation of villages and towns, followed by the contraction of the fourteenth and fifteenth centuries, can be attributed, at least in part, to slight but significant shifts in the levels of temperature and rainfall. An earlier and more dramatic dissimilarity from our present climate is well attested in the Bronze Age between the 6th millennium BC, and the 3rd millennium BC, when average land temperatures were 2°-3°C higher than today's figures and the sea was 2°C warmer. As a result oak, elm and lime trees were growing in Britain up to 1000 feet higher than the present limit. (The drop in the average temperature is about 3°C per 1000 feet of height). Clearly, such considerations are vital in the interpretation of our excavated sites and the understanding of their economy, the character of housing and the recreation of life on and around the site.

The changes in the flora and particularly in woodland species may record the clearance of forest and the expansion of agriculture, changes which may be reflected in the composition of the buried soils of the site. Such changes may be paralleled and supported by an increase in domesticated animal bones, a corresponding decrease in the bones of wild species and the first appearance of querns on the site. Conversely, an increase in woodland or scrub species in the pollen spectrum may indicate a reversion to forest, paralleling shrinkage or temporary abandonment of the settlement.

An introduction to pollen analysis will be found in Brothwell and Higgs, 1969, Chapter 14 and RESCUE has recently published a booklet *First Aid for Seeds* (Renfrew, Monk and Murphy, 1976) which concisely describes the preservation of seeds in archaeological deposits, sampling, flotation and the storage for specialist analysis. It is essential reading for excavators.

Analysis of the animal bones from a site will, of course, give information about the meat eaten by the inhabitants, but it may go further and throw an unexpected light on the marketing of the meat, or, by implication, the comparative poverty of the consumers. For instance, if all the meat bones are from butcher's joints it is probable that the animals were slaughtered elsewhere, as is the practice today; but if the remains include horns, skulls, hooves and so on, the animals probably came into the settlement or town 'on the hoof'. Sometimes a change in the practice can be observed. For example, the meat sold in the centre of a Roman town in its heyday may all be butchered, with the horns going elsewhere in the town to be made into handles, the hooves to be made into glue, the hides into leather and so forth. Later, in the town's decline, contracted and with a changed economy, live animals may well be sold, perhaps bartered, in the market. The poorer a community, the more it will exploit every scrap of the animal, just as in recent times, no part of the family pig was wasted, and the evidence will appear in the rubbish pits. Sometimes variations of the animal contents of rubbish pits within communities can point to differing social strata. On the site of the Blackfriars in Worcester three pits, all datable by pottery to the period 1480-1560, showed marked variations in their bone content, one of them containing bones from older animals, whose meat would be tougher and less palatable, together with less variety of species. Though the deductions cannot be certain, the implications are that the households using this pit were poorer or had, at least, less attractive meat, than the families using the other two pits (Chaplin in Barker et al., 1970). Such analysis and reasoning can of course be extended into much wider fields.

The character of animal diseases detectable in surviving bone is also of great interest, though here again, the more samples which can be examined from the region the sounder will be the conclusions drawn from them — one could hardly postulate a disastrous murrain from two individuals.

In a long and well-stratified sample the introduction of new strains of animals may be detected. Does this reflect an immigrant community, or simply good husbandry? Here other varieties of evidence would have to be brought to bear. If the introduction of the new variety coincided with the introduction of a new type of pottery the case for immigrants would be strengthened; and so on. Clearly, once again, the larger and more carefully dug and recorded the sample, the more valid and illuminating will be the deductions which can be drawn from it.

Many of these scientific disciplines are still in the data-collecting stages, since it is only recently that their potential has been realised by archaeologists. It is incumbent on those of us who dig to help to develop and refine these techniques through the closest possible cooperation with their practitioners.

The study of building materials

Many archaeological sites, particularly, though not exclusively, in towns, consist of or contain large areas of hard-core foundations, pebble surfaces, rubble spreads, clay floors, post-sockets and other remnants of former structures. The study of these layers and features from the structural point of view is an unexploited source of information supplementing that obtained from the study of the soils formed naturally in and around the site. For example, it may be very difficult to determine the length of time that a pebble floor was in use, especially in aceramic periods. Exhaustive tests on the wearing capacity of surfaces of all kinds made in the course of research into road construction enable close estimates to be made of the length of time taken to wear facets on pebbles of varying hardness. Equally, long term experiments on the wear of paving stones, stone stair treads and thresholds make close estimates of wear-time on these features available. While there will always, in archaeological terms, be imponderables, such as the estimated numbers of persons using a surface per day, any experimentally proven figures are better than guess-work as a basis for argument. Similarly, an analysis of the load-bearing capacity of the various surfaces assumed to be foundations may avoid interpretations which are impractical or even ludicrous.

On the other hand, a half-metre thick layer of make-up on one of the sites at Wroxeter was shown by the materials engineer who was consulted to have been laid wet, as a slurry, rather like pre-mixed concrete. In this form, its load-bearing capacity would be considerably increased, so that it can be assumed that it was laid as a deliberate foundation for the timber structure subsequently built on it, and not as an accumulation of soil and debris fortuitously used.

When a post or a sill-beam supporting a building rests on the ground, the area under and round the timber becomes permanently compacted. This compaction can be measured by simple methods dependent upon the differential penetration of the surface by a probe. In this way the existence of former buildings may be demonstrated (see the forthcoming report on the excavation of the Baths Basilica at Wroxeter).

Another example of the sort of information which may be sought from the study of the behaviour of materials is one from the same excavation at Wroxeter, where a large fragment of masonry, apparently part of a window embrasure, had fallen from one of the walls of the baths basilica, apparently that of the clerestory, and embedded itself in a sequence of sandy and pebble floors. By measuring the degree of compaction at a number of points under and around the fallen masonry, and then by weighing the fragment, it is hoped to be able to calculate the height from which it fell. As it is part of a window this should give the approximate height of the clerestory windows above the ground.

Though the information supplied by the study of the materials used on our sites may not always be very precise, this approach, coupled with that of the natural soil scientist (exemplified in Limbrey, 1975), should add considerably to our understanding of their stratigraphic development and the intentions of past builders.

12

Synthesis: The History of the Site

The ultimate aim of an excavation is to draw together the very varied strands of evidence into a coherent whole: the sequence of structural and natural events which have taken place on the site from the earliest occupation (or before) up to the present day. To this structural framework is added all the converging cultural, economic, domestic, and environmental evidence which can be detected and assessed.

It has been suggested in Chapter 5 that we shall approach the truth about the site more closely if we attempt to identify and explain the origin of every observable feature. In doing so we impose on ourselves a discipline that prevents us from ignoring awkward or inconvenient features. Similarly the use of a formal matrix or graph, such as that described on pp. 198-199, compels us to consider the relative positions of all layers and features and not simply to take a broad view of the more important or extensive.

Another exercise, which helps to clarify thinking at the later, synthetic stage of the excavation, is to take at random, or at 50 to 100 year intervals, a number of dates which fall within the known period of occupation of the site and to write descriptions or, better, make sketches of the *whole* site at those times. This ensures that every part of the site will be considered as part of the continuum of occupation and not just those structures which can be given relatively firm dates. There will, inevitably, be a good deal of uncertainty about the nature of the open spaces round buildings, and, more particularly, the survival of old buildings when new ones are erected. Usually we tend to simplify and rationalise the periods of occupation of our sites, partly because it is easier to describe and particularly to illustrate these periods as a series of complete rebuildings across the site. However, as an almost cursory glance at a group of farm buildings, a small village, or an area in a town centre, will show, the situation is in reality kaleidoscopic, with single buildings being replaced while older buildings on each side remain, and with the infilling of gardens or vacant plots, the demolition of old buildings and their sites left open, to say nothing of repairs and extensions, such as kitchens or garages, to existing buildings, and more ephemeral structures, like garden sheds, coming and going at even shorter intervals.

Such a kaleidoscopic, one might almost say contrapuntal, interpretation of an excavation is not easy to achieve, mainly due to the limitations of our ability to date precisely the building and demolition of structures. Another major cause of difficulty in phasing is the impossibility of demonstrating horizontal relationships unambiguously across the site. For example one may be able to say that both Buildings IV and V are earlier than III, and demonstrate this by means of a feature matrix, but one may not be able to demonstrate the chronological relationship of IV and V to each other, if they have no common horizontal stratigraphy beyond their mutual relationship to III. Under these circumstances, alternative phase diagrams and plans would be necessary. However, if the site contains dozens of buildings, the permutations and combinations, all possible but none demonstrable, might be endless, and difficult to describe and illustrate without an unwieldy proliferation of phases and sub-phases. This detailed illustration would not only be tedious and potentially confusing, but also exceedingly costly. Yet what is the alternative? Certainly not simplification in the name of tidiness or economy. If we are to approach a true description of the site (and this must be the first aim of any excavation) we must interpret and present the evidence as fully as we can, even if this means the loss of a strong story line such as the celebrated narrative introduction to the Maiden Castle report (Wheeler, 1943).

Archaeological evidence and historical documents

The relationship between archaeology and documented history has been the subject of a good deal of heart-searching in recent years. Perhaps the two most thoughtful and cogent discussions of the subject are Wainwright's (1962) and Dymond's (1974). There is no room here to summarize their arguments and the reader is referred to the books as a whole.

The establishment of the relationships between the archaeological evidence from an excavated site and historical documents relating to that site is full of pitfalls and must be approached with caution. It is only too easy to equate drastic changes in the archaeological evidence, such as rebuilding after burning, or abandonment of the site, with well-documented historical incidents. However, not every fire in south-eastern Britain in the mid-first century was due to Boudicca, nor every fourteenth-century village abandonment to the Black Death. On many sites, it would be very difficult indeed to detect the date and impact of the Norman Conquest. Building techniques, house styles and pottery types remain the same, or change progressively throughout the period. Perhaps only on defensive sites such as Sulgrave (B. K. Davison, personal communication) where a ring-work is imposed on an apparently undefended domestic complex, could a sudden and radical political change be postulated, though the cumulative evidence from fieldwork and excavation of castles would undoubtedly point to a new intensity in fortification and a change in military structures. However, as Davison has pointed out (1969) it cannot be shown that the new types of fortification (motte and bailey castles) were introduced from elsewhere, so that on purely archaeological grounds one could postulate an English conquest of Normandy (or a conquest of England and Normandy by a third party).

Perhaps the most thoroughly integrated study of a settlement by excavation and by examination of the documentary sources is that of Store Valby (Steensberg, 1975), where a mass of evidence relating not only to the excavated farms, their buildings and their furniture has been adduced, but where, by a close study of the registers of births, marriages and deaths, ownership, tenancies and the relationships and social standing of generations of farmers have been correlated with the buildings they lived in and worked from. In this case, as in that of so many deserted village sites, the archaeological evidence was often tenuous and ambiguous, and here the documentary descriptions of the farms at various periods illuminated the fieldwork and enabled more well-founded interpretations to be made than could have emerged with either form of evidence alone. The weakness of the excavation, as the author admits, was the paucity of environmental evidence and the summary treatment of the animal bones, of which there were insufficient for a full statistical analysis. The work remains a model of its kind, however, as yet unequalled by any British excavation.

A model interpretation

Another most illuminating interpretative study of a settlement site is that of the Glastonbury Lake Village by D. L. Clarke (1972). In this reconsideration of Bulleid and Gray's excavations carried out between 1892 and 1907 (published 1911 and 1917) the objective was 'simply to explore the old data in new ways' (*ibid*, 802). The method used was 'the erection of a set of alternative models, explicitly justified and derived from many sources, embodying alternative reasonable assumptions and then the explicit testing between the alternatives of their consequences for predictive accuracy and goodness of fit, by using skilfully devised experiments in the field or upon the recorded observations' (*ibid*, 801).

It is significant that the excavation chosen by Clarke is not only one of the few of a *complete* settlement available, but that in addition, being waterlogged, the retrieval of organic material and objects was very high, supplementing by many whole factors the information which would have been achieved if the site had been dry. The same study carried out on a partial excavation of a much-eroded or otherwise damaged site would have started with so much less information that the potential results would have been a good deal less trustworthy. As Clarke himself said: 'No archaeological study can be any better than the reliability of the observations upon which it is based and the assumptions that frame the development of its analysis and interpretation.' To my mind, the reliability of evidence from settlement sites depends on quantity and the size of the sample, as well as on the accuracy of the observations made on the spot.

Another distinct advantage that the Glastonbury site has for analysis and study of this kind is that the settlement was a multiple of structures which were repeatedly reproduced. There were none of the more or less violent changes of occupation and use which characterize many sites or parts of sites. On the one hand, we have the type of site which, by reason of the comparative homogeneity of its development, allows the stages of that development to be more easily compared one with another, and its relationships with its economic and cultural territory to be more confidently predicted. Such sites include some deserted medieval villages (Wharram Percy will, eventually, no doubt, provide a classic example for the Glastonbury type of analysis): extensively excavated Saxon settlement sites, such as Chalton (Addyman, Leigh and Hughes, 1972) and Mucking (Jones, 1974), and prehistoric sites such as hill-forts where one of the most pressing problems is the relationship of defended settlements to their contemporary valley counterparts. In a slightly varied way cemeteries excavated on a large scale would also lend themselves to statistical analysis and model building. On the other hand, towns, whether Roman or later, are more difficult, because of the multiplicity of structural types, the constant destruction of earlier deposits by later building and the consequent losses of artefacts as well as structural evidence. Nevertheless, at Novgorod, the area of the town excavated in the 1950s and '60s was more or less homogeneous in its development and would allow just the sort of analysis demonstrated by Clarke (Thompson, 1967).

Clarke's Glastonbury paper, which is more concerned with the direct results of excavations than many of the other applications of analytical archaeology, is essential reading for would-be directors.

The convergence of varying kinds of evidence: an example

This example, again taken from the motte and bailey castle site at Hen Domen, Montgomery, demonstrates in a microcosm how a number of different techniques can be made to converge on one problem, each, in its own way, reinforcing the others.

It had been noticed that the outer ditches and ramparts of the castle bailey apparently overlay (and were therefore later than) slight traces of ridge and furrow in the field north of the site (A on fig. 7). Since even relatively datable early ridge and furrow is rare, especially on the Welsh border, the possibility that this field system was pre-Norman was of great interest. When trowelling of a small area under the rampart revealed a buried soil which itself covered plough furrows cut into the undisturbed boulder clay, it was decided to contour survey the adjacent field and to examine the evidence buried under the rampart. At the same time, the documentary evidence was re-examined.

The various techniques used are here listed for convenience:

Field work: the field adjacent to the site was photographed in various lights, including car headlights, in order to observe the slight undulations of the ground in the greatest detail. It was then contour surveyed on a grid with 1 metre intervals and the contours were drawn at 20cm. vertical intervals. The visible ridges and furrows were plotted by interpolation.

Computer print out: the grid of readings was fed into a computer which was programmed to draw the resultant contours in a three-dimensional print-out. This was more objective than drawing by eye, and necessary because there was some scepticism about the existence of the field system (fig. 6).

Excavation: a 20m. length of the rampart was trowelled down to the buried soil and its surface contour surveyed at 2cm. vertical intervals. This demonstrated the existence of ridge and furrow buried under the rampart. The buried soil was removed and the visible plough furrows plotted. Amorphous holes dug through the buried soil and into the underlying subsoil were interpreted as places where bushes or small trees had been removed.

Pollen analysis: samples of the soil buried under the rampart were sent for pollen analysis. The botanist concerned was not told at the time the implications of what he might find. As a result of the analysis he deduced that the pollen indicated that the area in which the rampart was built was open land, which had been used for arable agriculture, perhaps for cereals. The abandonment had been of several years' duration and the area had perhaps been used for rough grazing.

Carbon 14 dating: A sample of charcoal from the buried soil was dated by the laboratory at Birmingham to AD 980 ± 290.

Finds: the only find from the buried soil was a fragment of Roman pottery carved into an amulet (?) and incised with what appears to be a letter A. As pottery was virtually unknown on the Welsh border between *c.* AD 400 and *c.* AD 1100, the Roman sherd would have been an object of considerable curiosity, worthy, in an aceramic period, of being carved into an amulet.

Documentary evidence: Domesday Book (fol. 254, a, 1.) is explicit that Roger, Earl of Shrewsbury, built a castle, which he called Montgomery, in an area of waste which had formerly contained 22 vills but which, in the time of Edward the Confessor, had been a hunting ground for three Saxon thegns. Roger was made Earl of Shrewsbury in 1070 or 1071, so that the castle (which can be shown to be Hen Domen) was built then or shortly afterwards.

It will be seen that any one or two facets of this evidence, taken independently, would be suggestive but not conclusive, whereas together they provide incontrovertible proof of a ridged field system, probably belonging to a Saxon vill, and abandoned before the Norman Conquest. The evidence is published in full in Barker and Lawson, 1971.

The more varied the forms of evidence which can be adduced in our investigations the richer and more unequivocal will be the results. There is now an enormous variety of aids at our disposal. By understanding their potential through discussion with the specialists who use them and by prior planning we must learn to deploy these techniques to the greatest advantage.

A much more intensive, and perhaps the best, example of intergrated landscape archaeology is C.C. Taylor's study of Whiteparish in Wiltshire (Taylor, 1967), which the reader is urged to study.

All excavations are local history

However widespread the remifications of an excavation may ultimately prove to be, initially it is a piece of local history, embedded in the immediate landscape, and relating to the area around it. Even sites of the remoter prehistoric periods were settled by men influenced by at least some, and perhaps many, of the factors which influenced Anglo-Savon farmers and medieval traders. The gulf which separates so many local historians from archaeologists (and archaeologists from local historians) is regrettable and unhelpful to both. The undocumented and the documented history of a parish or a district must be seen as a continuum from geological times to the present, and though we may be interested in one period more than others, we shall stultify our work if we do not see it in its broadest context. The excavator has therefore to see his site from two points of view, one vertically though time as part of the development of settlement, agriculture, industry, religion or architecture — the cultural pattern of the area; and the other horizontally through space, when the site is seen as one of a contemporary group or series of related groups, which may cover the whole of a continent. The legionary fortresses at Gloucester or Lincoln are facets of the local histories of those cities, they are also examples of a type of fortification which once covered most of the known world. These are obvious examples, and the excavators of these cities see their fortresses in both contexts. But how many pagan Saxon cemeteries, or open Iron-Age settlements are related by their excavators to the siting of the nearby medieval village or its Saxon predecessor, or the expansion and contraction of settlement in the periods before and after those being dug?

Another element of landscape study often neglected by archaeologists is the geographical development of the area, whether natural or influenced by man. For example, the rise or fall of the water table due to deforestation or afforestation, to a programme of land drainage or the development of bog may be crucial in the siting of villages and their wells and springs, or in the pattern or character of their agriculture. Similarly, the study of the courses of rivers and streams may be of the utmost importance to the archaeologist. Until comparatively recently, the Roman city of Wroxeter was thought to have lost as much as a quarter of its area through erosion by the River Severn. A geographer, David Pannett, working independently of archaeology, has shown that the river has hardly changed its course in the last 5000 years, so that the remains of the city are intact. Recent excavation on the eastern defences overlooking the river strongly supports this view, which has revolutionary implications for the siting of the legionary fortresses which underlie the civil settlement, for the siting of the Roman river crossing, the ultimate size of the city, and many other problems.

There is little doubt that consultation with local historians and geographers could add yet another dimension to the understanding of an excavation.

Works of art as archaeological evidence

From the sculpture and cave-paintings of Palaeolithic times onwards, works of art can be of great assistance in the interpretation of contemporary archaeological evidence. There is little need to stress the value of Egyptian tomb-painting, Greek sculpture or Roman wall painting in the understanding of the material remans of these civilisations. There are fewer survivals of art from very early times, in north-western Europe, but medieval and later drawings and paintings of towns with their defences, individual buildings, markets, workshops, fields, animals and implements can all be helpful in the understanding of excavated remains, while figure paintings and carvings, in particular those on tombs, can elucidate problems of dress ornament and detail.

The chief difficulty in the use of works of art as interpretative evidence is to determine whether or not the depiction is contemporary with the incident depicted, it it makes use of traditional forms, or alternatively, whether the work sets a traditional scene in dress and surroundings contemporary with the artist. Many Anglo-Saxon illuminated manuscripts use architectural backgrounds which can be traced back to Byzantine or Roman models, so that it would be unwise to use them as evidence for Anglo-Saxon building styles. Conversely, it was common practice for later painters from Masaccio onward to set Biblical scenes in their own landscapes, towns, and buildings, so that the soldiers guarding Christ's tomb in a painting by Mantegna are a better guide to fifteenth-century Italian uniform than to first-century Roman, and the dresses in a Nottingham alabaster, the alter vases shown in a fifteenth-century alterpiece, or the farming practices in a book of hours or on a misericord are likely to be up-to-date rather than historical.

On the other hand, tomb effigies may be added much later than the burials of the persons they commemorate. The effigy, in Shrewsbury Abbey, of Roger de Montgomery, who died in 1094, is dressed in the armour of a thirteenth-century knight. If we did not know this from the external evidence of many other thirteenth-century carvings we might well take this sculpture as evidence of Roger's dress.

In the later Renaissance and in the seventeenth and eighteenth centuries, painting became increasingly naturalistic, culminating in Canaletto's use of the *camera obscura*. As a result, the paintings and drawings of these centuries are a rich source of information on contemporary buildings, dress, furniture and pottery.

As an example fig. 69 is a remarkable sixteenth century engraving which seems

69 Giulio Campagnola (1482-c.1515), *The Old Shepherd* engraving (Ashmolean Museum, Oxford).

seems to show a timber castle standing on a motte or natural mound surrounded by a ditch. If this is so, it is one of the few realistic contemporary representations of a timber castle. The Bayeux Tapestry castles straddle the dividing line between the descriptive and the decorative, while most other illustrations of castles such as the magnificent series in *Les Très Riches Heures du Duc de Berry*, are of stone buildings.

The engraving shows a somewhat ramshackle, perhaps roofed, bridge leading from a gate tower over the ditch to a complex of buildings which includes a great hall, ? two towers (the second just appearing over the roof of the hall) and other roofed buildings, one with a louvred smoke outlet, perhaps surrounding an inner courtyard. The construction throughout is of vertical timbers which appear to have rotted characteristically at their lower ends. The buildings are of two storeys, with the upper storeys jettied. There is a suggestion of a postern towards the right hand side of the nearest building and perhaps a garde-robe structure at the opposite end. The hall has two chimneys. On the extreme right is a complicated jettied structure apparently built out over a valley.

The question is, of course, how fanciful is this drawing, and how far can it be used as a guide in the interpretation of a timber castle excavation? On the one hand, the careful realism of the shepherd, dressed in contemporary clothes, inspires confidence in the castle's authenticity. On the other hand, some of the structural details are dubious and impractical. The impression given is that the castle is not imaginary, or derived from a long line of other background drawings, but is of a building known to the artist, though drawn, as buildings so often are, without an understanding of structural principles, so that it does not stand up too well to architectural scrutiny. Nevertheless, since we have so little to guide us, it should not be discarded altogether. The general layout, with its piling of buildings together on the mound, is borne out by surviving stone castles and the excavated evidence, so far as it goes, of timber castles. (For example, the bailey at Hen Domen was crowded with buildings, some of them certainly of two storeys.)

Such a drawing may suggest solutions to otherwise intractable interpretative problems, though the dangers of arguing from one individual example to another are obvious, and it may be contended that a timber castle in Italy is minimally relevant to one in England or Wales.

Used critically, however, contemporary illustrations can be another and other- wise unparalleled form of evidence, especially helpful in areas where the written evidence fails.

A recent and most interesting example of the use of sculpture and painting in the interpretation of excavated evidence will be found in 'The Trelleborg House Reconsidered' (Schmidt, 1973).

13

Publication—an Obligation

At the time of writing, we are in the midst of a debate on the nature of archaeological publication. There is a consensus of opinion that an excavation is not finished until a full report is published or the evidence made available in another form. Some would go further and say that an unpublished excavated site has been destroyed or mutilated as surely as if it had been bulldozed. The problem of publication has become more serious as the number of excavations has increased in the face of the accelerating destruction of sites. It has been argued that, since the rate of destruction will probably slow down by the end of the century as development of all kinds slows and because by then most of our vulnerable sites will have gone, we should concentrate on retrieving and recording evidence from our vanishing sites, and leave full publication for later, when there is less pressure. Though in theory this argument may have something to commend it, it would not work in practice because publication is not an abstract activity based entirely on record cards, drawings, photographs and a roomful of finds, but relies also on an intimate knowledge of the site and its context, and on the contemplation of the ground itself at the time of excavation. Thus it follows that the director and his assistants are the only ones who can write a full report. Publication by committees, or by postgraduates who have never seen the sites they are publishing, or posthumous publication by professional ghost writers is better than nothing but falls short of the ideal of swift publication by the persons responsible for the excavation, which should become the norm.

There is no doubt that the marshalling of the evidence, the crystallization of the results and the physical writing of the report are very different activities from the fieldwork which produced the evidence in the first place, and that a considerable number of excavators find writing tedious.

Only recently has it been realised that it probably takes as many man-hours to prepare an excavation for publication as it did to dig the site in the first place.

Provisional planning, not only for money, but for *time* for post-excavation, pre-publication work should therefore be made before the excavation begins. The director must resist pressure to over-excavate, to go on from one site to the next, piling up a backlog of reports which will seem to grow as it recedes in time. Only thus can he fulfil his academic responsibilities to the site and his moral obligation to all those who have worked on it.

What to publish, and where?

Ideally, all the evidence should be published, in the manner of Pitt Rivers. But, in these days of complex and detailed excavations and high printing costs, only very small digs can be published in their entirety; most have to be summarized to a greater or lesser degree and unpublished information stored where it will be accessible to other workers.

There are three chief categories of reader interested in the publication of excavations. First there are those who are not only concerned with the results, but who may (perhaps should) wish to test the validity of the results by assessing all, or any part, of the evidence. They will include other archaeologists, specialists in the archaeological sciences, and hopefully, historians, geographers, archaeology students and others.

The second category will be members of the general archaeological public who are primarily interested in the results and the methods employed to achieve them, together with a summary of the evidence. The sort of people I have in mind are the members of the national and local archaeological societies, especially those who have contributed funds towards the excavation, volunteers on excavations, teachers of history, members of extramural classes and so forth.

The third category is the general public (including, particularly, children), most of whom have a latent interest in the subject which can be brought out and developed by concise and interesting publications coupled with good museum displays and exhibitions. This last group is by no means the least important since from them, the taxpayers, British archaeology derives most of its funds, and from their children will derive the next generation of archaeologists.

In this context it is important to remember that Pitt Rivers' great volumes were written for and distributed only to those other workers whom he thought would be interested in them:

> I have adhered to my plan of printing this volume, like the last, privately, although I have been urged by some to publish it. The numerous letters which I have received from this country and the Continent, afford ample evidence that the last volume has been appreciated by actual workers, for whose benefit alone it is intended: but it would be unreasonable to expect that a work of so much detail should interest the general public, or even those who care only for the results, without taking trouble to inquire into the means by which the

evidence has been obtained. For the same reason I have not been lavish in my presentations of the volumes, but have retained a certain number for future distribution.

The circle of the General's archaeological acquaintances was comparatively small. Now interest in the major excavations is worldwide and the problem of supplying more than a lengthy summary of results is more difficult, either being prohibitively expensive or involving the enquirer in a journey to London, Copenhagen, Los Angeles, or wherever the records are stored.

The tradition of publishing excavations to the highest possible standards of typography and printing, such as is found in HMSO volumes, the Research Reports of the Society of Antiquaries, *Archaeologia*, or the major national or period journals, is one that dies hard. It is undeniable that such volumes are a joy to handle and sometimes a pleasure to read; nevertheless, the present scale of archaeological fieldwork and the vastly increasing costs of printing deny such lavish treatment to all but the few, and therefore cheaper but workmanlike methods are being brought into use. One of the most successful innovations in this field has been the production of British Archaeological Reports, a private venture into the field of archaeological publishing. These volumes are in A4 size, which, though inconvenient in book shelves, allows larger-scale illustrations than the conventional quarto. They are printed lithographically from plates made direct from perfect typescripts, which are usually produced on electric typewriters with larger and more elegant typefaces than manual machines. Since it is incumbent on the author to produce the finished typescript, together with the illustrations, the work of the printers is minimized, thus speeding-up production and cutting costs such as those of type-setting. The resulting volumes are clear and serviceable, and though not as elegant as conventional productions, they provide a fast and economical means of publication, and one which, unlike the usual channels, pays royalties to the author. Nevertheless it is impracticable, even in BAR volumes, to publish all the evidence from large and highly detailed excavations so that other methods of information dissemination, storage and retrieval are actively being discussed.

In October 1975 the Department of the Environment published *Principles of Publication in Rescue Archaeology*, a report by a working party of the Ancient Monuments Board for England Committee for Rescue Archaeology. This paper discusses the crises in publication, particularly with reference to rescue excavations, though its conclusions and recommendations apply in many respects to all excavation publications.

As the report is readily available from the Department of the Environment, it need not be extensively summarized here. However, some of its arguments and conclusions are so crucial that they are worth repeating. The paper defines the successive levels of recording used in excavations thus:

The results of excavation are successively, in practice, refined through four levels of records, as follows:

Data

Level	Site descriptions	Loose material
Level I	The site itself and general notes, old letters, previous accounts, etc.	Excavated finds
Level II	Site note-books, recording forms, drawings, sound-recorded tapes.	Finds records, X-rays photographs, negatives colour transparencies.
Level III	Full illustration and description of all structural and strati-graphical relaionships.	Classified finds-lists and finds-drawings, and all specialist analyses.
Level IV	Synthesised descriptions with supporting data.	Selected finds and specialist reports relevant to synthesis.

It goes on to define what the working party sees as the future objectives for the organisation of this material:

Although publication at Level III, i.e. in full detail, has not yet become an economic impossibility for small excavations, we are agreed that, *provided certain conditions are fulfilled*, refined publication at Level IV should be the objective in future for all rescue excavations and indeed, for archaeological excavations in general. The conditions, which are essential, are:

that all the original records of the excavation, properly organised and curated, are housed in readily accessible form in a permanent archive.

that data at what we have described as Level III are readily available on request.

This presupposes an archive with duplication and, if possible, computer print-out facilities and equally demands from the excavator a high standard of preparation of Level III data, equal to that required for publication itself. The Level III record is the one which is often only cursorily treated at present.

Appendix I summarizes its recommendations for the storage and availability of excavated data thus:

SUMMARY OF RECOMMENDED ARRANGEMENTS FOR STORAGE AND AVAILABILITY OF EXCAVATION DATA

(See paragraph 2.8)

Level	Site Descriptions	Loose Material	Availability
I	The site itself and general notes, old letters, previous accounts, etc.	Excavated finds	Storage in museums.
II	Site note-books, recording forms, drawings, sound-recorded tapes	Finds records, X-rays, photographs, negatives, colour transparancies	Available for inspection inspection at museum or regional or national archive
III	Full illustration and description of all structural and relationships	Classified finds - lists and finds - drawings, and all analyses	Publication in journal or occasional papers, as required, or available as duplicates, mircrofiche, microfilm or computer print-out
IV	Synthesises descriptions with supporting data	Selected finds and specialist reports relevant to synthesis	Publication in multiple copies

One solution not mentioned in the report lies in the availability of rapid and comparatively cheap photographic reproductions. If the site is photographed vertically in colour negatives as described in Chapter 9, a complete mosaic of the site can be obtained for the cost of the prints. If, in addition, the drawings are microfilmed, a complete set, to any scale, can be produced, again for the price of the prints, or the whole site can be examined, by microfilm reader. The published report could be reduced, in microfiche form, to a small package. A reader in any country, equipped with this, or a copy of the published report, who adds to it stereoscopic cover in colour together with copies of all the plans and finds distribution plots will have a complete record of the excavation at minimal cost, without the necessity of travelling to the central archive.

In recent years the debate over publication has tended to crystallize over the value of microfiche as a substitute for, or a supplement to, written reports, published in the traditional manner. While there is no question that microfiche is cheaper than traditional printing, it has one or two fundamental disadvantages. Drawings on microfiche cannot be enlarged bigger than the screen of the micro-fiche reader, a much smaller size than that of a fold-out drawing, though 35mm. microfilm, mounted as slides projected on to a screen would overcome this objection. It would also be necessary to use colour film if the original drawings were in more than one colour. Comparison between one or more drawings is difficult if only one reader is available, and the publication of very large, detailed excavations in a series of joining sheets with interpretative sheets for comparison would be impossible in microfiche. There is also no substitute for transparent overlays, exemplified so well in *The Future of London's Past* (Biddle, Hudson and Heighway, 1973). Over and above these technicalities, the majority of archaeo-logists consulted by the writer would rather read books in the train or by the fire or in bed.

It will be interesting to see if these attitudes change, as microfiche reading machines become, as some predict, household furniture.

An alternative to microfiche which has not, I think, been previously suggested, is that used to produce *The Compact Edition of the Oxford English Dictionary*. In this edition, four pages of the original are reduced photographically to the size of one of the original pages. The resulting type-size can be read comfortably with a reading lens. An advantage of this method, especially for photo-litho printed books, is that the texts of lists, highly-detailed reports to which reference might need to be made while reading the main text, and other matter which would otherwise be microfiched could all be bound together in a single volume. It is much cheaper and less trouble to use a magnifying glass from time to time than to resort to a microfiche reader.

Publication of long-term excavations presents a particular problem: whether to wait until the excavation is finished before publishing all but short interim reports (when the task may be overwhelmingly large) or to publish a series of 'final' reports on each stage of the excavation, reports which may prove to be invalid in important aspects as the excavation proceeds. The dilemma is accentuated if the excavation is examining all the periods of the site's occupation simultaneously, by means of trenches or areas which cut through all the occupation deposits. This may happen as the result of a policy decision, or may be unavoidable, in for instance a town, where excavation is perforce piecemeal as sites become available, or where a site is too big to be dug as a whole.

If, however, the site is being dug either as a whole or in large areas, it is possible to publish a series of fascicules which can ultimately be bound together to form a complete record, and in which subsequent modification by later discoveries is reduced to a minimum. In such fascicules the observed evidence must be kept strictly apart from the interpretation, so that ultimately all the evidence can be viewed as a whole without interpretive modifications which may by then be out-of-date. In the case of deeply stratified sites, the observed evidence of the latest

layers, once they have been removed, cannot be altered by any subsequent work
— it is only the interpretation which may be changed. Even here, it is unlikely
that plans of buildings and other structures will be affected, nor will the relative
dating, since the latest structures must be the latest, whatever their date. The
variables are the absolute dates, which may well be affected by underlying finds,
and the analysis and interpretation of pottery and small finds, and to some extent
animal and other bones, since it will not be clear, until the excavation is finished,
what proportions of these are residual. Work on the layers immediately underlying those removed can often throw light on the meaning of the overlying layers
and structures by showing their derivation — the rubble from a demolished
building, the upcast of a ditch, a spread of burnt debris and so on — but since the
fascicule relating to the upper layers is unlikely to be published before the next
layers are examined, or at least seen, any particularly relevant information in
those layers can be incorporated. There is a considerable advantage, too, in
publishing all the excavations from a town or other major development area as
fascicules, even if the work is not carried out under one aegis. In this way, piecemeal publication, to differing standards in different formats, and in journals of
widely varying circulation, will be avoided.

The lay-out of the report

The published report should be laid out in a logical and developing sequence
which leads the reader from the general (that is, the site's region, area and immediate surroundings) through the particular (the excavation itself, with its
details of structures, finds and other *minutiae*) back to the general (the significance of the results in the region, the country, perhaps the continent, even world).

It should not be assumed that the reader will know where the site is, or even
whereabouts in the country the county in which it is situated lies, so that it is
a good general rule to set the scene for, say, a Japanese reader rather than a
member of one's local society. A series of maps should therefore be given to
provide an increasingly enlarged view of the site and its setting, rather like a
series of stills from a spacecraft entering the atmosphere and homing on the
centre of the excavation. Grinsell, Rahtz and Price-Williams, 1974, show such a
series in their fig. 1. It could be extended by adding a plan of the site in its
immediate context, with its surrounding relief, fields, routes and so forth, together with a plan of the site itself, preferably contoured (their fig. 2), showing
the excavated areas.

Similarly, the text and illustrations of the excavation should follow a logical
sequence, leading the reader from the reasons the excavation was undertaken to
the methods employed. Both of these aspects are important if the report is to be
properly understood and assessed. The evidence exposed by the excavation should
be described with as little interpretation as possible. It is virtually impossible to
exclude all interpretation, explicit or implicit, from a description of the features,

layers and their relationships — the very use of words such as post-hole, floor, or hearth imply a considerable degree of interpretation — but the more objective the primary evidence can be the better.

The illustrations

Since the results of excavation are above all visual — we record, after all, very little which we cannot see — it follows that the illustrations form the core of the report, from which the text, descriptive or interpretative, stems. Once the plan of the report has been decided it is probably simplest and most effective to prepare all the illustrations, both drawings and photographs, arrange them in a logical and coherent sequence, and write the text as a commentary on them. If the drawings are very large it will be helpful, if money is available, to make reductions so that they can easily be handled, or mounted on a wall or display board.

Since with litho reproductions, now increasingly being used, drawings are usually cheaper and photographs are no more expensive to reproduce per page than text, which still requires typesetting (if it is not merely typewritten), the number of drawings can be increased relative to the text, and since one drawing is traditionally worth 1000 words, more information can be published more cheaply than with line-block methods.

Ideally, the drawings should lead the reader through the stages of the excavation like a carefully planned guided tour, and, so far as possible the field drawings should be published, redrawn, without interpretation. Any interpretations such as descriptive labels, outlines of buildings, the relationship of features and so on should be clearly distinguishable from the initial evidence on which they are based. A merely interpretative series of drawings presents the reader with a *fait accompli* which he has no chance of evaluating.

However, there is an intermediate form of illustration which can be misleading. This is the 'edited' field drawing, in which elements which the excavator cannot understand or does not wish to include are omitted. It may consist of little more than 'cleaning up' the areas round floors or walls or other features, or emphasising lines of stones, or edges of floors or groups of postholes to make them stand out more clearly, or it may go further and eliminate anomalous or awkward features which do not fit into the interpretative pattern. Allied to this is the rationalisation of features, so that they become a little more in line, or rectangular, or circular or whatever. All distortions of this kind should be rigorously avoided, and all the interpretive drawings kept separate from the evidence, either as distinct drawings, or as transparent overlays, so that the interpretation can be directly compared with the evidence (figs. 70-1; 76-7).

All published plans should be related to a key plan near the beginning of the report, so that the relationships of one drawing to another can easily be found. Similarly the positions of all published sections should be easily locatable on a master plan, if necessary a separate one from that which locates the plan drawings. If the site is large and detailed the drawings of the evidence will have to be

Archaeological   Disturbance

Line of Wall

33 32
+
19 18

VI

19 18
+

Fig. 70 shows part of the uppermost excavated surface within the precinct of the baths basilica at Wroxeter Roman City. All the visible evidence has been recorded. North is at the top of the plan. The grid points are 10m. apart.

That evidence which is considered to be structural has been redrawn in fig. 71

Trench

32 31
18 17

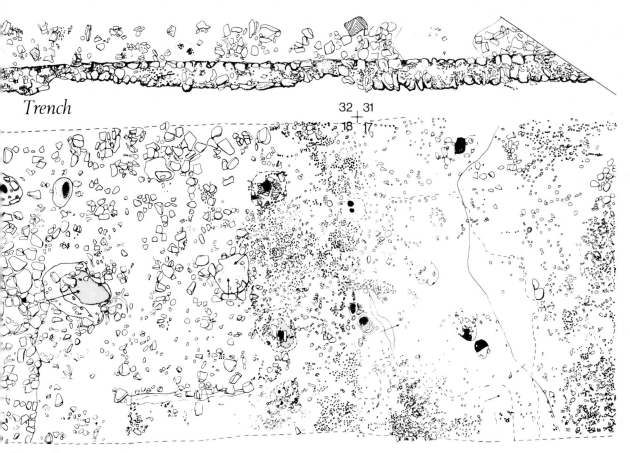

ological   Trench

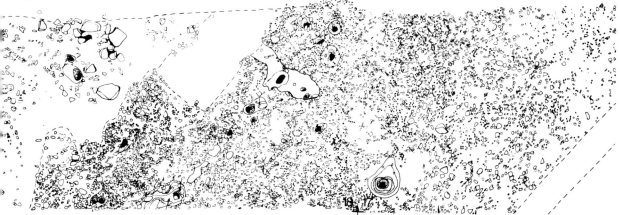

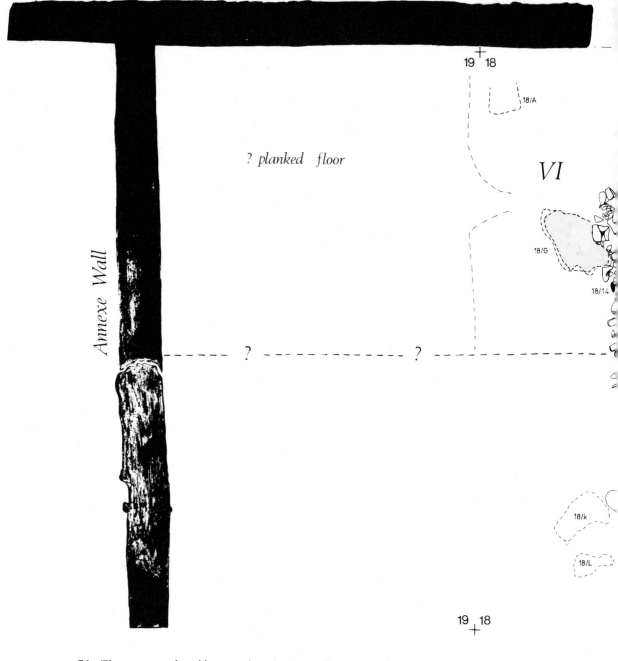

Annexe Wall

? planked floor

19 $+$ 18

18/A

VI

18/G

18/14

19 $+$ 18

18/k

18/L

71 The structural evidence from fig. 70 consists of a worn sandstone area 18/15 flanked by two depressions 18/F and 18/G, opposite a break in the precinct wall, all lying within an area of unworn rubble (see Fig. 71) whose limits are shown by the broken line. At the eastern end of this area a pebble surface 18/D is flanked by stakeholes 18/21, 18/5, 17/31, 18/22, 18/6, 17/7, 17/28 and 17/29. The function of the other post-sockets 18/A, 18/2, 18/B, 18/C, 17/30 and 18/E is not clear.

The evidence suggests a rectangular framed building leaning-to against the still-standing precinct wall. The horizontal timbers of the building bounded the rubble area, and there were three entrances, one through the

? planked floor

18/2

18/B

18/C

18/21

32 31
18 17

17/31

?

18/5

18/D

18/E

18/F

18/18

18/15

18/6

17/7

18/22

17/30

17/28

17/29

18/4

H

18/I

18/J

18/9

18/11

18 17

precinct wall to the north, one opposite it, paved and perhaps flanked by two large posts, 18/G and 18/F, and one to the east, pebble floored and with a funnel-shaped porch. The worn sandstone of the southern entrance contrasts with the

unworn rubble of the rest of the interior, suggesting that the building had a planked floor which protected the rubble hard-core from wear.

Slight differences in the rubble west of the central entrances suggest a partition

here.

The features south of this building are considered to belong to a separate structure.

published in a series of smaller areas, each drawing including an overlap with its neighbour in order to show their interrelationship clearly. In such cases, the plan drawings should all be published at the same scale so that the plan of the whole site can be fitted together like a jigsaw. It is also helpful if the sections are published at the same scale as they are then more easily and directly relatable to the plans. It should also be made quite clear which way the sections run, if necessary publishing them reversed for comparison with other sections. For example the drawings of two faces of a trench cut through a ditch should be published with one reversed so that they can be directly compared.

It would be highly desirable for all plans and sections to be published in colour, and with the technological advances now being made in litho printing this may soon be possible. In the meantime, however, black and white keys in various forms have to be used, either by repeated symbols or by varied tones of hatching, stippling, cross-hatching or shading. The more naturalistic drawings are, the more closely they will represent the observed evidence. While it is impossible to reproduce every nuance of surface of a layer or section, the sort of stylized section drawing common during the last 30 years (and reproduced together with a more naturalistic section in Grinsell, Rahtz and Price Williams, 1974, p.42) eliminates significant detail such as tip-lines and is altogether too generalized to be adequately informative.

Photographs for publication should be chosen to illustrate aspects of the evidence not easily drawn. For example, oblique photographs can combine vertical and horizontal surfaces in a way difficult except in an isometric or axonometric drawing (see below, fig. 73), or by use of lighting may bring out a variety of textures, or changes in surface or level. They can also, by being panoramic, encompass whole buildings or groups of buildings in a glance, and ideally they should be reproduced opposite their related drawings and not isolated at the end of the report, where they are often printed sideways on to the page, so that comparison with the drawings is made doubly difficult. Here again, lithographic printing does not need glossy art paper (the main reason for segregation of plates of photographs), so making the typography simpler and more logical.

To sum up, the illustrations should be sufficiently comprehensive *and* comprehensible that the reader should be able to understand the excavation, its relative chronology and its structural interpretation with minimal help from the text.

Drawing for publication
The reader should consult the advice given in Grinsell, Rahtz and Price Williams, 1974, Chapter 3, which is not repeated here.

If the field drawings are clear, accurately related to the site grid and, preferably, built up in standard units for ease of handling, it should be possible to trace the final drawings from them direct, without intermediate stages. (Ideally, of course, the field drawings themselves ought to be published. This would require them not only to be of very high quality but compatible with each other in all respects of style, colour or keys. While this is not impossible, it does impose an even greater responsibility on the field draughtsmen in circumstances in which they already have a great deal to think about.)

Although Price Williams (*op.cit.*, 34) disparages the use of polyester film such as Permatrace for publication drawings, it is being increasingly used, and few printers, in my experience, are unwilling to accept drawings made on it. Pelikan T (not TT) ink should be used, though I have drawings made ten years ago using ordinary indian ink on plastic film which have not deteriorated. The important advantage of using translucent film for the final drawings is that the field drawings can be traced directly through it, which is much faster and more accurate than transferring them on to darwing paper. The interpretative drawings — overlays, underlays, details, isolated features — can also be traced with minimum difficulty.

Rapidograph, Leroy or other stylus pens are the most convenient, though they can produce rather wiry lines with a mechanical appearance if they are held vertically. If, on the other hand, they are used obliquely, as with an ordinary pen or pencil they will give a variety of line which gives life to the drawing. They should, of course, be held vertically if used with stencils.

Corrections to drawings on film can be made with a sharp razor blade held vertically, a small piece of damp cotton wool (buds on sticks sold for cleaning babies' ears are useful for removing details), or one of the special erasers made by Rotring/Pelikan. The size of pens used should be related to the intended reduction of the drawing. A stylus giving a line 0.1mm. thick on the drawing will give a line 0.05mm. thick if the drawing is reduced by 1:2. Most catalogues of draughtsmen's supplies give an illustration of pens and the lines they will produce so that it is easy to see by reference to the catalogue illustration if a line 0.05mm. thick will be adequate in the final reduction. Alternatively one can work the opposite way, choosing from the key to pen sizes the size of line or lines one thinks appropriate or minimal in the published drawing, and by scaling up choose the appropriate pen needed to produce that thickness again when the drawing is reduced.

A simple method of assessing the degree of reduction that a drawing will bear is to fix the drawing to a wall and retreat from it until it appears to be the size that it would be when reproduced. If it is intended, for instance, that it should fill a quarto page, hold a page of the appropriate size (or a copy of the relevant journal) at normal reading distance between the eye and the drawing and retreat until the drawing appears to be the same size as the page. This is the size it would be when reproduced, and it can be judged from this whether it should instead be a folder, or could be reduced even more, to take up, say, half a page. For small drawings, of finds, for example, or for parts of drawings, a reducing glass is useful to assess the effect of reduction.

If the detail disappears at the intended scale of reduction, either the drawing must be reproduced in a larger format, or it must be redrawn in simpler, bolder form. If it is a drawing of the evidence, the second solution is not recommended.

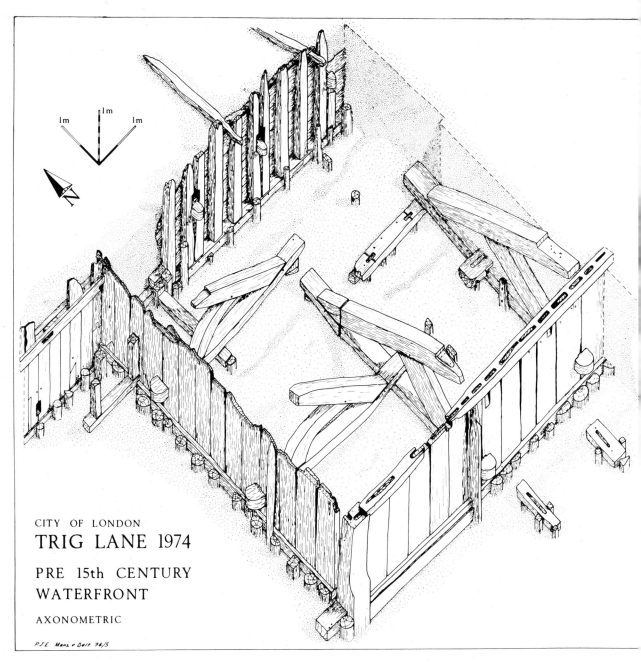

1m   1m   1m

N

CITY OF LONDON
TRIG LANE 1974
PRE 15th CENTURY WATERFRONT
AXONOMETRIC

PJE Meas + Delt 74/5

Since the excavation itself will normally be based on a rectilinear grid it is convenient to cover the drawing board with squared paper, which will represent the site grid, subdivided into millimetre squares. Not only is this used for positioning drawings and overlays, but obviates the need for drawing guidelines for lettering, scale-lines, borders, and so forth, thus saving a good deal of time.

All drawings on sheets of paper or film are two-dimensional. However, most sites, even most layers, are three dimensional and there are various ways of showing the third dimension on flat drawings. One is to superimpose contours. Sometimes, these can be drawn on the base drawing, especially if it is not very highly detailed, using dotted or dashed lines. If the contours so drawn would be lost in a maze of walls or pebbles it is better to print them as an overlay in another colour, such as blue, which will be distinct without being obtrusive. Hachuring is a common way of adding a three-dimensional element to plans, but has the disadvantage that if produces generalized slopes, lacking in subtlety. However it is easily read — there is no doubt of the way the slope runs, which is not always immediately apparent from contours.

Shading, either with stippling or with Letratone dry stencil sheets, can indicate hollows, scoops, post-holes and other irregularities. Stippling is more flexible and can show subtle undulations but takes a lot more time and skill than Letratone.

Arrows can be used to show slopes, either in conjunction with contours or form lines (which are conjectured contours), or to show the slopes of individual stones, tiles or the like (see Grimes, 1960, fig. 7).

Letratone or other forms of hatching and stippling can also be used to define areas of burning, or significant colour changes in the soil, floors, etc. If shading is used to indicate both three-dimensions and changes in colour or tone on the same drawing there is risk of confusion, so that it must be done with discretion and clear differentiation made in the attached key.

A more accurate, measurable way of drawing in three-dimensions is the isometric or axonometric drawing, in which measurements are either correct in any direction (isometric) or along one or more axes (axonometric). Graph paper, ruled with lines at say, 30° to the main axis, is available, which makes axonometric drawing fairly painless. Before one can draw axonometrically one has to have both vertical and horizontal drawings of the surfaces, walls, pits or other features on the site. Examples of axonometric drawings can be seen in Grimes, 1968, fig. 1, Barker, 1970, fig. 17, Grinsell, Rahtz, Price Williams, 1974, figs. 5 and 6. A fine example is reproduced here as fig. 73.

Isometric and axonometric drawings are undoubtedly the best ways of demonstrating relationships which would be difficult to read from a series of plans and vertical sections, or elevations. Though they take time to construct, they condense a great deal of measurable information in one drawing, and thus avoid pages of description. Fig. 72 shows an example from a recent excavation in London which illustrates the point admirably.

73 Sharpley Pool Furnace, Astley, Worcestershire: axonometric projection. This fine drawing combines the plans and sections drawn in the field into one 'three-dimensional' drawing in which the furnace is viewed as if from above obliquely. This form of drawing has the advantage over perspective drawing that the measurements are to scale along the main axes, which in this case are at 45° to each other, though a 60° – 30° alignment is sometimes more structurally revealing.

This is the site of a very early blast furnace, probably built by Andrew Yarranton about 1651. It lies in the valley of a small stream which is made to flow round the furnace in channels cut into the solid rock (A, A on the drawing). A large water-wheel set in the channel at B drove a bellows at C.

SHARPLEY POOL FURNACE
Astley, Worcestershire.
Axonometric projection at one to twenty.
Key:

mortar
bedrock
wood
flood deposits – sand, silt, clay.
spot level, metres above sea-level.
   „   „   on water surface.

September 76   Richard Lea

one metre intervals

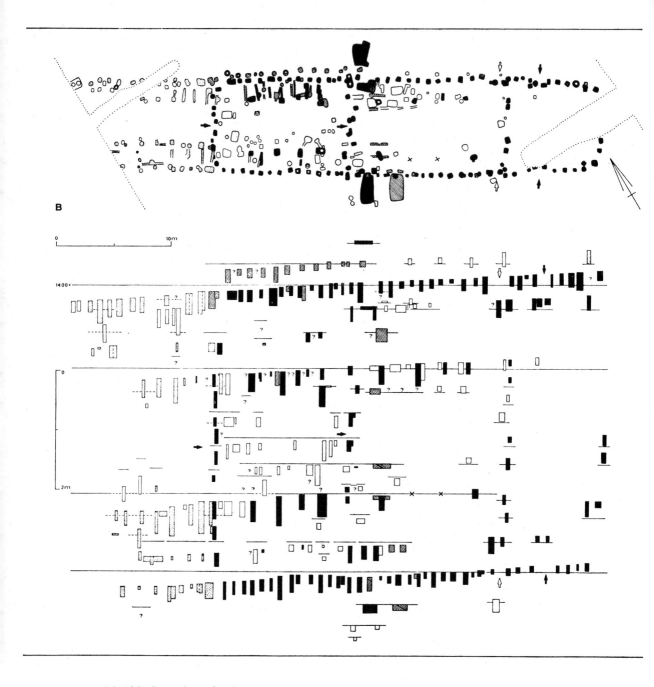

74 This is a plan of a long-house of Wijster type, at Ede, Holland, with living quarters at one end and stalls for cattle at the other (see van Es, 1967 for details of the type). The house has been rebuilt at least once. The lower drawing is a diagrammatic representation of the depths of the post-holes, shown in a way which enables their relationship with the plan and each other to be seen at a glance. A refinement would be to draw the post-hole sections realistically instead of diagrammatically.

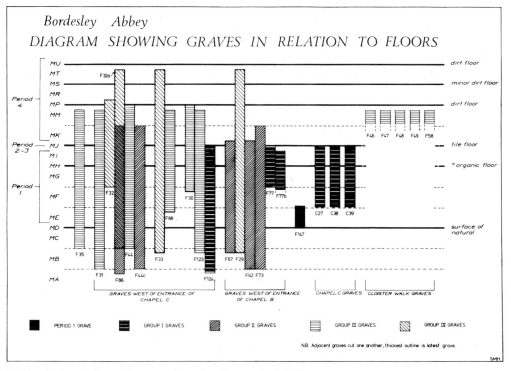

75 Bordesley Abbey: diagram showing graves in relation to floors. This is an attempt to show the vertical relationships (based on measurements taken) between the floor-levels of different periods in the South Transept, the levels from which graves were inserted, and the depths to which they were dug.

The use of diagrams in publication

Well thought-out and clearly drawn diagrams will make the report much easier to use and understand. For example, it is often essential to the assessment of a post-hole building to include the dimensions of the post-holes. If there are hundreds, perhaps thousands, of these in a large excavation, lists of dimensions would be cumbersome and sheets of sections difficult to relate to a structure whose plan was on another page. One way of presenting the information graphically in a style which is directly relateable to the plan is shown in fig. 74.

A refinement of this method would be to draw the sections or profiles of the post-holes (together, if necessary, with their post-pits) in diagrammatic form alongside the plan. In this case all post-holes and pits should be sectioned in at least one common plane, so that the published sections would be comparable.

The matrix proposed by Edward Harris and variants on it provide a useful diagrammatic way of demonstrating the inter-relationship of the stratigraphic units of the site or its constituent parts (above p. 199) and the relationship of finds one to another, or of fragments of the same vessels can best be demonstrated diagrammatically.

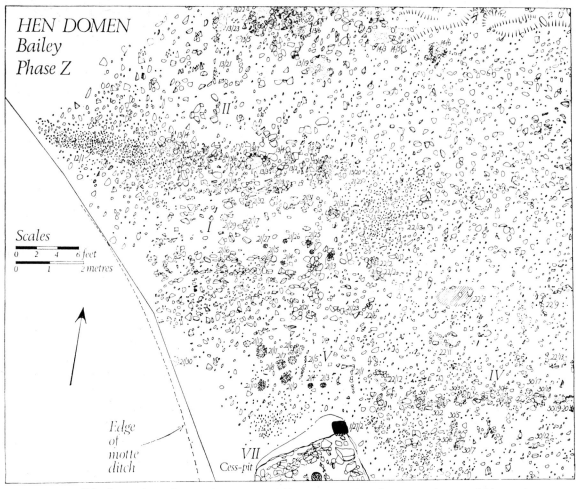

HEN DOMEN
Bailey
Phase Z

II

I

Scales

0 2 4 6 feet
0   1   2 metres

V

IV

VII
Cess-pit

Edge
of
motte
ditch

76 *above* Plan of part of the uppermost layers in the north-west corner of the bailey at Hen Domen, Montgomery, showing distribution of stones and post-sockets.

77 *right* Interpretative drawing of Building I extracted from fig. 76, showing the position of major post-

sockets, pebble surfaces and etc. The structural significance of these features is a further step not yet fully understood.

The comparative depth of a series of graves and the levels from which they were cut are illustrated graphically in fig. 75, which presents the information more concisely than in any other way.

In the publication of the finds themselves and of environmental evidence, histograms, graphs and other diagrams are commonplace and there is no need to enlarge on their use here.

Lettering

There is little doubt that Letraset or other types of dry transfer lettering are the quickest and most elegant way to letter drawings and diagrams, but they are very expensive. Stencils, such as Uno, Rotring, or Leroy are perfectly adequate, if properly used, though the larger sizes are less satisfactory than the smaller. Many draughtsmen compromise, using Letraset for titling and stencils for labelling,

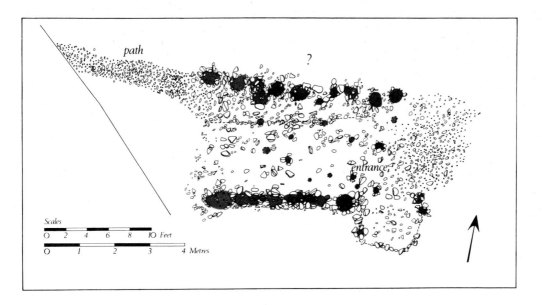

feature numbers and so on. Whichever methods are used, the results can be inelegant and clumsy if the spacing between the letters, words and lines is not right. Letraset have introduced a method of spacing called 'spacematic' which helps to position the letters, but ultimately it is best to learn the elements of proportional spacing. It may be argued that it is the truth of the evidence and the interpretation which matter and that well-proportioned lettering is merely a luxury or even a distraction; and it may even be argued that an inaccurate field drawing, beautifully redrawn and elegantly lettered can mislead even more than a poor drawing, since it inspires misplaced confidence. I would prefer accurate field drawings, faithfully redrawn and well lettered.

Alternative interpretative drawings
Interpretative drawings will almost always be abstractions from the total evidence, leaving out those features which the excavator considers to be inessential and linking those features which he believes to be related (figs. 70-1; 76-7). Sometimes the same field evidence will allow a number of alternative interpretations to be made. These may be included on one drawing by the use of different conventions for each suggested interpretation. If this is not feasible or if it would be unnecessarily confusing, each alternative should have its own drawing.

The text

There is no need to repeat the advice in Grinsell, Rahtz and Price Williams (1974), Chapter 4, on such matters as the arrangement of the text, descriptions of finds and specialist reports.

I believe that the director of the excavation should read the whole report, including those parts not written by him, right through as though he were reading it for the first time from the point of view of an interested worker in another discipline. Only thus will he discover logical inconsistencies in the arguments, or see whether the figures and photographs are effective illustrations of these arguments. He should follow up every reference to see that it is adequate, and where necessary is cross-referred to other examples. The illustrations should be referred to the pages in the text which they illustrate and specialists' reports integrated into the main text by means of cross-references. In other words, the text should be a coherent whole, one that can be read straight through with understanding and without the frustration of loose ends and logical inconsistencies.

The English used should be as clear and free of jargon as possible. It should also be unambiguous. As George Orwell said in another context, 'write so as to make your meaning inescapable'. The writers of excavation reports should be brought up not on other excavation reports but on the short stories of Graham Greene and the novels of Georges Simenon.

Interim reports

Since most of the local regional and national journals are published annually, full publication of even a short excavation usually takes a year or more to appear after it is written. The greater delay in the publication of longer or larger excavations is notorious and often is as long as 10-15 years after the completion of the report. Such delays are not only frustrating for all those who are interested in the site and the results, but the time-lag stultifies and retards the development of archaeology itself. If publication of the results of medical or engineering research were similarly delayed progress in these sciences would be decades behind the position in which they are now.

Interim reports help to relieve the situation by making summaries of the results of excavations quickly available. The limitations of interim reports are threefold. First, because they are short, they compress, simplify and therefore distort much of the evidence especially by making positive that which may be only probable. Second, because they are concise they may be used as definitive by historians, geographers, teachers and others who either cannot wait for the full report (which, after all, may never appear) or who have no time to read it when ultimately it is in print. Thirdly, publication of an interim report tends to weaken the director's resolve to publish a full report since there is a feeling that duty has been done, at least in part. In addition, all interim reports should perhaps carry the warning: '*The results published in this report are subject to drastic revision in the light of next season's work/criticism from my colleagues/analysis of the pottery/coins/finds/ or the results of someone else's work on a similar site. Do not therefore rely too heavily on them for your thesis/text-book/forthcoming world history/television series.*'

A deficiency of almost all interim reports is that they carry little information regarding the techniques used to recover the results which are summarized so that dissemination of new methods or refinements of old ones is slow and intermittent. If no plan of the excavation is given the information can be highly ambiguous. One reads that 'The excavation showed that a phase of timber building datable to the twelfth-century was followed by two periods of stone buildings. Occupation of the site continued into the fourteenth and fifteenth centuries.' This may simply mean that a post-hole containing a twelfth century cooking-pot rim was overlain by two fragments of wall, which were covered by a layer containing fourteenth - fifteenth-century pottery.

It follows that interim reports should be short, but not too short. They should be full enough to give the reader an outline not only of the results achieved but of the methods used in achieving them and they should give some indication of the reliability and anticipated permanence of the assertions made in the text. On the maxim that one illustration is worth 1,000 words (and is cheaper to print) plans and sections should be included where possible. If the uninterpreted evidence can be included, so much the better, since it offers the reader a chance to make his own assessment.

Interim reports, being by definition ephemeral, should be published as cheaply and distributed as widely as possible. Litho pamphlets or news-sheets are satisfactory since they are cheaper than publication in county or national journals and can be included in the mailing of the journals. In this way the essential interim 'throwaway' nature of the report is preserved. On the other hand, the short summaries of current work published annually in the major period publications *Britannia, Medieval* and *Post-Medieval Archaeology* and by the Inspectorate of Ancient Monuments and the Council for British Archaeology are useful handlists of work in progress. They are particularly valuable where long-term projects are concerned and we should draw a distinction between interim reports on completed excavations and those on excavations which extend over a number of years. In the latter case, it must be made clear that further work may radically alter previous results in a way less likely with completed digs.

Another, and very valuable, form of interim report is that designed for the general, archaeologically interested, public. A good example is the booklet called *Interim*, the bulletin of the York Archaeological Trust, which contains conventional interim reports interleaved with articles on aspects of ancient York, specialized archaeological techniques, archaeological philosophy and politics and even profiles of members of the Trust.

Such publications can do only good, especially since by far the largest financial supporter of British archaeology is the tax-payer, and it is right and proper that he should see how his money is being spent. There is a ready market for the short, cheap, easily read, well-illustrated pamphlet or booklet which describes work in progress in simple terms (without obscurantist jargon such as '. . . successive sub-phasing of activity is discernible', encountered in one recent interim).

Unfortunately excavation and its associated disciplines are becoming so complex that it is not easy to write simply about most sites. Interim reports written for the public should therefore perhaps be in two parts — the first, a clear and simply written summary of results to date written with a bright twelve-year old in mind; the second part, a fuller account which describes the basic evidence on which the first part is based. In this way children, and adults, who simply want to be told what has been found, can find the answers without searching through a mass of information which presupposes a basic knowledge of classical or medieval history or the techniques of building construction. On the other hand, many visitors to sites are very much more experienced and knowledgable than we sometimes guess, and these require more than take-it-or-leave-it statements. Such two-level reports may achieve the best of both worlds.

Data storage as an alternative to conventional publication

The quantity of data recovered from a large, highly detailed excavation is enormous and quite beyond publication in the traditional manner. It has already been suggested (above p. 226) that drawings can be stored conveniently in the form of microfilm, and in this way are readily available to those who wish to consult them. In the same way the negatives of photographs both in black and white and in colour pose no problem of storage. If in addition the record cards of features and finds are microfilmed they too can be stored and reproduced cheaply and conveniently. Since the number of workers wishing to consult the primary records of an excavation is never likely to be great, microfilm storage will probably be adequate for most sites. However, the data from excavations carried out by one of the larger urban units, for instance, may be stored conveniently on tape or punched card if it is anticipated that cross-referencing between sites will be frequent. Certainly the finds from a complex of related sites will need to be stored in a form that gives swift and flexible retrieval, perhaps more so than data referring to excavated features.

However, concern over the inadequacies of conventional pottery publication has been growing for some years, since it has become increasingly obvious that there is no agreed terminology for forms, fabrics, inclusive colours, textures and so forth, nor is there any agreed criterion for assessing the quantities of pottery found either in the excavation as a whole or in its component contexts.

The Medieval Pottery Research Group, formed in 1975, is concerned not only to examine and rationalize, where possible, the publication of medieval pottery but is also concerned with the wider aspects of pottery analysis and interpretation, and its technology, economics and social history.

The quantities of material now being produced by the larger units, particularly the urban units, demand more precisely defined descriptions and a nationally (if not internationally) agreed criteria for analysis. At the time of writing these criteria are still being formulated.

Pottery and small finds publication

Conventions for the drawing of pottery and small finds for publication have evolved in slightly different ways in Britain, America and the continent of Europe. There is a tendency to use more photography in the publication of pottery in Europe and the convention of using a 1:4 scale is not so commonly held.

The conventional methods of drawing pottery and small finds for publication are extensively covered in Grinsell, Rahtz and Price Williams, 1974, 46-53, and in the articles quoted by them in their bibliography, Piggott and Hope-Taylor, 1965, Hope-Taylor, 1966 and 1967, Kewick, 1971, Terrell, J., 1971 and Trump, 1971. While much of the advice given there is useful, it is rather too rigid, and this could result in the production of unnecessarily stylized drawings. Ruled horizontal lines representing rilling or carination may be justified in precisely thrown or moulded classical pottery, but the majority of the pottery discovered on excavations in Britain is anything but rigidly symmetrical and the drawings should be as truthful as possible, reproducing wavy rims, uneven bases or misshapen handles just as they are.

If stamped decoration wanders round the shoulder of the pot it should be drawn thus, and there is no reason why textures, if they are marked, should not be indicated. The purpose of the published drawing is to illustrate the find as closely as possible — over-stylized drawing will merely mislead. There is some justification for the argument which suggests that all pottery publication is a waste of time and space, since the drawings and photographs can never be anything more than a general guide to shape and decoration, and that the excavator

78 There is some controversy regarding the use of stippling versus hatching in pottery drawing. This example shows that when necessary, both can be used on the same drawing.

seeking parallels must handle the pottery himself. How often one sees in reports simple rims which appear to be similar to one another or to pottery which one has dug up, but when they are handled and compared their texture, surface, and whole character are unmistakably different.

Pottery publication thus may be seen as a guide to the styles of pottery from a site and little more. However this is an extreme view, and there is no doubt that many drawings, particularly of decorated pots, such as those from pagan Saxon cemeteries, form corpora indispensable for the study of their type.

It is essential that the angle of the rim should be accurately aligned so that the top of the rim is horizontal or a highly misleading impression of the pot size may be given. If the rim-sherd is not long enough to enable an accurate estimate of the angle to be made, this should be stated in the accompanying catalogue in the text. The same remarks apply to the rim-diameter. A simple series of concentric arcs will provide a guide to diameters (Terrell, 1971) but if the rim-sherd is short large errors are possible.

It has become conventional to publish pottery at a scale of 1:4 except in special cases where the drawings would either be too big for the page or too small to show necessary detail adequately. By using this common scale comparison of pottery from different sites is made easier. In the drawing of both pottery and small finds there is a controversy regarding the use of stippling as distinct from hatching or shading. My own view is that techniques should not be rigid, and that use should be made of whatever method will best depict the character and texture of the object. There is no reason at all why stippling and hatching should not be used on the same drawing since they are not mutually exclusive techniques (fig. 78).

Small finds, such as brooches, pins, buckles and so on should almost without exception be drawn at twice life-size. This makes the drawing of detail much easier and more accurate. In the case of very small objects such as intaglios 4:1 may be a more appropriate enlargement. It is important that the object be carefully studied before being drawn, preferably in discussion with the person responsible for writing-up the finds. It is disconcerting to realize, after the drawing is complete, that the object has been drawn upside-down perhaps with some zoomorphic abstraction missed by the draughtsman who was not examining the object from the point of view of the meaning of the decoration, or that the object has been drawn sideways-on because the draughtsman did not realize its function. If a small find is complex it may be necessary to draw two or three views, together with one or more sections chosen to illustrate its structure of function more clearly. Finds drawings should be combined with photographs in the full illustration of objects. With litho printing, drawings and photographs can be published on the same page, so that direct comparison is possible. Photographs of objects should be taken to show those aspects which are difficult to draw, such as textures, and colour in the case of important finds. Oblique photographs give a three-dimensional view of the object, often difficult to convey in a drawing, and

than page after page of rim-sherd drawings. Roman sites in particular produce
in all cases the lighting of photographs is of crucial importance. Iron objects
are often best drawn from X-rays since there is little point in publishing shapeless
lumps of iron oxide when inside lurks a recognizable artifact which X-rays will
reveal. Other metal finds often yield a wealth of detail under X-rays and ultra-
violet or infra-red light will sometimes reveal patterns, writing or other essential
information on organic materials. It is therefore wise to delay the final drawings
of objects if scientific examination is likely to produce aspects of detail which
should be incorporated in the publication.

Catalogues of illustrated sherds and small finds should not be unnecessarily
verbose. It will save much space if they are as concise as possible and printed
in smaller type than the main text. There is little point in describing a rim form
or jug shape in words if the drawings clearly show this information. On the other
hand textures and colours must be described. Here there is a great deal of confusion because most descriptions are purely subjective, 'buff' to one writer being
'light red' to another. If one gives a sherd to six different people and asks them
to write a description of it, there is little doubt that six totally different descriptions will be given. An attempt to standardize the descriptions of colours has been
made by the production of a Pottery Colour Chart (Webster, 1970). This was
developed by Dr Graham Webster in conjunction with Mr Christopher Simmons
of Messrs Reeves Ltd, and is a simplified and specialized version of a soil colour
chart. While it is a very helpful step forward, it cannot solve all the problems of
colour description particularly with glazed medieval pottery where differential
firing and incomplete glazing may produce a dozen or more colours on one pot.

Nothing is more daunting to the non-specialist reader of excavation reports
vast quantities of sherds all of which should be published if the report is not
simply to contain a selection of those that the excavator thought significant at
the time. In order to cut down labour, in both drawing and printing, and repeated
costs of publishing the same or very similar pots every time they are dug up, it
would seem sensible to construct and publish a corpus of at least the Roman
and medieval pottery of each region, and, if pottery of other periods is plentiful,
of these as well. If this publication was in loose-leaf or in some other cumulative
form it could be extended and inter-leaved as material became available. There
should then be no need for individual pottery reports of any elaboration to be
published in reports of excavations in the region. If pottery from an excavation
was unprecedented, it would go into the corpus in its appropriate place. If it was
all paralleled by material already in the corpus, reference to this would be all
that was required. Ultimately, if the quantities became great enough computer
storage of the information could be considered. In the case of the projected
long-term excavations of large Roman sites, computer storage should perhaps
be implemented at an early stage before the quantities of material become un-
manageable.

14

The Theoretical Reconstruction of Buildings

The most valid, and sometimes the most dramatic, way of assessing our interpretative assumptions is to simulate the conditions which we believe produced the excavated evidence and to test the results against our observations. Such experiments can range from small-scale work on the techniques of working metal to large scale agricultural or house-construction projects. The subject has recently been dealt with at length by Coles (1973, revised edition 1979) so that there is no need to expand on it here. In addition, there is a new journal, the *Bulletin of Experimental Archaeology*, whose first issue appeared in 1980, produced by the Department of Adult Education of the University of Southampton, which summarizes recent experimental research, with details of whom to contact and where further information can be obtained.

It is worth adding, however, that intense observation of the effects of natural agencies, such as rain, wind, frost, worms, etc., on the site which one is currently excavating will often throw light on problems encountered only a short while before. This applies particularly to long-term excavations, where continuous monitoring of the deterioration of the site due to exposure should be routine.

The scope for archaeological experiment is almost unlimited, though it is, at present, inadequately financed and receives little official encouragement, even though it promises to make more valid the results of excavations costing tens of thousands of pounds.

The publication of the outlines of walls or the patterns of post-holes which appear to be the plans of buildings is the minimum duty of the excavator. But, so long as the observed evidence is kept firmly separated from the stages of interpretation, it can only be helpful and stimulating to the reader to discuss the form and construction of the buildings represented by the plans, and where feasible, to illustrate the discussion with tentative elevations and sections. Such attempts are criticized by many archaeologists and architects with the argument that they tend to crystallize one out of the many possible reconstructions which might be based on the evidence as found in the ground. It is seldom possible to deduce anything whatever about the roof construction from the plan and therefore the 'reconstruction' becomes less reliable the further it rises above the ground. Nevertheless the attempt should be made. The conscious effort to translate a pattern of timber-slots or post-holes into a three-dimensional entity is a salutary one, bringing home the limitations of archaeology but also forcing one to think practically, in terms of structures that would stand up. For this reason it is of great value for the excavator to consult an architect on the feasibility of the reconstruction he attempts. Only thus will he avoid some of the ludicrous mistakes which have been made in the past, where a few moments with pencil and paper would have shown the suggested forms and structures to be highly unlikely.

Where two or three variant reconstructions are possible for one ground plan, all should be included, with a note indicating the degree of probability of each. Sometimes archaeologist and architect will disagree fundamentally, in which case both views, with their supporting arguments, should be published.

Reconstructions may be on paper only, may be scale models or full-size simulations. Elevations and sections, or axonometric reconstructions are, of course, very valuable for stimulating discussion, posing questions, such as the possible height of walls or the run-off and disposal of rain water, which might not otherwise be considered in detail, and releasing the imagination from the two dimensional plane. Scale models go further in that they demand a fully three-dimensional appraisal of the building. But in neither of these cases is there the necessity of solving structural problems. Almost anything can be made to look viable on paper, and balsa wood and glue can by-pass many problems of weight, stress, loading and the nature of joints.

Paper reconstructions include pictorial representations such as those made famous by the late Alan Sorrell. These do not attempt to suggest solutions to structural difficulties (which they are often accused of glossing over) but are far more evocative of place and period than formal elevations and sections. They are therefore more suitable for short reports for the general public, museum displays and dioramas, text-books and the like. This does not mean that they should ever be inaccurate, mere flights of fancy. They should be capable of standing up to rigorous criticism, or should not be made at all. However, by their very nature they will be largely conjectural, and the accompanying text should make this clear. The difficulty is that drawings of this kind, if well done, are convincing even if wrong, and may perpetuate errors for generations. How many reconstruction drawings of timber castles have only a tool shed or two in the bailey? Yet it is clear from almost every excavation carried out on a castle bailey that they were packed with buildings.

Often theoretical buildings are erected on the flimsiest evidence; a dozen post-holes in a rectangular pattern can be made to carry many kinds of superstructure. The most useful reconstructions, therefore, whether on paper or in

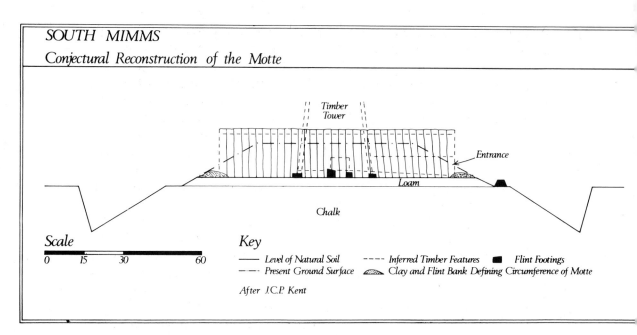

SOUTH MIMMS

Conjectural Reconstruction of the Motte

Timber
Tower

Entrance

Loam

Chalk

Scale

0   15   30   60

Key

—— Level of Natural Soil   - - - - Inferred Timber Features   ■ Flint Footings
—·—· Present Ground Surface   Clay and Flint Bank Defining Circumference of Motte

After J.C.P. Kent

79 The Motte at South Mimms. This diagrammatic section shows how the shape of the motte of South Mimms before excavation gave little hint of the extraordinary form which the defences originally took. Excavation (by Dr. J.P.C. Kent) showed that a tapering timber tower (rather like the 12th Century church tower at Pembridge, Herefordshire) rose above a vertical circular palisade which acted as a revettment to earth piled between it and the tower. Access to the tower was by means of a tunnel.

three dimensions, as models or full-scale simulations, will be those based on highly detailed excavated evidence.

Where an excavation has revealed evidence for timber-framed buildings resting on ground-sills, the structure can assume any of the forms known from existing or postulated framed buildings. In such cases, the evidence is usually minimal, and the scope for creativity maximal. However, where post-hole buildings are discovered, any reconstruction or simulation must fit the evidence without distortion, and too often only one of a number of possible reconstructions is described and illustrated and, often also, non-existent post-holes are adduced to support the chosen argument, while other, awkwardly placed but existing ones, are discarded.

Recently published perspective or axonometric drawings include a series of Anglo-Saxon houses at Maxey (Addyman, 1964), the Arthurian period hall at South Cadbury (Alcock, 1972) and Anglo-Saxon houses at Chalton (Addyman, Leigh and Hughes, 1972).

At South Mimms, Dr John Kent demonstrated that the timber tower of the motte was, contrary to expectations based on other excavated examples, a massive tapered framed tower (not unlike the twelfth-century tower of the church at Pembridge, Herefordshire) which had had the motte piled round its base. This mound was itself revetted by a circular palisade, so that in fact no earth was visible, the tower rising from the centre of what must have appeared from the outside to be a solid wall of wood (Kent, personal communication, fig. 79).

On the other hand, at Lismahon, Dr Dudley Waterman showed that the motte there carried a small bipartite hall, not unlike one of the houses of a medieval village, to which was attached a small four-post look-out tower (Waterman, 1959). No two timber castles could have been more different. Their paper reconstructions, though perhaps not accurate in every detail, bring home the point in a way that ground plans never do.

In none of the eleventh-century town houses in Antwerp (van der Walle, 1961) is there any attempt to illustrate more than one of a number of possible roof constructions. For example, the cantilevered aisled roof structure of the Antwerp house, may; on German parallels, have had the cantilevers as a continuation of the tie-beam and not as separate lower projections. But the important thing is that these drawings should be published and discussed.

At Goltho, however, Beresford (1975) has made a suggestion regarding roof-jointing which is based strictly on the excavated evidence. As in so many cases in which buildings are founded on post-holes or post-pads, the wall posts were clearly not in a straight line and therefore the posts could not have been mortised into a straight wall-plate. Beresford has postulated that 'reversed assembly' was used in which 'a tie-beam was mortised on to paired studs with a post-head mortise and tenon joint; (the wall plate) would then have been dowelled on to the upper sides of the tie-beams' (*ibid*. fig. 19 and p. 41). Precisely this problem had to be faced in the full-scale simulation of the Wroxeter house built at Avoncroft Museum of Buildings, Bromsgrove, where a similar conclusion was reached purely empirically (fig. 85).

Because roof construction is one of the chief diagnostic features used by students of vernacular architecture, the almost complete lack in excavations of all but ground plans makes it difficult to bridge the gap between the excavator and the architectural historian.

A number of fundamental premisses are nevertheless beginning to emerge as a result of the experiments in reconstruction now being made and the discussions and disputes which these experiments have generated. One is that it must be remembered and assumed that the buildings whose plans we recover by excavation were, almost without exception, constructed by men with great experience, building within a long tradition, and that therefore the styles of the buildings and the forms of their structures were the most efficient, and most convenient and the most closely adapted to their builder's needs. Whether we are dealing with a wattle-and-daub hut or a Saxon palace it is highly unlikely that the building we excavate is the first of its kind to have been built. It is more likely to be an example taken from a very long sequence. Since no-one, except under extreme circumstances, builds inefficiently, risking the whole structure collapsing, which at best is a waste of valuable time and work, or at worst fatal, it must be assumed that the buildings we recover were, by and large, the best that could be built at that time, and the most fitted for their purpose. The Indian tepee and the Bedouin tent leave little archaeological trace but are marvellously adapted to the way of life of their inhabitants. These are the portable houses of nomads. At the other extreme, it would be no use building an inefficient, carelessly thatched roof on a house in the Hebrides — the first strong breeze would remove it. Even without previous experience, builders of houses, mills, barns, haystacks, even pigsties would quickly evolve efficient structures from sheer practical necessity. Almost without exception the builders of the structures we excavate were working within traditions which embodied thousands of years' experience. We should therefore be wary of dismissing as inefficient or 'jerry built' structural evidence which, at first sight, does not seem to be explicable in terms of buildings with which we are familiar. We should rather take the opposite view, that all the evidence we find is to be explained in terms of efficiency, or practicability for the particular structure, given the materials available to the builder. This is not to say that all excavated structures are architectural masterpieces, but that only a small minority are likely to have been dangerously ramshackle when they were put up, even though the plan of post- or stake-holes may look incoherent.

There is little doubt, too, that the buildings whose traces we excavate were often more elaborate, more highly finished and more structurally sound than the excavation implies. This is evident if we look at examples where, through water-logging, above-ground timbers which would normally have rotted, are preserved. A good example is shown in figs. 80 and 81, from recent excavations in York, where it would be highly unlikely that we should postulate so massive and well-founded a structure from the evidence of the post-holes alone, if they were all that had survived. Another good example comes from the Husterknupp, a defensive site in Germany in which a motte-like mound buried the remains of an earlier building at ground-level. It was highly significant that the posts of this earlier building were unworked tree-trunks below ground, whereas above ground, the visible posts were squared and chamfered. If only the post-holes, full of earth, had been found, as would be the case on the great majority of sites, one would almost certainly have reconstructed the building as having walls of unworked timber — no-one would have been likely to have drawn the walls which we know to have been there but for which there would have been no evidence. Similarly, if no stave churches survived in Norway, who would dare on the basis of a cross-shaped plan alone, to erect a great pagoda-like structure bristling with dragons at every corner? He would be laughed out of court.

As a result, therefore, of the inevitable paucity of the excavated evidence, we are likely to under-interpret, to err on the safe side, and to produce 'reconstructions' which are simpler and less sophisticated than the actual buildings were.

Paper reconstructions of stone buildings are usually based on more than a ground plan or a series of robber trenches. Where the structures are preserved for a significant height above the original ground level, reconstruction will naturally be more reliable, though, again, roof structures will be largely conjectural or based on other known examples. A recent carefully argued pair of reconstructions are those of the amphitheatres at Chester where evidence survived for both a timber and a stone phase (N.J. Sunter *in* Thompson, 1976). A famous surviving fragment of wall, the Old Work, at Wroxeter has been carefully examined by Paul Woodfield and the suggested reconstruction published (Webster and Woodfield, 1966). On a smaller scale the successive stone and timber-framed buildings which stood on the Town Wall of Shrewsbury in Pride Hill have been conjecturally restored by Philip Clarke (Carver, forthcoming) and the successive phases of the pre-Conquest Church at Deerhurst are being recovered and drawn isometrically (Taylor and Rahtz).

In recent years, an increasing number of full-scale simulations of timber build-ings have been attempted. These range from Iron Age houses at Avoncroft and the prehistoric experimental farm at Little Butser, Hampshire (Reynolds, 1979), Saxon Grubenhauser at the Open Air Museum, Singleton, Sussex and at West Stow in Suffolk, to the most ambitious, the rampart and gateway and the granary at the Lunt Roman Fort, Coventry (Hobley, 1973). Though none of these simulations is demonstrably accurate their undertaking is of the greatest importance. Initiators of such projects lay themselves open to criticism, but by doing so raise questions which would not otherwise get off the ground either metaphorically or literally.

While questions of detail will always be disputed some of the disputes generated have been fundamental. One of the most important is that of the gatehouse at the Lunt where the controversy centres on whether it is ever feasible or sensible to rear post-hole structures.

Deep post-holes imply that the posts were ground-fast, that is that they were meant to stand on their own, otherwise there would be little point in digging such deep holes. On the other hand, an increasing number of sites produce post-holes which are not and could never have been deep enough to support their posts. This implies that the posts merely stood in these sockets (or alternatively, on stone post-pads) and were framed in some way to the horizontals, whether wall-plates, ground-sills or tie-beams, which made up the rest of the structural skeleton. Structures of this kind thave been excavated from the Roman and medieval periods, in particular from Hen Domen, Montgomery (Barker, 1969a). An attempt to simulate one such structure in order better to understand its method of construction was made at the Avoncroft Museum of Buildings, Bromsgrove where a bow-sided late Roman building excavated at Wroxeter Roman City was built, or at least begun, in 1975. The plan upon which the reconstruction was based was exceptionally detailed (fig. 83) so that it was hoped that a good deal would be learnt about the internal arrangements when the partitions and floors were built. Two photographs (figs. 86 and 87) show the building under construc-tion. In retrospect it was probably a mistake to build the roof before the walls

80 *above* Part of a water-logged timber structure excavated by the York Archaeological Trust. The remains consist of three sill-beams pinned to the ground by short vertical pegs or posts. 81B and C *opposite* are a plan and section respectively of the timbers shown in fig. 80. A is a plan of the pegs and posts which were driven into the ground, and which would have formed post-holes if all the wood had rotted. The upper surface of sill-beam 1 is slotted, presumably to take horizontal weather-boarding or a wattle wall. Beam 2 forms a threshold leading to a heavily-planked floor, perhaps of a passage. It happens that these remains were preserved by waterlogging, but this is of course exceptional. On the majority of sites only the post-holes would remain.

81A shows what one would find of this structure on a non-waterlogged site, and is a dramatic illustration not only of what is lost when timbers rot but of the amount we may be justified in restoring to sites where post-holes are all that are found.

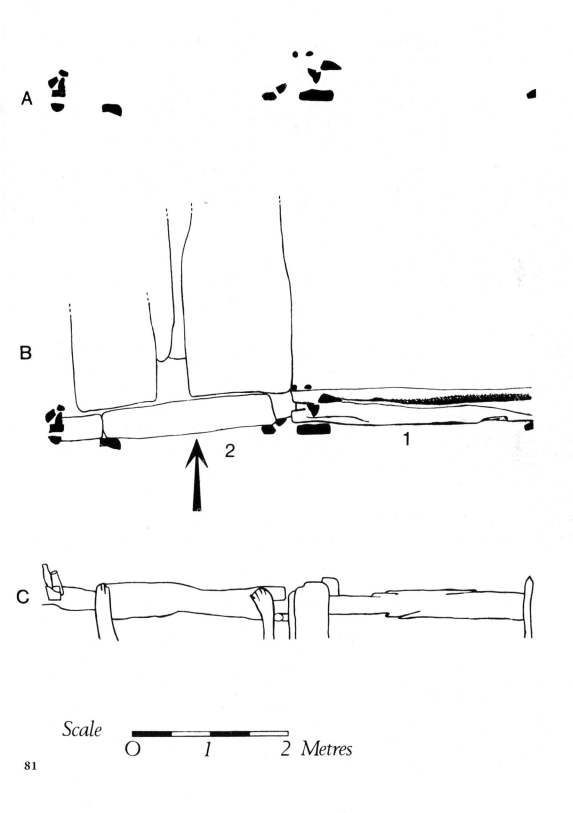

Scale

O   1   2 Metres

WROXETER · Site 68 · Phase Z

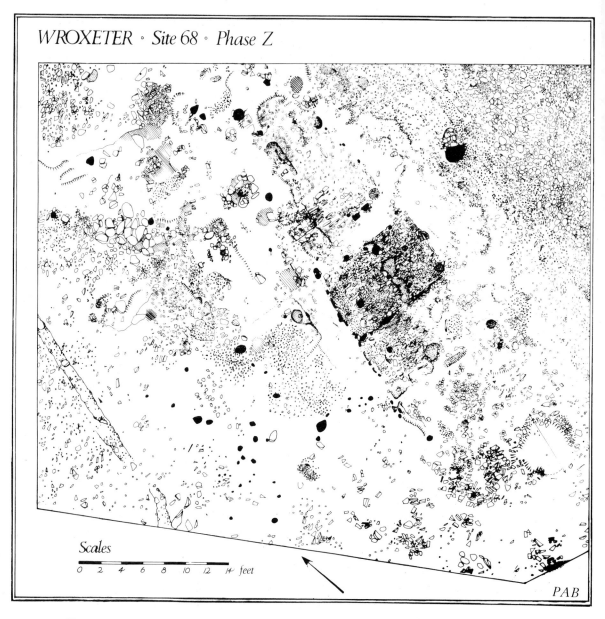

Scales

0   2   4   6   8   10   12   14 feet

PAB

82 Wroxeter, Baths Basilica Building I. This building was revealed when the ploughsoil was removed and the upper-most archaeological layers were cleaned simply by re-moving the humic soil and leaving all stones, tiles, clay etc. The maximum depth of the post-sockets was 2-3cm. so that it was clear that none of the posts had been sunk into the ground and that they could not have stood independently. Some of the post and stake holes were packed round with tiles and pottery which projected above the floor levels. Since, if the plough had touched them, they would have been displaced, it was apparent that this was the last struc-ture built on this part of the site before its abandonment and that, contrary to previous opinion, it had not suffered plough damage.

were more firmly braced and cladded, though the building was stable enough in ordinary bad weather. However, the exceptional gales of the night of 2 January 1976, when winds reached some 70-80 mph in Worcestershire, demolished the structure and it has not yet been rebuilt. Enough was learnt however to show that buildings of this size, some 40ft (12.5m.) long, were perfectly practicable without either massive sill-beams or with their posts ground-fast.

Other notable reconstructions or simulations are those at Lejre in Denmark where a group of Iron Age houses has stood for some years, and been used for short experiments in living under quasi-Iron Age conditions. A most interesting experiment was carried out at Lejre when one of the houses was deliberately burnt down. The whole episode was filmed and the temperatures which were reached in various parts of the house were recorded. The fire lasted a frighteningly short time and was a vivid reminder of the climax of Njal's Saga, when the hero is burnt alive in his house by his enemies.

Six months after the fire the site was excavated and the plan of the remains drawn (see Coles, 1973, figs. 9-11). As Coles says, 'The correlation of the plans was quite remarkable. . . . door frames, partitions and flooring could be recognised, if with difficulty.' Experiments such as this give us greater confidence in the interpretation of slight and ephemeral traces of structures, interpretations which we should otherwise have to make almost solely on intuition.

The building of a variety of full-scale models, and their observed destruction, either by fire or demolition, or by the much longer processes of natural decay, is very laborious, but will in the future be one of the most important ways in which we shall deepen our understanding of the excavated evidence.

Most of us dig out of insatiable curiosity coupled with the, perhaps arrogant, conviction that by dissecting ancient sites we can understand them. The subtle flanks of an ancient earthwork, embedded in the landscape like a half-submerged sculpture by Henry Moore, or the dark green contrapuntal tracery of a cropmark seen from the air, give us a powerful *frisson* of discovery and recognition and an overwhelming desire to know what it means.

Man is, after all, the only animal which realizes that it has a past, and that it can consciously study it. And one of the principal ways in which we can get back into that past is by excavation, the first-hand study of the material evidence.

While we all acknowledge Wheeler's dictum that we should dig up people, not things, archaeologically we can only get at the people of the past through the things that they left, chiefly the debris of their buildings, their domestic rubbish, and, sometimes more closely, their own skeletal remains. So we spend weeks cleaning cobbled surfaces which were always deep in mud when they were in use, or conscientiously collect and docket scraps of pottery which were discarded by their owners without a second thought. And what Roger de Montgomery would think if he saw us at Hen Domen lovingly dissecting his soldiers' sewage

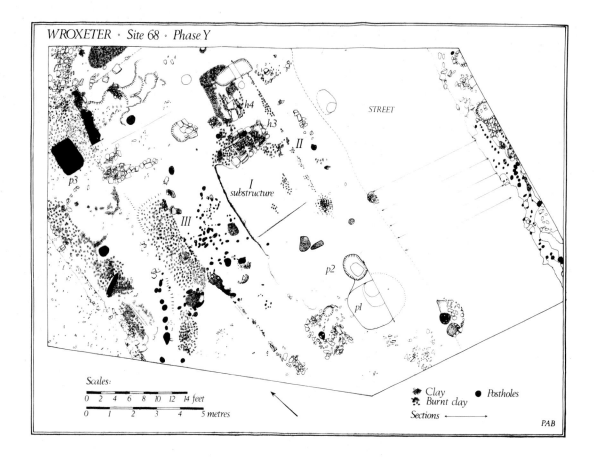

WROXETER · Site 68 · Phase Y

h4

h3

II

STREET

p3

I
substructure

III

p2

p1

Scales:

0 2 4 6 8 10 12 14 *feet*

0 1 2 3 4 5 *metres*

Clay
Burnt clay
Postholes

Sections

PAB

83 Removal of a few centimetres of deposits over the area revealed traces of two earlier buildings on the same alignment. One was revealed only by a curving edge of burnt clay (II), the other by a mass of stake-holes and a hearth (III).

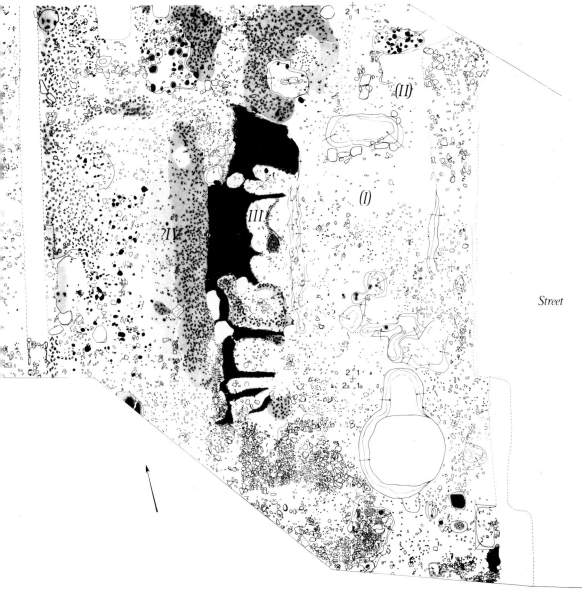

84 Removal of the uppermost layers, again only a centimetre or two thick, revealed more evidence of building III, this time in the form of colour-differentiated soils and a burnt area. There was evidence also of a fourth building (IV on plan) which appeared as two longitudinal areas of burnt clay.

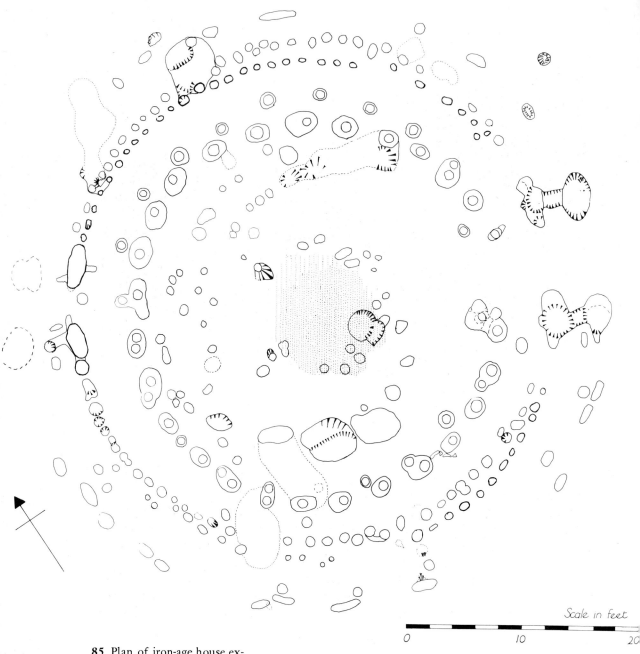

85 Plan of iron-age house excavated at Pimperne, Dorset by Professor Dennis Harding in 1961.

Scale in feet

0   10   20

86 Full-scale reconstruction
of the Pimperne house (by
P.J. Reynolds and J. Langley
at Butser Ancient Farm Project, Hampshire).

and packing it into little polythene bags we can barely guess.

Yet the sum total of all this apparently ludicrous activity, integrated by means
of all the converging skills and techniques of analysis and synthesis we can muster,
gives us, so long as we keep our heads, and do not get bogged down in mathemati-
cal or linguistic abstractions, a panoramic view of the past obtainable in no other
way. More than that, it enables us individually to put down deep roots in our
landscape — or townscape — to realize our place in the continuum of history, and,
by sympathetic direction, teaching and example, to help others to do the same.

Appendix

Treasure Hunting and Metal Detectors

The sale of metal detectors for treasure hunting is now widespread and its defenders claim the right to pursue what they see as a harmless hobby and invoke the freedom of the individual as an argument. Many claim that since they obtain the prior permission of the landowner, and give or sell any objects they find to a museum, complaints by archaeologists are unjustified and are prompted chiefly by sour grapes and professional jealousy.

I do not intend here to discuss the legal or moral issues which often confuse the purely archaeological arguments, but to show that any treasure hunting on an archaeological site is indefensible on purely archaeological grounds. I have shown elsewhere in this book that the digging of holes (even quite large holes) in archaeological sites produces fragmented, often distorted evidence which can rarely be understood (Chap. 4). The same arguments have even more force when applied to the tiny holes dug at the prompting of a metal detector. Many of these holes may produce nothing more significant than a modern horseshoe, a fragment of farm machinery or a nail. But the purpose of treasure hunting is primarily to find archaeological objects which have a market or intrinsic value. It is hard to think of any such object of metal which is not also potentially valuable as a piece of archaeological evidence. A coin, or a group of coins, an object such as a brooch, an arrow or spearhead, a fragment of harness of a finger-ring are all likely to be datable and to yield a great deal of information about the people who lost them, but only if they can be closely related to their position in the site and to all the other objects used and lost in the settlement, farm, temple, fort or whatever the site was that was being searched. An object of any kind divorced from its context loses almost all its value as evidence. To say that a coin came from a certain depth and a particular point in a field is simply not good enough. If the coin is to yield its full potential information about the dating and economy of the site we need to know precisely its relationship to the stratigraphy, the layers in or under which it was found. It follows that we need to know a great deal about the stratigraphy of the whole site, or at least a large part of it, before we can understand what the coins or other objects mean and that there is no chance whatever of recovering that information in a hole six inches square, or even three feet square. Only the most meticulous trowelling and accurate recording of the occupation layers in which the objects were embedded will provide the necessary contexts, and, as the rest of this book attempts to show, excavation has to be extensive if it is to be properly understood. Thus there can never be an archaeological justification for treasure hunting, or the use of a metal detector to find and dig out objects from archaeological sites.

If it is argued that the objects dug up were not from an archaeological site, the onus of proof of this must lie with the treasure hunter, since there is no way that a field can be shown *not* to contain, or be part of, an archaeological site, without very extensive geophysical survey and excavation. In other words, the treasure hunter either knows beforehand that an archaeological site is there, or he is digging blind, in which case he cannot know that it is not there.

Glossary

aceramic — without pottery; used of periods, both historic and prehistoric, in which pottery is not used, usually in contrast with other preceding or succeeding periods, or neighbouring contemporary cultures, in which pottery is used.

anaerobic — without air: used to describe conditions, such as waterlogging, where there is insufficient oxygen for bacterial or fungal growth, so that organic materials reach a state of equilibrium beyond which they do not decay.

balk (baulk) — a strip of an archaeological site left undug to form a barrow-run, or to provide vertical *sections* (q.v.)

froth flotation — by adding a detergent to the water in which the soil samples are agitated, light-weight materials such as seeds and charcoal fragments can be more easily separated from the *matrix* (q.v.)

hachure — a tapering line (tadpole) used to indicate the direction of a slope on the survey of an earthwork. The *hachure* points downhill and its length is related to the steepness of the slope. See Taylor, 1974 for excellent examples of hachured surveys.

isometric and axonometric projection (see figs. 72 and 73) — In these projections the plan and elevations are combined to give a 'three-dimensional' view, on which correct measurements can be taken either in any direction (isometric) or along two or three axes (axonometric).

levelling — In the context of this book, levelling means to establish the height above site datum of a number of points (spot heights) which will either record the level of the surface of a feature or layer, or enable a contour survey to be constructed.

magnetometer — an instrument for the measurement of changes in the magnetism of the earth's surface. By picking up anomalies in the earth's magnetism it can detect the presence of kilns, hearths, pits, ditches, etc.

matrix — 1. The mass of material such as mud, enclosing waterlogged vegetable remains; clay containing flints, etc.

2. by extension, the word is used to describe a pro-forma of rectangles used to construct a table of the relationship of features one to another (See p. 198).

micro-climate — the specifically local climate brought about by hills, slopes, woodland, lakes or other features of the landscape which modify the general climate of the region.

micro-podsol — a podsol is formed when water leaches dissolved chemicals through the uppermost layers of the soil, changing their appearance and often precipitating salts at a lower level, where they may, for instance form an *iron-pan*. The effect has often misled excavators into believing that they have found floors, etc., though the process is entirely natural. See Limbrey, 1975, 137-145.

mortice — a hole, usually rectangular, cut into a beam or plank, to take a *tenon*, which is a projection cut on the end of another beam and inserted into the *mortice* so that they can be joined together.

motte — a motte is a castle mound, usually of earth, but sometimes of stone. Attached to it may be one or more *baileys*, which are enclosures surrounded by ramparts or stone walls.

Munsell Colour Chart — a book of colour samples, each perforated with a hole through which the colour of the soil or other material can be compared with the standard sample which has a code denoting its hue and tone.

photogrammetry — the use of an overlapping stereoscopic mosaic of photographs to produce (usually with the aid of a mechanical plotter) a contour survey.

planum — a method of digging in which horizontal slices are removed either from the whole site, or from specific features, in order to reveal a succession of plans.

pollen spectrum — the diagram resulting from the analysis of the pollen from a column of peat or other soil.

post-hole (abbrev. ph); *post-pipe*; *post-pit* — in this book the term post-hole is used to mean the void or soil-filled mould where a post has stood. Some archaeologists use the term *post-pipe* to mean the same thing. *Post-pit* is used here to mean the pit dug to take a post. The pit is usually, though not always, bigger than its associated post-hole.

protohistoric — the earliest historic periods, that is, those early periods which have documentary evidence, often minimal, relating to them.

resistivity meter — a machine which measures the electrical resistivity of the earth between two probes. Since the resistivity of the soil changes with humidity, humus content, etc. the machine can detect pits, ditches, roads, floors, etc.

robber trench — the trench left (usually backfilled) by the labourers who have 'robbed' out a wall either completely or of its facing stone.

section — as here used, means the stratification revealed by the cutting of a trench or other vertical face through an archaeological site.

sleeper-beam; *sill-beam*; *cill-beam*; *ground-sill* — a horizontal foundation beam of wood, either lying directly on the ground or in a *timber-slot*, q.v.

solifluction — the downhill movement of saturated soil.

stratification — the successive layers, either natural or man-made, which make up the surface of the earth, and which, in this context, are revealed by an excavation.

stratigraphy — the scientific description of stratification.

timber-slot — a trench dug to contain a horizontal beam. See *sleeper-beam*.

vivianite — ferrosoferric phosphate, a white powder which forms in some buried soils and on iron objects. It turns a characteristic blue on contact with air.

Bibliography

Adams, J.M. (1969), 'Mapping with a third dimension', *Geographical Magazine* XLIII, No. 1, 45-49

Describes and illustrates anaglyphic mapping with red and green contours (spectacles provided). There is an impressive anaglyph chart of the bed of part of the Indian Ocean which demonstrates the possibilities of the method. (An adjacent article 'After Aberfan — analysis of the Welsh Valleys' by Wayne K.D. Davies shows the possibilities of using anaglyphic photography.)

Addyman, P. (1964), 'Dark Age Settlements at Maxey, Northants', *Med. Archaeol*, VIII

Addyman, P., Leigh, D., and Hughes, M.J., *Anglo-Saxon Houses at Chalton, Hampshire*, Medieval Archaeology, XVI,-1972 13 - 32

Alcock, L. (1972), *By South Cadbury is that Camelot*, London

Alexander, J. (1970), *The Directing of Archaeological Excavations*, London

Aston, M. and Rowley, R.T. (1974), *Landscape Archaeology*, London

Atkinson, R.J.C. (1953), *Field Archaeology*, 2nd edition, London

Atkinson, R.J.C. (1957), 'Worms and Weathering', *Antiquity*, 31

Barker, P.A. (1958) 'Moated Enclosure at Watling Street Grange, Oakengates, Emergency Excavations, 1958' *Shrops. Archaeol. Trans.* LVI, Part I, 21-25

Baker, P.A. (1961), 'A Pottery Sequence from Brockhurst Castle, Church Stretton, 1959', *Shrops. Arch. Trans.* LVII, Part I, 63-80

Barker, P.A. (1964), 'Excavations on the Moated site at Shifnal', *Shrops. Archaeol Trans.* LVII, Part III, 194-205

Barker, P.A. (1966), 'The Deserted Medieval Hamelt at Braggington', *Shrops. Archaeol. Trans.* LVIII, Part II, 122-39

Barker, P.A. (1969a), 'Hen Domen, Montgomery: Excavations 1960-7', *Chateau Gaillard* III, 15-27

Barker, P.A. (1969b), 'Some aspects of the excavation of timber buildings', *World Archaeol.* I, No. 2, 220-35

Barker, P.A. *et. al.* (1970), 'The Origins of Worcester', *Trans. Worcestershire Archaeol. Soc.*, Third Series, 2, 1968-9

Barker, P.A. (1970), *The medieval pottery of Shropshire from the Conquest to 1400*, Shropshire Archaeological Society

Barker, P.A. and Lawson, J. (1971), 'A pre-Norman field system at Hen Domen, Montgomery', *Medieval Archaeology*, XV, 58-72

Barker, P.A. (1975), 'Excavations on the site of the Baths Basilica at Wroxeter, An interim report'. *Britannia*. VI, 106-17

Benson, D. and Miles, D. (1974) *The Upper Thames Valley: an archaeological survey of the river gravels*, Oxford
    A model of fieldwork publication combining the results of aerial photography, excavation and surface finds

Beresford, M. and Hurst, J.G. (1971), *Deserted Medieval Villiages*

Bersu, G. (1940), 'Excavations at Little Woodbury', *Proc. Prehist. Soc.* VI, 30-111

Bersu, G. (1949), 'A Promontory Fort on the Shore of Ramsey Bay, Isle of Man', *Antiquaries Journal*, Vol. XXIX, January-April, 62-79

Bersu, G. (1977), edited by C.A. Ralegh Radford, *Three Iron Age Round Houses in the Isle of Man*, The Manx Museum and the National Trust.
    The report on a remarkable series of excavations carried out under armed guard while Bersu, with other 'enemy aliens', was interned in the Isle of Man during the Second World War

Beutiner-Jannaech, J. (1954), 'Use of Infra-red Photography in Archaeological Work', *American Antiquity*, 20, 84, Salt Lake City

Beveridge, W.I.B. (1950) *The Art of Scientific Investigation*, London

Biddle, M. and B. Kjølbye-. (1969), 'Metres, areas and robbing', *World Archaeology* I (2), 208-19

Biddle, M. (Winchester Interim Reports), *Arch. Journ.* CXIX, (1962), 150-94; *Antiq. Journ.* XLIV (1964), 188-219; XLV (1965); 230-64; XLVI (1966), 308-22; XLVII, (1967), 251-79; XLVIII, (1968), 250-84; XLIX, (1969), 295-329; (1970), 277-326; LII, (1972), 93-131; LV (1975) 96-126

Biek, L. (1963), *Archaeology and the Microscope*, London

Binford, S.R. and L.R. (eds.) (1968), *New Perspectives in Archaeology*, Chicago
    A symposium of essays reflecting the statistical approaches to archaeology being developed in the 1960s in America

Binford, L.R. (1972), *An Archaeological Perspective*, New York and London
    A collection of essays by one of the founders of the 'New Archaeology' linked by slightly embarrassing autobiographical passages

Bonnichsen, Robson (1972), 'Millie's Camp: an experiment in archaeology', *World Archaeology*, 4, 277-91
    An illuminating exercise in the interpretation of a deserted Indian camp site, checked by subsequent reference to the recent occupants, and demonstrating the fallibility of some of our 'common sense' reasoning. A useful bibliography of similar analogies is appended

Bowen, H.C. (1970), *Ancient Fields*, London

Bracegirdle, B. (1970), *Photography for Books and Reports*

Bradley, R. (1970), 'The Excavation of a Beaker Settlement at Belle Tout, East Sussex, England', *Proc. Prehist. Soc.*, XXXVI, 312-379

Bradley, R. (1976), 'Maumbury Rings, Dorchester: The Excavations of 1908-1913', *Archaeologia*, CV, 1-98

Brothwell, D. (1963), *Digging up Bones*, London

Brothwell, D. and Brothwell, P. (1969), *Food in Antiquity*, London

Brothwell, D. and Higgs, E. eds. (1969), *Science in Archaeology*, London

Browne, D. (1975), *Teach Yourself Archaeology*, London

Bruce-Mitford, R.L.S. (ed.) (1956), *Recent Archaeological Excavations in Britain*, London

Contains the first published account of the development of the techniques of excavation used at Wharram Percy

Bruce-Mitford, R.L.S. 1974

Buckland, P.C. (1974), 'Archaeology and Environment in York', *Journal of Archaeological Science*, 1974, 1, 303-16

Bushe-Fox (1913, 1914, 1916), *Excavations on the Site of the Roman Town at Wroxeter, Shropshire, in 1912*

Second Report on the Excavations on the Site of the Roman Town at Wroxeter, Shropshire in 1913

Third Report on the Excavations on the Site of the Roman Town at Wroxeter, Shropshire in 1916 Society of Antiquaries

Carver, M.O.H. (1981), 'Sampling Towns: an optimistic strategy' in Clack and Haselgrove (eds), *Approaches to the Urban Past*, Durham. Contains a useful bibliography

Case, H. (1952), 'The Excavation of Two Round Barrows at Poole, Dorset', *Proc. of the Prehistoric Society*, N.S. XVIII, 148-59

Casey, J. (1974), 'The Interpretation of Romano-British Site Finds', *Coins and the Archaeologist*, British Archaeological Reports, 4, 37-51

A salutary article on the misuse of coin evidence due to misunderstanding of the historic and economic background

Cherry, J.F., Gamble, C., and Shennan, S, (1978), *Sampling in Contemporary British Archaeology,* Oxford

Papers stemming from a conference held at Southampton in 1977. Many of the papers take a fundamentally different stance on excavation from that taken in this book and it is therefore required reading for those wishing to achieve a balanced view

Clack, P., and Haselgrove, S (eds) (1981), *Approaches to the Urban Past*, Durham

Clark, G. (1957), *Archaeology and Society*, 3rd edition, London

Clarke, D.L. (1968), *Analytical Archaeology*, London

The best introduction to statistical methods of archaeological analysis

Clarke, D.L. (ed) (1972), *Models in Archaeology*, London

Coles, J. (1972), *Field Archaeology in Britain*, London

Coles, J. (1973), *Archaeology by Experiment*, Hutchinson

Coles, J. (1979), *Experimental Archaeology*, London

Collingwood, R.G. (1939), *An Autobiography*, Oxford

Conlon, V.M. (1973), *Camera Techniques in Archaeology*, London

Cook, S.F., and Heizer, R.F. (1965), *Studies on the Chemical Analysis of Archaeological Sites*, University of California Press

Cooke, F.B.M. and Wacher, J.S. 'Photogrammetric Surveying at Wanborough, Wilts', *Antiquity*, 44

    A description of vertical photography on a fourth-century AD excavation using a turret similar to that described in Nylen 1964

Cookson, M.B. (1954), *Photography for Archaeologists*, London

Cornwall, I. (1956), *Bones for the Archaeologist*, London

Cornwall, I. (1958), *Soils for the Archaeologist*, London

Council for British Archaeology (1970) *Handbook of Scientific Aids and Evidence for Archaeologists*, London

    With bibliographies for each subject

Crawford, O.G.S. (1953), *Archaeology in the Field*, London

Cunliffe, B. (1973), 'Chalton, Hants, The Evolution of a Landscape', *Antiq. Journal* LIII, Part II, 173-90

Daniel, G. (1950), *A Hundred Years of Archaeology*, London

Daniel, G. (1967), *The Origins and Growth of Archaeology*, Harmondsworth

Daniel, G. (1976), *A Hundred and Fifty Years of Archaeology*, Cambridge

Darwin, C. (1881), *The Formation of Vegetable Mould Through the Action of Worms with Observations on their Habits* (republished by Faber and Faber London, 1945, under the title *Darwin on Humus and the Earthworm*, with an introduction by Sir Albert Howard)

Davison, B.K. (1969), Early Earthwork Castles: A New Model, *Chateau Gaillard III*, Chichester, 37, ff.

de Bono, E. (1970), *Lateral Thinking: a textbook of creativity*, London

de Bouard, M. (1975), *Manuel d'archeologie medievale*, Paris

    A study of medieval archaeology in France by one of her most respected elder statesmen

Department of the Environment (1975), *Principles of Publication in Rescue Archaeology*, H.M.S.O.

Dimbleby, G. (1967), *Plants and Archaeology*, London

Dimbleby, G. (1978), *The Scientific Treatment of Material from Rescue Excavations*, Department of the Environment

    Although principally concerned (through its terms of reference) with rescue archaeology, the recommendations of the report apply equally to all excavated material, however recovered

Doran, J. (1970), 'Systems theory, computer simulations and archaeology', *World Archaeology*, I, No. 3, February, 289-98

Dowman, E.A. (1970), *Conservation in Field Archaeology*, London

Dymond, D.P. (1974), *Archaeology and History – a plea for reconciliation*, London

Ellison, A. (1981), *A Policy for Archaeological Investigation in Wessex*, Salisbury
A clear and logical analysis of the massive destruction of the Wessex landscape together with proposals for period-based projects designed to examine those problems which are deemed to be the most urgent or which have, in the past, received least attention

Es, W.A. van, (1967), 'Wijster: a Native Village beyond the Imperial Frontier 150-425 AD', *Palaeohistoria* XI
An exemplary report on the excavation of a village of timber buildings.

Es, W.A. van, (1969), 'Excavations at Dorestad, a Pre-preliminary Report: 1967-68', *Berichten van de Rijksdienst Voor het Oudheidkundig Bodemonderzoek*

Farrugia, J.P., Duper, R., Luning, J., Stehli, P. (1973), 'Untersuchunger zur Neolithischen Besiedlung der Aldenhovener Platte', *Bonner Jahrbucher, 226-56*
Describes and illustrates the large-scale machine stripping of a linear pottery settlement with examples of feature and find recording cards.

Fasham, P.J., Schadla-Hall, R.T., Shennan, S.J., and Bates, P.J. (1980), *Fieldwalking for Archaeologists*, Andover, Hampshire
A clear and concise guide

Fleming, S. (1976), *Dating in Archaeology: A Guide to Scientific Techniques.*

Flond, R. (1973), *An Introduction to Quantitative Methods for Historians*, London

Fowler, E. (ed). (1972), *Field Survey in British Archaeology*, London

Fowler, P.J. (ed). (1972), *Archaeology and the Landscape*, London

Fowler, P.J. (ed). (1972), *Responsibility and Safeguards in Archaeological Excavation*, Council for British Archaeology

Fowler, E. (ed). (1972a), *Field Survey in British Archaeology*, London

Fowler, P.J. (ed). (1972b), *Responsibility and Safeguards in Archaeology Excavation*, Council for British Archaeology

Fowler, P.J. (1977), *Approaches to Archaeology*, London
A successor to Piggott's *Approach to Archaeology*, 1959, which reviews the changes in British archaeology in the last 18 years, and looks forward to the next decade.

Fox and Hope (1891), Fox (1892), Fox and Hope (1893), *Excavations on the site of the Roman City of Silchester, Hants*, (in 1890, 1891, 1892) London

Fox, Aileen and Cyril (1960), 'Wandsdyke Reconsidered', *Archaeol. Journal*, CXV, 1-48
A reassessment of a famous linear earthwork based on intensive observation and a study of the historical evidence

Fox, Sir Cyril (1952), *The Personality of Britain: Its influence on inhabitant and invader in prehistoric and early historic times*, Cardiff
Though written before the full impact of aerial photography on settlement

patterns was realized this is still a classic archaeological geography

Fox, Sir Cyril (1955), *Offa's Dyke*,
   A classic field study of a linear earthwork. Though some questions remain unanswered (and some unasked) it is probable that little more can be discovered about the dyke without excavation (though see Hill, 1970)

Fox and Hope, (1891), Fox, (1892), Fox and Hope, (1893), *Excavations at Silchester, Hants 1890, 1891, 1892*, Society of Antiquaries

Frere, S.S. (1959), 'Excavations at Verulamium, 1958', *Antiq. Journal* XXXIX, 1-18

Frere, S.S. (1971), *Verulamium Excavations* I, Oxford

Fryer, D.H. (1971), *Surveying for archaeologists*, 4th edition, Durham

Gardin, J.G. (1966), *Code pour l'analyse des poteries medievales*, Université de Caen
   An attempt to codify all possible characteristics of medieval pottery, so that a punch-card system (and subsequently computer storage) can be developed. The publication demonstrates the vast range of characteristics for which entries are required if all variants are to be recorded

Giffen, van (1958), 'Prehistorische Hausformen auf Sandboden in den Niederlanden', *Germania*, jaargang 36, 36-7

Gillam, J.P. (1957, sec. ed. 1968), *Types of Roman Coarse Pottery Vessels in Northern Britain*

Goodyear, F.H. (1971), *Archaeological Site Science*, London

Grimes, W.F. (1960), *Excavations on Defence Sites, 1939-1945*, I, H.M.S.O.

Grimes, W.F. (1968), *The Excavation of Roman and Medieval London*, London

Grinsell, L., Rahtz, P., D. Price Williams, (1974), *The Preparation of Archaeological Reports*, Revised edition, London
   This revised and enlarged edition replaces that of 1966

Guilbert, G. (1973), 'Moel y Gaer, A progress report', *Current Archaeology* 37, March, 38-44

Guerreschi, A. (1973), 'A mechanical sieve for archaeological excavations', *Antiquity*, XLVII, 187, September

Haggett, P. (1965), *Location Analysis in Human Geography*, London

Hamilton, J.R.C. (1956), *Excavations at Jarlshof, Shetland*, H.M.S.O.
   A multi-period site excavated and published in exemplary style

Hanson, N.R., (1967), 'Observation and Interpretation' in (ed. S. Morgenbesser) *Philosophy of Science Today*, New York

Harris, E.C. (1975), 'The Stratigraphic Sequence: a question of time', *World Archaeology*, Vol. 7, No. 1 June, 109-21

Harris, E.C. (1979), *Principles of Archaeological Stratigraphy*, London
   A fundamental statement of the laws of stratigraphy and the ways in which they may be applied and understood.

Hassall, T.G. (1971), 'Excavations at Oxford', *Oxoniensia*, 36

Hatt, G. (1957), 'Nørre Fjand, an Early Iron Age Village in West Jutland', *Arkaeol.*

Kunsthist, Skr. Dan. Vid. Selsk. 2, No. 2. Copenhagen

Hawkes, C.F.C. (1948), 'Britons, Romans and Saxons in and around Salisbury and Cranborne Chase', *Archaeol. Journal*, CIV, 27-81

Hayfield, C. (1980), *Fieldwalking as a method of Archaeological Research*, Department of the Environment
   A collection of highly suggestive papers from a conference held in 1976

Hayward, J.A. (1968), 'Unshored Excavations are Killers', *The British Journal of Occupational Safety*, Vol. 7, No. 85, Autumn
   A very useful survey with check list of safety questions

Heizer, R.F. and Graham, J.A. (1967), *A Guide to Field Methods in Archaeology*, California
   A comprehensive exposition of American methods with a very extensive but unclassified and uncritical bibliography

Hill, D. (1974), 'The inter-relation of Offa's and Wat's Dykes', *Antiquity*, XLVIII, 192, 309-312

Hirst, S. (1976), *Recording on Excavations I, the Written Record*, RESCUE publication No. 7, Hertford

Hobley, B. (1973), 'Excavations at "The Lunt" Roman Military Site, Baginton, Warwickshire 1968-71, Second Interim Report', *Trans. Birm, and Warwicks, Archaeol. Soc.* Vol. 85, 1972

Hodges, H. (1970), *Technology in the Ancient World*, Harmondsworth

Hodson, Kendall and Tautu (eds). (1971), *Mathematics in the Archaeological and Historical Sciences*, Edinburgh

Hogg, A.H.A. (1981), *Surveying for Archaeologists and other Fieldworkers*, London
   A highly detailed handbook supplementing instruction in the field (which it or any other manual cannot replace)

Hope-Taylor, B. (1966), 'Archaeological Draughtsmanship, II', *Antiquity*, XL

Hope-Taylor, B. (1967), 'Archaeological Draughtsmanship III', *Antiquity*, XLI

Hope-Taylor, B. (1977), *Yeavering, An Anglo-British centre of early Northumbria*, London, H.M.S.O.

Hurst, J.G. (1956), 'Deserted Medieval Villages and the Excavation at Wharram Percy, Yorkshire', in Bruce-Mitford, R.L.S. (ed.), *Recent Archaeological Excavations in Great Britain*, London

Hurst, J.G. (1969), 'Medieval Britain in 1968', *Med. Archaeol,* XIII, 252-3

Hurst, J.G. (ed.) (1974), *Medieval Pottery from Excavations*, London

Hurst, J.G. (ed.) (1979), *Wharram, A Study of Settlement on the Yorkshire Wolds*, Society for Medieval Archaeology Monograph No. 8

Jankuhn, H. (1969), 'Vor- und Fruhgeschichte vom Neolithikum bis der Volker-wanderingszeit', *Deutsche Agrargeschichte*, I, Verlag Eugen Ulmer
   Contains many plans of settlement sites

Jeffries, J.S. (1977), *Excavation Records. Techniques in use by the Central Excavation Unit*, Department of the Environment

Jones, M.U. *et. al* (1968), 'Crop-mark Sites at Mucking, Essex', *Antiquaries Journal*, XLVIII, Part II 210-30

Jones, M.U. (1974), 'Excavations at Mucking, Essex: A second interim report', *Antiquaries Journal*, LIV, Pt. II 183-99

Joukowsky, M. (1980), *A Complete Manual of Field Archaeology*, New Jersey
Contains an exhaustive and very useful bibliography. However, the text has a number of fundamental weaknesses which invalidate much of its advice

Kenrick, P. (1971), 'Aids to the drawing of finds', *Antiquity*, XLV

Kenyon, K.M. (1964), *Beginning in Archaeology*, London

Kjølbye-Biddle, B. (1975), 'A Cathedral Cemetery: problems in excavation and interpretation, *World Archaeology*, Vol. 7, No. 1

Lamb, H.H. (1971), 'Britain's Worsening Winters', *The Times*, 30 January, London

Lamb, H.H. (1972), *Climate, Present, Past and Future*, London

Lapinskas, P. (1975), 'Flotation Machine', *M3 Archaeology 1974*, ed. Fasham, Winchester

Leigh, D and others, (1972), *First Aid for Finds*, Worcester

Limbrey, S. (2975), *Soil Science and Archaeology*, London

Mackie, E. *et al* (1971), 'Thoughts on radio-carbon dating', *Antiquity*, XLV, No. 179, 197-204

Mason, J.F.A. and Barker, P.A. (1961), 'The Norman Castle at Quatford', *Trans. Shrops, Archaeol, Soc.* LVII, Pt. I, 37-62

Matthews, S.K. (1968), *Photography in Archaeology and Art*, London

Medawar, P.B. (1969), *Induction and Intuition in Scientific Thought*

Megaw, J.V.S., ed. (1979), *Signposts for Archaeological Publication*, Council for British Archaeology, London

Morgan, J.W.W. (1975), 'The Preservation of Timber', *Timber Grower, 55*

Musson, C.R. (1971), In *Durrington Walls, Excavations 1966-1968*. Report of the Research Committee, Society of Antiquaries of London XXIX, 363-77 London

Nørlund, P. (1948), *Trelleborg*, Copenhagen

Nylen, E. (1964), 'A Turret for Vertical Photography', *Antikvariskt Arkiv*, XXIV

Olsen, O. (1968), 'Om at Udgrave Stolpehuller', *Nationalmuseets Arbijdsmark*
Describes the techniques, including those for enhancing soil colour differences, used to re-excavate post-holes at the Viking fortresses of Trelleborg and Fyrkat

Olsen, Ol. and Crumlin-Pedersen, O. (1968), *The Skuldelev Ships*, Copenhagen
Demonstrates methods of excavating and particularly of recording (photogrammetrically) surfaces on which it is impossible or undesirable to walk

Ordnance Survey (1963), *Field Archaeology, Some Notes for Beginners*, 4th edition, H.M.S.O., London (5th ed. in preparation)

Orton, C. (1980) *Mathematics in Archaeology*, London
A splendidly lucid exposition for the semi-numerate of the uses of mathematics in archaeology

Panton, *et al* (1958), 'The Clarendon Hotel, Oxford' *Oxoniensia*, XXIII, 1.129

Petch, D.F. (1911), 'Earthmoving machines and their employment on archaeological excavations', *Journal of the Chester Archaeological Society*

Petrie, W.M.F. (1904), *Methods and Aims in Archaeology*, London

Piggott, S. (1959), *Approach to Archaeology*, London

Piggott, S. and Hope-Taylor, B. (1965), 'Archaeological Draughtsmanship: Principles and Practice', *Antiquity*, XXXIX, 5-8

Pitt Rivers, A.H.L.F. (1887-98), *Excavations in Cranborne Chase*, 4 vols. London

Plenderlieth, H.J. (1956), *The Conservation of Antiquities and works of Art*

Pryor, F. (1974), *Earthmoving on Open Archaeological Sites*, Nene Valley Archaeol. Handbook I

Pyddoke, E. (ed.) (1963), *The Scientist and Archaeology*, London

Rahtz, P.A. (1964), 'Saxon and Medieval Palaces at Cheddar', *Medieval Archaeology*, VI-VII 53-66 and forthcoming H.M.S.O. volume

Rahtz, P.A. (1969) *Excavations at King John's Hunting Lodge, Writtle Essex. 1955-57*, Society for Medieval Archaeology Monograph Series 3, London
> An exemplary report on a rescue excavation of a complex moated site with only tenuous evidence of some of the major buildings.

Rahtz, P.A. (ed), (1974), *Rescue Archaeology*, Harmondsworth

Rahtz, P.A. (1975), 'How Likely is Likely?', *Antiquity*, XLIX, 59-61

Rahtz, P.A. (1979), *The Saxon and Medieval Palaces at Cheddar*, B.A.R. British Series 65, Oxford

Rahtz, P.A. and Hirst, S. (1975), *Bordesley Abbey*, Oxford

Raikes, R. (1911), *Water, Weather and Prehistory*, London

Renfrew, C. (ed.) (1974), *British Prehistory, A New Outline*, London

Renfrew, T.M., Monk, M, and Murphy, P. (1976), *First Aid for Seeds*, Hertford

Reynolds, P. (1979), *Iron Age Farm*, London

Rodwell, W. and K. (1973), 'Rivenhall (Church)', *Current Archaeol.*, 36

Rodwell, K. (1976), 'The Archaeological Investigation of Hadstock Church, Essex, An Interim Report', *Antiq. Journal*, LVI, Part I, 55-71

Rodwell, W. (1982), *The Archaeology of the English Church*, London

Royal Society, (1965), *The Preparation of Scientific Papers*, London

Ryder, M.L. (1969), *Animal Bones in Archaeology*, Oxford

St. Joseph, J.K.S. (ed.) (1966), *The Uses of Air Photography*, London

Schmidt, H. (1973), 'The Trelleborg House reconsidered', *Med. Archaeol.* XVII, 52-77

Simmons, H.C. (1969), *Archaeological Photography*, London

Slosson, E.E. (1928), 'The Science of the City Dump', *Snapshots of Science* in Raport and Wright, 1963, *Archaeology*, New York
> A very early example of the view that archaeology began yesterday

Sorrell, A. (1973, 'The Artist and Reconstruction', *Current Archaeology*, 41, November, 177-81
> A valuable statement by the late Alan Sorrell on the aims and methods of the archaeological artist

Steensberg, A. (1968), *Atlas over Borups Agre*, Copenhagen
>   The record of an astounding piece of fieldwork in which the positions of about a million stones and boulders were plotted to demonstrate the pattern of field systems over an area of some 72 hectares

Steensberg, A. (1952), *Farms and Water Mills in Denmark during 2000 Years* Copenhagen
>   Contains reports of the excavations of three major sites, Bølle, Pebringe and Aså and a smaller site, Nødskovlede. These excavations, made between 1938 and 1940 mark a turning point in the development of medieval archaeology

Steensberg, A. (1975), *Store Valby*, Copenhagen

Strong, D.E. (ed.) (1973), *Archaeological Theory and Practice*, Seminar Press

Taylor, C.C. (1967), 'Whiteparish', *Wilts Archaeol. Magazine*, 62, 79-102

Taylor, C.C. (1974), *Fieldwork in Medieval Archaeology*, London

Taylor, C.C. (1975), *Fields in the English Landscape*, London

Terrell, J. (1971), 'Potsherd rim angles: a simple device', *Antiquity*, XLV

Thompson, F.H. (1976), 'The Excavation of the Roman Amphitheatre at Chester' *Archaeologia*, MCMLXXVI

Thompson, M.W. (1967), *Novgorod the Great, Excavations at the Medieval City*, 1951-62

Trump, D.H. (1971), 'Aids to drawing: sherd radii', *Antiquity*, XLV

Tylecote, R.F. (1962), *Metallurgy in Archaeology*, London

Ucko, P.J. and Dimbleby, G.W. (eds.) (1969), *The demonstration and exploitation of plants and animals*, London

Wade, K. (1974), 'Whither Anglo-Saxon Archaeology?', in Rowley, ed., *Anglo-Saxon Settlement and Landscape*, Oxford

Wainwright, F.T. (1962) *Archaeology and Place-Names and History*, London

Wainwright, J.G. (1971), *Durrington Walls, Excavations, 1966-1968*, Report of the Research Committee, Society of Antiquaries of London, XXIX

Walle, A. van de, (1961), 'Excavations in the Ancient Centre of Antwerp', *Med. Archaeol.*, V, 123-136, Fig. 36
>   These important excavations show how slight the traces of town houses may be and how walls may simply be built of wattling without corner posts (Fig. 35)

Waterman, D.M. (1959), 'Excavations at Lismahon, co. Down', *Med. Archaeol*, III, 139-76

Webster, G. (1970), *Pottery Colour Chart*, RESCUE, Worcester

Webster, G. (1974), *Practical Archaeology*, 2nd edition, London

Webster, G. (ed.) (1976), *Romano-British Coarse Pottery. A Student's Guide*, London, 3rd edition

Webster, G. and Woodfield, P. (1966), 'The Old Work at the Public Baths at Wroxeter', *Antiq. Journal*, XLVI, 234, 237

Webster, P. (1975), 'Roman and Iron-Age Tankards in Western Britain', *Bulletin of the Board of Celtic Studies*, XXVI, 231-6

Wells, C. (1964), *Bones, Bodies, and Disease*, London

Wheeler, R.E.M. (Sir) (1943), 'Maiden Castle, Dorset', *Society of Antiquaries*, London

> A classic excavation report. The first part of the report, in particular, is a model of exposition

Wheeler, R.E.M. (Sir) (154), *Archaeology from the Earth*, Oxford

> Reprints in Pelican Books, 1956 and 1961

Williams, D. (1973), 'Flotation at Siraf', *Antiquity*, XLVII, 188, December

Williams, J.C.C. (1969), *Simple Photogrammetry*, Academic Press

> A useful introduction to photogrammetry

Wilson, D. Gay (1973), 'An open letter to archaeologists', *Antiquity*, 47, No. 188, December, 264-8

> A plea for archaeologists to understand the limitations and difficulties of scientific techniques

Wilson, D.R. (ed.) (1975), *Aerial Reconnaissance for Archaeology*, C.B.A. Research Report no. 12

Wilson, D.R. (1982), *Air Photo Interpretation for Archaeologists*, London

Wincklemann, W. (1958), 'Die Ausgrabungen in der fruhmittelalterlichen Siedlung bei Warendorf, *Neue Ausgrabungen in Deutschland*, 492-517

Woolley, L. (1930), *Digging up the Past*, London, Penguin ed. 1954

Young, C.J., (ed) (1980), *Guidelines for the Processing and Publication of Roman Pottery from Excavations*, Department of the Environment

> An attempt by the DoE and the Study Group for Roman-British Pottery to create and bring into use common standards for examining and recording the masses of pottery commonly found on Romano-British sites

Index

Page numbers in *italics* indicate those on which illustrations appear

Abdon, Shropshire
  House sites at   39
Aceramic periods   137, 180-2
Acton Scott, Shropshire
  Greek coins from   178
Adderley, Shropshire
  Pottery from   178
Addyman, P.V.   256
Alcock, L.   34
Alexander, J.   160
Anglo-Saxon Coins   178, 190
  Pottery   177
  Sunken floored huts   136
  Palaces   20, 88, 89
Antwerp
  Town houses at   257
Archaeological units   32

Astley, Sharpley Pool
  Furnace   *242, 243*
Aston, M.   28, 31
Atkinson, D.   205
Atkinson, R.J.C.   45, 121-5, 151, 160

Balks   84
Barrows (burial mounds)   32, 56
Barton, K.J.   38
Bayeux Tapestry
  Castles on   224
Beckford, Worcs.   *72, 73*
Belle Tout, Sussex   *174, 175*
Beresford, G.   257
Beresford, M.W.   21, 119
Bersu, G.   16, 20

Beveridge, W.I.B.   144
Biddle, M.   21, 84, 231
  and Kjølbye-Biddle, B.   151, 195
Biek, L.   116
Binford, L.R.   188
Binford, S.R.   188
Bones
  Animal   43, 100, 113, 146, 182, 188, 208, 214
  Fluorine etc. dating of   208
Bonnichsen, R.   195
Bono, de, E.   193
Bordesley Abbey   31, 45, *62, 63, 64, 65, 245*
Bradley, R.   14, 174
Bradphys restivity machine   35

Bridgwater, N. 120
British Archaeological Reports
    228
Britnell, W. 73, 74
Bronze Age hut 56
    linear ditch *73*
Brothwell, D. 100, 116, 207,
    208
Bruce-Mitford, R.L.S. 97
Brushes, brushing 71, 82
Buckland, P.C. 213
Bushe-Fox, J.P. 15
Butler, L. 59

Caerwent 15
Campagnola, G.,
    engraving of timber castle by
    224
Cannington, cemetery at *102*
Carver, M.O.H. 39, 42, 59, 259
Case, H. 16
Casey, J. 190
Cemeteries, graves, burials 32,
    73, 100, *101*, *102*, 103, 104
Chalton, Hampshire 41, 220
Champion, T. 41
Chaplin, R. 214
Cheddar, Anglo-Saxon palace at
    20, 89
    Coins from, 178
Cherry, J.F. 42
Chester, reconstruction of
    amphitheatre at, 259
Clack, P. 39
Clarendon Hotel, Oxford 59
Clarke, D.L. 183, 220
Climatic changes 213
Coins 38, 66, 81, 95, 133, 137,
    139, 176, 178, 179, 190
    Cleaning of, 189
    Dating by, 197-200
Coles, J. 31, 74, 94, 131, 151,
    254, 263
Collingwood, R.G. 42, 43
Computers, use in archaeology
    29, 31, 147, 150, 187
Conservation, conservators 96,
    97, 98, 99, 100
Construction trenches 57, 195
Corbridge 14
Cornwall. I. 116
Council for British Archaeology,
    Insurance scheme 109
Crop Marks 27, 34, 35, 36, 40,
    53, 131-3, 137
Cunliffe, B.W. 33

Daniel, G. 13
Darwin, C. 117
Dating 197-203
    Dendrochronology 190, 192
    211
    Fluorine etc, dating of bone

208
    Methods 38, 42, 43
    Obsidian 207
    Radio Carbon 192, 207, 211,
    221
    Thermo-luminescence 207
    Thermo-remanent magnetism
    207
Davison, B.K. 218, 219
Dendrochronology 190, 192, 211
Deserted medieval villages 32, 39,
    40, 43, 44, 56
    Wharram Percy 21
Dimbleby, G. 208
Ditches 121, 123, 131, 132, 134
    City ditch at Worcester 137
Documentary evidence 12, 27,
    32, 36, 37, 218, 219, 221
Dorestad 44, 129, 133, *135*
Dowsing 51, 132
Drawings for publication 233-47
Duncot, Shropshire, Roman Fort
    35
Durrington Walls 133, 206
Dymond, D.P. 218

Earthworks 27, 28, 31, 32, 35,
    38, *39*, 52, 137
    Medieval fish ponds 45
    Mottes 43-4, 56, 219, 256-8
    Ringworks 43
Earthworms, worm action 95,
    117, 121-5, 132
Ede, Holland
    Long House at, *244*
Ellison, A. 42
Environmental Evidence 208,
    210-15, 221
Es, W.A. van 44, 74, 129, 131,
    133, 134, 244; *back endpapers*

Fasham, P.J. 35
Farrugia, J.P. 74
Fields 28
    Names 32, 40
    Systems 30, 31, 73, 220
Fieldwork 27-36, 40, 220
    Field walking 32, 33, 35
Flotation, for environmental
    evidence 142, 212-15
Fluorine etc, dating of bones 208
Forster, E.M. 146
Fosse Way 52
Foundation trenches 58
Fowler, P.J. 82, 109
Fox, Sir Cyril 52
Fox, G.E. (and Hope) 15
Frere, S.S. 21
Froth flotation 212
Fryer, D.H. 31, 151
Fyrkat, Denmark 41, 78

Gamble, C. 42

Gardin, J.G. 177
Geology 27, 118
Geophysical prospecting
    see Surveying
Giffen, van 16
Glastonbury Lake Village, model
    interpretation of 219, 220
Gloucester 26, 31, 222
Golson, J. 21
Goltho, medieval house at 257
Gray, H. St George 14
Gray, M. 45
Greenwell, Canon 13
Gregg, A. 143
Grimes, W.F. 241
Grinsell, L. 36, 232, 238, 241,
    247, 251
Guerreschi, A. 212
Guilbert, G.C. 115

Haggett, P. 174
Hanson, N.R. 143
Harris, E. 154, 201, *202*, *203*,
    245
Haselgrove, S. 39
Hassall, T. 59
Hastings 38
Hatt, G. 16, 20, 87
Haverfield, F. 14
Hawkes, C.F.C. 14
Health and Safety at Work Act,
    1974 82, 109, 110
Heighway, C. 231
Hen Domen, Montgomery *30*,
    31, 39, 44, *46*, *47*, *48*, *49*,
    54, *85*, *86*, 99, 112, 122, 130,
    259
    Aceramic period at 180
    Building I, plan and inter-
    pretation *246*, *247*
    Figure of eight hasps from 176
    Pre-Norman field system at
    29, 220-2
    Coins at 190
Higgs, E. 116, 207, 208, 214
Hill, D. 52
Hill Forts 44
Hirst, S. 45
History and archaeology 218,
    219, 221-23
Hobley, B. 44, 259
Hoes, used for excavation 133,
    134
Hope-Taylor, B. 9, 20, 88, 136,
    251
Hudson, D. 231
Hurst, J.G. 21, 59, 119, 177
Hurst, T. *161*, *162*, *163*
Husterknupp, The, Germany
    Medieval building at 258

Ideal excavation 41
Interim Reports 21

Iron Age   Glastonbury Lake
    Village
    Model interpretation of   219
    Pottery   185
    Settlement   73
    Simulation of Iron Age houses,
        Lejre   263

Janssen, excavations at Dorestad
    133
Jenks, E.   59
Jericho   50
Jerusalem   50
Jones, M.U.   33, 103, 131, 133

Kent, J.P.C.   256, 257
Kenyon, Dame K.   50, 160
Kjølbye-Biddle, B.   66, 104
Kuper, R.   74

Lamb, H.H.   213
Lapinskas, P.   212
'Lateral' thinking   193
Lawson, J.   31, 221
Lea, R.   242, 243
Leigh, D. (and others)   96, 97
Lejre, Denmark
    Simulations of Iron Age houses
        263
Limbrey, L.   82, 116, 120, 121,
    131, 160, 216
Lincoln   26, 31, 222
Lismahon, motte at   257
Little Butser, Hampshire
    Prehistoric experimental farm
        at   259
London   26, 148, 149, 161, 162,
    163, 240
Luning, J.   74

Machinery, earth moving   51, 73,
    74-5, 107, 127, 128, 130,
    133, 135, 136, 141
    Machine digging at Worcester
        137
Mackie, E.   211
Magnetometer surveys
    see Surveying
Maiden Castle   218
Maps   28, 31-3,
    Distribution   129
Maxey   256
Medawar, P.B.   143
Medieval Building at the Huster-
        knupp   258
    Coins   179, 190
    House at Goltho   257
    Long houses   56, 119
    Manor house   56
    Pottery   177
    Settlements   128
Metal detectors   268
Millie's Camp, Interpretation of

deserted Indian site   195
Microfiche   230
Microfilm   230
Moats   38
Mobius Network   132
Moel-y-Gaer, rectangular timber
    building at   113, 114, 115
Monk, M.   212, 214
Montgomery, Roger de, effigy of
    in Shrewsbury Abbey   223
Morgan, W.W.   89, 91
Mucking, Essex   220
Munsell Soil Colour Chart   120
Murphy, P.   212, 214
Museums   12, 36, 99, 100, 147
    Avoncroft Museum of
        Buildings, Bromsgrove
        257, 259
    Singleton, Sussex   259
Musson, C.R.   206

Nørlund, P.   78, 94
Nørre Fjand   16, 17, 18, 19, 20
Novgorod   190, 220

Olsen, O.   78, 94
    and Crumlin-Pederson, O.   99
Orton, C.   174

Panton, W.   59
Pebringe   59
Penetrometer   78
Petch, D.F.   74
Petrie, F.   14
Photography   118, 140, 142,
    146, 150, 160-72
    Aerial Journal of   33
    For publication   233, 238
    Oblique   132, 166
    Of burials   100, 103
    Of small finds   97, 98
    Photogrammetry   28, 65,
        142, 170
    Polaroid   97, 170
    Site   138
    Stereo   28, 31, 100, 104, 159,
        169
    Using coloured filters   78
    Vertical   100, 104, 132, 160,
        164, 170, 171, 172
Pits, see Post-holes
Pitt Rivers, Lieut.-General   Front
    endpapers, 13, 14, 173, 227
Plans, planning   15, 24, 25, 84,
    85, 91, 92, 118, 139, 150,
    151, 152, 154, 156-60
    Drawing frames for   154, 155
    Of burials and cemeteries
        103, 104
Planum excavation   80, 117,
    133, 134
    Method of excavating post-
        holes and pits   92

Post-holes, stake-holes and pits
    59, 65, 77, 78, 79, 80, 81, 84,
    87, 88, 89, 91-94, 108, 116-18,
    120, 121, 123, 131, 132, 136,
    144, 159, 174, 175
Pottery   37, 40, 52, 66, 100,
    113, 124, 132, 137, 139,
    140, 146, 205
    Aceramic periods   179-81
    Glazes   184
    Iron Age and Roman tankards
        185
    Recording of   173-91
    Residual pottery   181
Price-Williams, D.   36, 232, 238,
    241, 247, 251
Problems and strategies   37-67
Pryor, F.   74
Publication
    Drawing for   233-47
    Levels of   228-32
    Of post-holes   244
    Photography for   233, 238

Radiocarbon dating   192, 207,
    211, 221
Rahtz, P.A.   20, 36, 45, 59, 89,
    112, 126, 178, 188, 206,
    232, 238, 241, 247, 251, 259
Recording   142, 143-72, 173-91
    Record cards   101, 103, 120,
        139, 142, 146, 147, 148,
        149, 150
    Pottery   173-91
    Small finds   173-5, 185-91
Renfrew, C.   175, 211, 212-14
Renow, S. Frontispiece, 71,
    171-2, 194
Rescue excavation   28, 126-42
Research excavation   129-31
Residual pottery   181
Resistivity surveys   34, 51
Reynolds, P.J.   133
Robber trenches   58, 66, 118,
    195
Roman
    Environmental evidence from
        sewer at York   213
    Field boundaries   73
    Forts   32, 35, 38, 44
    Lunt, The   44, 259
    Pottery   177, 178, 185
    Roads   52
    Villa   56, 178
    See also Wroxeter
Rotherley, Romano-British
    village plan Front endpapers
Rowley, R.T.   28, 31, 39

Safety precautions   109, 140
St Joseph, J.K.S.   34
Sample, sampling   15, 24, 37,
    39, 42-5, 53, 55, 56, 210, 211

Environmental 98
Soil sampling 35, 103, 117, 118
Trial excavation 43, 50
Trenching 38, 44, 45, 51, 54, 118, 132
Sanctuary, The, Wiltshire 206
Sand and gravel sites 73, 130-36
Schmidt, H. 225
Scollar, I. 132
Sections 15, 44, 77, 78, 81, 82, 84, 87, 88, 92, 93, 118, 130, *138*, 140, 150, 160
Cumulative 57, 82, *83*, *86*, 87, 92, 93, 94
Ditch 44-5, *46-9*, 160
Horizontal 136
Segontium, Hasp from 176
Settlements 32
Anglo-Saxon 136
Iron Age *73*, 219
Roman Iron Age *back end-papers*
Medieval 138
Romano-British *front end-papers*
Shelters, Excavation 105
Shennan, S. 42
Sherratt, N. 207
Shifnal 45
Shrewsbury, Pride Hill Chambers, Merchant's House 259
Sieves and sieving 81, 142, 212-15
Silchester 15, 24
Silting 121, 124
Simmons, C. 253
Skudelev ship excavation, Roskilde 99
Small finds 94-100, 113, 137, 139, 146
Photography of 97, 98
Recording 108, 159, 173-75 185-91
Waterlogged 98, 99
Soils 116-21
Analysis 118
Colour enhancement 94, 103, 145
Excavation of plough soil suggested 133
Soil sampling 35, 103, 117, 118
Tannin in 120
Sonar scanning 35
Sorrell, A. 255
South Mimms, motte at *256*
Spades, used for top soil stripping 133, *135*
Spoil, spoil heaps 50, 69, 107, 108, 142
Stake-holes, *see* Post-holes
Stamford, St Martin's *67*

Steensberg, A. 16, 20, 21, 59 219
Stehli, P. 74
Stonehenge 123
Store Valby 20, *22*, *23*, 219
Strategies 37-67
Stratification 51, 59, 200, *201*
Subsoil 51, 75, 80, 87, 121, 124-5, 133, 136
Sulgrave 218
Sunter 259
Surveying 84, 140, 142, 151
Contour 28, *29*, 31, 87,
Geophysical 34, 35, 45, 50, 51, 54, 130, 132
Hachures 31
Sutton Hoo Ship Burial 97, 182

Taylor, C.C. 28, 31, 222
Taylor, H.M. 59, 259
Terminus ante quem 177, 197-99
Terminus post quem 38, 81, 177-79, 188, *196*, 197-99
Terrell, J. 251, 252
Thermo-luminescence 207, 211
Thermo-remanent magnetism 207, 211
Thompson, M.W. 190, 220
Timber, rates of decay 89-91
Toms, G. 59
Tools 69ff.
Treasure hunting 268
Trelleborg, Denmark 41, 78, 94, 225
Tres Riches Heures du Duc de Berry, Les
Castles in 224
Trial Excavation 43, 50
Trenching 45, 51, 54, 118, 132
Trowel, trowelling 69, 75-7, 81, 82, 121, 130, 133
in salvage excavation 137
Trump, D.H. 251

Urban archaeology 53, 56, 128

Verulamium 21
Vowlan, Isle of Man 20, *24*, *25*

Wade, K. 40
Wainwright, F.T. 218
Wainwright, J.G. 133
Walle, A. van de 257
Warendorf, Medieval settlement at 128
Washford, Worcestershire, Fishponds at 45
Waterman, D. 257
Weathering, of subsoils 124-5, 145
Webster, G. 160, 184, 253

Webster, P. 185
West Stow, Suffolk
Reconstructed buildings at 259
Wharram Percy 21, 59
Deserted Medieval village at *119*, 220
Wheeler, Sir Mortimer 13, 15, 160, 218
Whiteparish, Wiltshire 222
Wijster, Holland 131, *back end-papers*
Long House type *244*
Williams, D. 212
Wilson, D. 33, 34, 132
Wilson, Mrs D.S. 210
Winchester 21, 84, 104
Old and New Minsters 66
Wincklemann, W. 128
Woodfield, P. 259
Woodhenge 206
Woolley, Sir Leonard 14
Worcester 137, 140
Anglo Saxon and Medieval coins from 190
Animal bones from 214
City Wall 137
Friars Gate 137
Talbot Street *138*, *139*
Worms and worm action, *see* Earthworm
Wroxeter (Viroconium)
Frontispiece, 15, 44, 70, 81, 113, 124
A ceramic period of, 180
Building IV *234*, *235*, *236*, *237*
Building materials at, 215, 216
Building plans *262*, *264*, *265*
Drawing of find from *title page*
Erosion by River Severn 222
Gravel Street at 153
Human skulls 205
Interpretative example from *194*
Pottery at 41-2, 173
Rebuilding of City Centre 204
Reconstruction of Old Work 259
Simulation of Building I 197, 257, 259

Yeavering, Anglo-Saxon palaces at 9, 20, 88, 136
York 26
Environmental evidence from Roman sewer 213
Preserved timber structure at *260*, *261*